Making a Difference *in* Patients' Lives

Emotional Experience in the Therapeutic Setting

SANDRA BUECHLER

Routledge
Taylor & Francis Group
New York   London

"Clearances" from *Opened Ground: Selected Poems 1966-1996* by Seamus Heaney. Copyright © 1998 by Seamus Heaney. Reprinted by permission of Farrar, Straus and Giroux, LLC.

"The Writer" from *The Mind-Reader,* copyright © 1971 and renewed 1999 by Richard Wilbur, reprinted by permission of Harcourt, Inc.

"Something I've Not Done" from *Writings to an Unfinished Accompaniment,* copyright ©1979 by W.S. Merwin. Reprinted by permission of the Wylie Agency.

Routledge
Taylor & Francis Group
270 Madison Avenue
New York, NY 10016

Routledge
Taylor & Francis Group
27 Church Road
Hove, East Sussex BN3 2FA

© 2008 by Taylor & Francis Group, LLC
Routledge is an imprint of Taylor & Francis Group, an Informa business

International Standard Book Number-13: 978-0-88163-494-5 (Softcover) 978-0-88163-443-3 (Hardcover)

Visit the Taylor & Francis Web site at
http://www.taylorandfrancis.com

and the Routledge Web site at
http://www.routledge.com

For Daphne, Isaac, their parents, and George

Contents

Introduction
Meaningfully Impacting Patients' Lives

In the preface to her biography of Frieda Fromm-Reichmann, Hornstein (2000) describes the analyst's well documented devotion:

> She was willing to try practically anything that might help them, which
> was a great deal more than most other psychiatrists were willing to do....
> 'She would have swung from the chandelier like Tarzan if she thought it
> would help,' Joanne Greenberg later observed. (xv–xvi)

Gail Hornstein's biography of Frieda Fromm-Reichmann is the moving story of one woman's determination to make a difference in the lives of her patients. When I read it I had the thought that Fromm-Reichmann's fierce will and clarity of purpose probably helped her remain hopeful, even when working with very severely disturbed patients. Personally, I have often felt calmed and centered by my own certainty that I will expend whatever effort the work with someone requires. But sheer determination is not enough. What else is needed for a clinician to have a meaningful impact on her patients' lives?

Making a Difference in Patients' Lives is my effort to formulate what emotion theory, interpersonal psychoanalysis, and my own clinical experience have taught me about having a significant emotional impact in treatment. The fundamental tenets of emotion theory can suggest much to the clinician. They have powerful implications for our understanding of therapeutic action.

I draw on both my own clinical experiences and treatment accounts contributed by others to explore the clinical relevance of concepts taken from emotion theory. What can its precepts tell us about how one person affects the way life feels to someone else? For example, in her moving personal chronicle (in Casey, 2001) Martha Manning writes about what made her own depression bearable:

> I kept going only for my daughter. Every morning, Keara stumbles semi-
> conscious into the bathroom and turns on the shower. Within the space

of thirty seconds she starts to sing. She starts out humming so softly that her voice blends with the spray as it bounces off the wall. And then she chooses her song—sometimes sweet and lyrical, sometimes loud and rocking. Each morning, when I had to face another day on two hours of sleep and absolutely no hope, I leaned against the bathroom door waiting for her to sing and let her voice invite me to try for one more day. (p. 266)

In her periodic bouts of depression Manning was haunted by her little girl's constant question, "Why are you so sad?" But she was also rescued, in a sense, by that little girl, whose song existed *alongside* everything else. Insight and other "techniques" failed, especially when they seemed to her like efforts to convince her she should feel better. But her daughter's aliveness existed alongside her depression and, by its very existence, modified it. Just as the emotion theorist would suggest, an emotion is most often modulated by another feeling. The most powerful regulator of an emotion is another feeling, because all emotions exist in a constantly changing system. The whole emotion system is altered with a shift in any one of its components. What can the clinician trying to have a powerful emotional impact learn from this story?

Each chapter of this book approaches the issue of the clinician's emotional impact from a different angle. The first chapter outlines some basic precepts about human feelings that emotion theory has researched, and then explores their potential clinical applications. For example, the already mentioned notion of how strong feelings modify one another might influence the clinician to focus more broadly on the patient's *whole* system of emotions. My own clinical experience has suggested to me that this approach is often useful. Over and over again, I have found that focusing on the patient's depression, for example, generally does not alter the depression. Human feelings such as sadness, fear, and rage are most often modified by *other emotions*, such as life's joys, curiosities, surprises, and passions. Consequently, I have found it more useful to focus on these feelings (or their absence).

We know, just from our own experience as human beings, that often nothing can diminish life's pain. In treatment, the therapist's efforts to avoid or minimize it can signal to the patient that the clinician is faint of heart. In addition to being capable of squarely facing pain, it may sometimes be necessary for the clinician to challenge culturally prevalent idealizations of eliminating hurtful feelings, through pharmaceutical or simple therapeutic methods. Emotion theory's precepts can suggest some bases for these challenges.

Throughout this book, I explore what my reading of some of the interpersonal analytic literature and emotion theory (as well as my clinical experience) suggests about the sources of treatment's emotional impact (the emotional aspect of therapeutic action). While analytic theories differ in how they understand therapeutic action, we know that to have lasting significance a treatment must engage forces with the power to affect the course of a human life. Poets, visual artists, philosophers, ecclesiastics, developmental researchers, and others have long searched for an understanding of what is powerful enough to truly affect life experience. It is my belief that one set of answers can be found in the feelings that form our bonds, our passions, our shared emotional experiences.

Thus, for example, Manning (quoted above) suffers from depressive emotions, but it is an interpersonally evoked feeling that also exists that enables her to bear them. Insight clarifies, but does not create this strength in her. It seems possible to me that insight about what helped her may make it easier to replicate the improvement. But what caused it to happen was joy and love.

I imagine that Keara's song tells her mother that this joy and love, too, exist. In other words, life goes on alongside depression. No one is telling Manning not to be depressed, that she doesn't have cause, or that she should handle things differently. No one is advising her to "pull up her socks" and tough it out. No one is preaching Stoicism. At the moment, at least, mood altering medications are not the answer, because how to get rid of the depression is not the question. At issue is *how to add something.*

I suggest that by maintaining her own balance and expressing her own feelings Keara offers her mother a basis for a renewed attachment to life. In each chapter, in a sense, I ask what the analyst can learn from this example and many other vignettes of human beings whose emotional experiences have been profoundly affected by the behavior of another.

The second chapter applies emotion theory and interpersonal analytic theory to our understanding of empathy in treatment. How can we envision empathic therapeutic action if we use ideas contributed by these theories? First, it seems to me, our conception of an empathic therapeutic stance would be likely to focus on the feelings that the analyst's presence *adds to* the patient's emotional experience.

Empathy, in this view, is not understood as necessarily involving mirroring or delimiting emotion. Using my own reading and clinical experience as guides I would suggest that it is often through the analyst's (and the patient's) struggle to *regain balance*, in unpredictable, previously unformulated ways, that emotional modifications occur for them both. What is added, in short, is the analyst's active emotional effort to discover how to be in relation to this patient. In terms of Hoffman's (1993) dialectic between what is preformulated or ritual in analysis and what is spontaneous, this understanding of empathy falls closer to the spontaneous end. In each treatment, in each hour, for each emotion, what constitutes empathy may radically differ.

Thus, for example, one patient begins each session with a heavy, accusatory silence. To me it seems to express her insistence that I provide for her, rather than the other way around. If I wait for her to "produce material" for analysis I am forcing her to submit to my rules. To her, this would signal that she has accepted them and, by extension, other sets of rules she opposes. What is an empathic response in this situation? One definition of empathy offered by my (*American Heritage*) dictionary mentions "vicarious identification." Does empathy with this patient require an identification with her feelings? Which feelings?

I am proposing an understanding of therapeutic empathy that emphasizes:

1. An empathic response often requires an *active emotional adjustment* of one person to the feelings of another.
2. Whatever adjustment the analyst makes to a patient is idiosyncratic to that analyst. In other words, how I adjust to Patient A is partially a product of who I am. It may especially depend on my own history of experience with the patient's predominating emotions. This is a fundamentally interpersonal point of view. Patient A would not get the same analysis from another analyst, because that other clinician would adjust differently to being with Patient A. My way of adjusting to Patient A reflects my own personal life experience and clinical experience. It is shaped by those who have influenced me, the events of my life, my character, my defenses, my values, and my theoretical beliefs. Unlike some traditional views of empathy that emphasize a sharing of feelings, this perspective highlights that the analyst, by remaining him or herself (with her characteristic ways of coping) may *provide telling contrasts and sources of emotional modulation*. For example, although Keara

is not an analyst, her song, undiminished, contrasts enough to tell her mother how different their states are (though this contrast may well be unintended and unformulated by Keara and her mother). Her song also provides feeling that could modify her mother's depression, merely through its existence, since the emotions of one person affect the other, and an emotion affects all the others in a person's system. Joy modifies sorrow partially by adding contrast. Contrast teaches and, potentially, regulates. For example, joining a child's tantrum may merely escalate it, with little gained. On the other hand, calm in the face of agitation illuminates and potentially modulates it. One person's calm can both point out the agitation of the other and help to regulate that agitation. Thus, an interpersonal emotional interaction potentially can interpret (or illuminate) *as well as* modify the patient's feeling state.

3. Frequently, empathy is most readily communicated through an action, rather than in words. Thus, with my initially silent patient (mentioned above), empathy might be expressed through a willingness to struggle with the situation. The *action* of struggling has the potential to provide a contrast that clarifies the patient's attitude as well as, possibly, modulating it. We often learn about responses we take for granted by watching someone else respond differently.

4. Often, I find, there is something for us both to learn from how we recover our emotional balance after an interaction with each other. This is especially true during "empathic failures" or "ruptures." We have a particularly rich opportunity to learn something about how we normally function and how we can adjust to each other emotionally at these points.

For example, with my initially silent patient, the question that occurs to me is, what would it take for each of us to regain a mostly curious emotional balance? I believe my own struggle in that direction could be informative and, possibly, mutative (for us both). If my patient and I can be curious about our opening gambit with each other we may learn something new and, perhaps even more importantly, the process of exploration itself will feel different enough to teach us something about our (usual) selves and each other.

The following five chapters honor the emotion theorist's fundamental belief that each emotion deserves to be understood as a different human experience. Our regret is not entirely the same as our shame or our guilt, although all three may have much in common. Analysts come into contact with every possible human feeling, in their patients and in themselves. Can we say anything about working with regretful moments? Is there some way empathic immersion in these experiences differs from work with intense shame, or anger, or sadness? It is especially important, in my view, to consider nuances of difference in our own and our patients' emotions. Too often we refer to countertransferential emotions as though they were inter-changeable. We write about disclosing "affect" as though it makes no difference which feeling it is. Recognizing that I am frustrated and not enraged helps me communicate with others and with myself, and to relate this moment with others I have known.

Shame and, even more frequently, the fear of shame can present special problems in treatment (and other life situations). It may inhibit all action, creating a stasis from which there may seem to be no escape. Often the person with stage fright is paralyzed because of the anticipation of the scathing reviews he or she will give his or her own performance if the show is allowed to go on. In the treatment microcosm I may find myself disclosing more than usual. I want to emphasize that this is *not* a predetermined recipe. I do not decide that a certain patient, who suffers from a fear of shame, needs me to self-disclose. Rather, in a generally unformulated way, *I find myself* unusually self-disclosing, and *then* become curious about why.

While self-disclosure by the analyst has been amply discussed in the recent literature (by Maroda, 1991, 1999, 2002; Renik, 1995, 1998; and many others) it is not usually considered an interpretation of the patient's fear of shame. I think its mutative effect often partially stems from the contrast between a patient silenced by the fear of shame and an analyst willing to be a "fool for love," (Buechler, 2004) that is, willing to speak and risk looking foolish. Finding myself dis-closing may, at times, be my (usually unformulated) way of *adjusting* to being with a patient in the grip of an intense fear of shame. Thus, I am adjusting to this patient, but I am doing it in a characteristically Sandra Buechler way, which has been shaped by countless personal and professional experiences.

For example, after considerable consideration I decide to tell a patient that I have frequently suffered from a sensation of nausea during our sessions. Nausea is a highly unusual response for me. I felt quite uncomfortable about telling him this, anticipating awk-wardness on both our parts. It felt as if I was saying that he made me sick. I could find no explanation of why this was occurring. When I introduced it (probably in a tentative voice) I am sure he knew how difficult this disclosure was for me. I think he understood that I was privileging our potential learning over our likely discomfort. My discomfort, the forms its expression took, and my actions certainly reflect attitudes and priorities shaped by my personal and professional life.

As is often the case, I felt that regaining my own mainly curious emotional balance necessitated the disclosure. I was off-kilter and conscious of it, without understanding why. My disclosure provoked a memorably intense mutual exploration. The shift in my countertransference was striking. Disgust yielded completely, and in its place many other feelings held sway.

Shame, regret, joy, sadness or depression, and anger are each considered in separate chapters. I believe it is crucial to think in emotion-specific terms when we write about the treatment exchange. What can we say about working with these feelings when each predominates? Is the nature of an empathic response to regret different, in any identifiable way, from an empathic response to sadness? While every clinical moment is unique, and every treatment pair its own interpersonal milieu, it seems probable that we can say something about what it feels like to respond to great joy, for example, when we encounter it in treatment.

The book's final chapters make up a special section on clinical training, where I consider how we can nurture the cognitive, emotional, and interpersonal strengths needed to treat patients using insights derived from emotion theory and interpersonal psychoanalysis. What is the "right stuff" to do this kind of work? Is it "born" or "made"? Are there ways to recognize candidates who can use their emotions well in clinical exchanges? What fosters the development of a capacity for empathic emotional relating as it is discussed in this book?

When termination of treatment with one of my patients approaches, I make it a point to reflect, with the patient, about our emotional experiences with each other. In particular, I ask what the patient thinks affected him or her most. A patient comes to mind, now, whose answer surprised me. I had felt that our several years of treatment had yielded limited results. True, he had become better able to speak up for himself with his partner and with his family. A man in his middle 30s when we first met, his professional and personal life was hobbled by obsessive rituals. Getting out of the house in the morning took hours. Washing was self-torture. In his bureaucratic job, there were always more forms to do than he could finish in a normal work day. Consequently, long, late hours of polishing every sentence were commonplace in his life. Reading a book or a newspaper had always been out of the question, because he could never be sure enough that he had read every word, so had to begin every page, over and over again, until he became too worn out to continue. Every aspect of his life was ruled by cruel exhausting repetitions.

When he decided to end our work I was more than a little puzzled and disturbed. Why at that point, when the rituals still held sway? Isn't diminishing their power what he came to me to do? Why quit now? He explained to me that this was, indeed, what he originally came to me to do. He had wanted to get rid of his obsessive rituals, and to be free to read and wash as others do. But over the course of our work together *his goals changed*. Of course, it still would be nice to further diminish the hold of the rituals. He would continue to work on that on his own. But he had been able to stop taking antidepressants for the first time in many years, and his sexual life was much improved. While the rituals were still there, his feelings about them had changed. They were an annoying, but not defining, part of his life and sense of self. He was much better than he had ever been at making more important decisions than how often to wash. He could decide about his priorities, his relationship, his career. He had a sense of how he became the person he is and could see his own strengths, not just the liabilities. He had more fun. He liked himself, and appreciated his own determination to create a decent life for himself and his partner. Referring again to his rituals he asked me, "Who doesn't have some handicaps?"

As much as anyone, this patient reinforced some precepts I had already learned from emotion theory and interpersonal psychoanalysis. While I had mastered these lessons in the abstract it took clinical experience to show me their application to human predicaments. Both theoretical frameworks include authors who especially prize curiosity, the capacity to be surprised, and openness to the new. Sullivan (1953), in fact, centered his definition of health on the basis of the capacity to learn from new experience. Later writers, such as Donnel Stern (1990) have highlighted the role of surprise and curiosity in treatment and the rest of life. So when the patient explained that his goals had evolved, I understood that he was, in a sense, less rigid than I was. Where is it written that the goals in the first session have to remain frozen? Where is it written that symptoms are more important than how a life *feels* to the person living it?

The patient had explained that, in the context of his evolving enjoyment of life, the troubling aspects felt different. In other words, because the emotions form a system, a change in the intensity of his joy changed all his other feelings.

Patients have taught me that making a difference can come in various forms. This complicates research into a treatment's course and outcome studies of its effectiveness. How can effectiveness be measured, if the patient's definition of progress is always evolving? But, although this complexity makes the study of therapeutic action more difficult, the vast array of ways a human life can be improved is a blessing for both clinician and patient. Emotion theory and interpersonal psychoanalysis can both be mined by the clinician for new ways to think about how to make a meaningful difference in patients' lives.

1

Basic Assumptions about Human Emotions*

I can tell it will be a hard session from the set of her jaw as she passes my chair on her way to the couch. Even before she has had time to lie down, her agitation has affected me. I register the jazzy staccato in her tone, like someone souped up on caffeine. I feel the music before I hear the words. She tries to smile but it comes out lopsided, half of her mouth reaching upward but the rest failing to follow. Her tension has already begun to invade me as she tries to settle. Like a cat about to spring, she seems to be in the air, even while lying still. Her squirm is Yeats' center that cannot hold.

Anna is a statuesque, raven-haired, middle-aged professional married woman. Something piercing about the eyes would help you single her out in a crowd. Coal black, they plead with you, even if you are a stranger.

Some days I feel I don't have what Anna needs. I wish I could side-step her intensity. But I might as well wish for wings.

On this particular Monday evening, her agitation preceding her, Anna remarks, "Rough weekend." I hear an accusation, as though I have already failed her. Or, perhaps, as though the previous Friday, I intentionally abandoned her to a bleak Saturday and Sunday. More softly, I hear her accusing me of having had a better weekend than hers, appropriating the only available peace for myself.

But for me, in this Monday hour, peace is a distant memory. I have to force myself to listen to Anna's words. I register that her husband (also) withdrew from her this weekend, preferring his work-strewn study. What feeling is rising in me? Is it contempt? Scorn? Am I ready to laugh at Anna for making herself into an absurd person singular,

---

* Mark Blechner, George Hammer, and Donnel B. Stern helped me develop this chapter.

the eternally unpopular misfit eating alone in the high school cafeteria? Is it glee that I am not her (today)? Do I want to mock her to distance myself from her ugly loneliness, or out of anger at her claim on me?

Only a few seconds of our endless session have passed. Anna is implacably winding herself up, agitation escalating as she prosecutes her husband for the moments he should have been humane and dropped his work in favor of her company. Is it already too late to hide my heart's affinity with her husband? I retreat to my own "study," that is, the relief of private thoughts. I grab on to a bit of theory here, an idea there, anything to save me from Anna's grasp.

Moments later, although I did not fall asleep, I seem to startle awake, hearing Anna describe lunch with a friend. She wonders if she shared too much about her "neglectful" husband in a bid to get her friend's sympathetic attention. More directly than usual, she asks my opinion. In sharing these confidences with her friend did she betray her husband? I feel caught red handed, as though *I* have committed the indiscretion. I feel I should have an answer, but, instead, my mind is absorbed in its calculations. Why are Anna's friend, husband, and analyst all so desperate to escape her?

Now I feel a strong pull to abandon myself to guilt. Maybe she is right and I don't care enough. Maybe I am too vested in being above her, different from her, away from her, to enter her feelings empathically. She is that kid in the playground nobody picks for their team.

Or maybe I just don't want to be stirred up today. Maybe I want to get through this last hour unruffled and lurch toward my own comforting dinner.

I begin to sink. Too many thoughts, wildly proliferating. Anna is the victim of everyone's indifference ... no, wait ... she is a bully ... but, really, she's lonely and scared ... but she puts everyone on the spot. It must be deliberate, hostile ... but, no, she feels like *she* submits to everyone else because she needs us so ... I am the bully ... no, wait, Anna is the bully....

Is it a neurotic need for control that now renders me calm? Is my calm the bad kind of countertransference, the old, sick kind we were not allowed when psychoanalysis and I were young?

A fork in the road. Of all I have already thought and felt what, if anything, should I tell Anna? Would disclosing be honesty or revenge? Mostly for her or mostly for me? Right or wrong? Proper analysis or wild analysis? And now I realize I am entering my version of *Anna's* conflict about disclosure. How much should she tell her friend and how much should I tell her? How do people ever know how much of their thoughts to share? Should it depend on what we think our motives for disclosure are? Or is the probable *impact* of the disclosure the only relevant question?

In this situation, regardless of what I decide about deliberate, verbal disclosure, I believe my calm itself expresses:

1. An emotion
2. A countertransference response
3. A comment
4. An enactment
5. A contrast to Anna's emotions
6. An interpretation of Anna's emotions

In responding "all of the above," I am making a number of assumptions about the emotions in the clinical interchange, and, more generally, in human interaction. In the remainder of this chapter, and throughout this book, I spell out these assumptions. Each clinician implicitly relies on a set of beliefs about how people cope with life's challenges and how they can use treatment to help them live more fully. I rely on faith in the power of one person's feelings to affect the emotions of another. Briefly, I explore how I can use my calm to help Anna recognize, and possibly modulate, her agitation.

Assumption 1

"… the emotions constitute the primary motivational system for human beings." (Izard, 1977, p.3)

A theory of human motivation based on drives is fundamentally different from a theory based on emotions. Drives generally evoke relatively fixed patterns of behavior and they have a cyclic quality, that is, an inevitable progression from build up of tension to discharge, and back to build up, and so on. Emotions, in contrast, are more varied, do not dictate specific behaviors, and are not necessarily cyclic. Consequently, seeing the emotions as our fundamental human motives leaves more room for individual variation. This may help us check the impulse to assume we understand why patients behaved as they did, when we may not have inquired enough about their feelings. We might be better able to continue a curious inquiry when we

think in terms of each of us having a vast personal history of emotions, combinations of emotions, and emotion-cognition patterns.

Thus, when I think about my session with Anna, my understanding is radically different if I focus on emotions rather than drives
(or any other motivational construct). Drive theory could lock me
in to seeing her as either enacting an inevitable Oedipal drama with
me, or as giving vent to aggression toward me. These are, of course,
two very real possibilities, and are potentially useful hypotheses. I
believe that I should not ignore them, but I can usefully add to them
with a theory of the emotions as the primary motivational system for
human beings. Seeing emotions as primary means to me that sexual
and aggressive impulses express two of the many emotionally shaped
motivational forces in human beings. Emotions such as fear, shame,
guilt, curiosity, and many others can make a sexual or aggressive
pull a very different experience. As is true for any other significant
aspect of being a human being, our interpersonal history (along with
our endowments) shapes our personal experience of these motives.

When I consider what might be fueling Anna's intense agitation,
I will hear differently if I come to the session with an outlook that
puts a wealth of interpersonal emotional experience at the helm. My
hearing can then be more open ended than if I believed in a closed
system of motivating forces. Putting the emotions in center stage
means that there can be an *infinite* variety of emotion-cognition patterns shaped partially by one's interpersonal history at play at any
particular moment. Thus, for example, if I see both Anna and myself
as driven, partially, by our loneliness, then for each of us our history
of being lonely is salient. A particular array of feelings, and feeling-
cognition combinations comes more strongly into play, as we make
each other lonelier in how we interact. My own memory of being
a lonely 7th grader is more relevant than usual when I am working. Anna's experience of being left alone as an infant shapes her
consciousness more powerfully than it generally does. Furthermore,
for one or both of us, loneliness is associated with anxiety that will
affect this moment in this session. On the other hand, if one of us
tends to get very curious about being lonely, that will have a different
impact. How loneliness tends to affect each of us cognitively may be
particularly salient in this session. For each of us, has loneliness frequently evoked moments of intense, sharp concentration or a confused, blank absentmindedness?

Understanding the emotions as the primary motivational system in human beings allows me to enter a session with a very flexible, yet orienting, theory. With this way of thinking I can hold all my motivational hypotheses lightly as I feel Anna out. I don't come into the session without *any* theory of what motivates people. While some might argue that such a clean slate is the best way to enter sessions, I believe it is difficult to perceive anything without some ready-made constructs. Just as it would be hard to see a circle without a concept of circularity, I would have trouble seeing loneliness as a driving force in a session unless I entered already understanding that human beings can be driven by gnawing loneliness.

So as I enter this session with Anna I assume she *could* be Oedipally jealous of my (presumed) better position with men. Or she *could* be aggressively punishing me with her demands. But she *could* also be driven by a powerful loneliness that was born in some of her early experiences in infancy, way before Oedipal triangles emerged. Or she *could* be feeling mainly intense, shameful social inadequacy, with its attendant memories, thoughts, connected emotions, and impact on consciousness. Her shame might have many profound sources, not just in her family experience, but in all walks of her interpersonal life. As she pushes for an answer from me (about whether she betrayed her husband by revealing his "neglect" to a friend) is she telling me how inadequate she has always felt about making these social judgments on her own?

From our field's inception analysts and patients have had endless battles about the appropriate limits of the analyst's role. With important (and sometimes egregious) exceptions, most of the time it has been patients who have wanted less talk and more action. Why is this so? I think one way we can understand the patients' wish for action is as an expression of their greater faith in action to evoke intense feelings. Perhaps, in a not-yet-articulated way, they hope that the analyst's disclosure, or direct advice, or concrete help, or the gift of a soothing phrase, will evoke in the patient feelings strong enough to have the power to heal. I think many treatment stalemates result from the patients' insistence on getting something that makes them feel substantially better, while the analyst can't or won't comply.

How can we formulate a theory that honors the infinite variety of interpersonal emotional experience that a particular patient may need, in order to profoundly change? More specifically, in the present context, I want my theory to help me toward a nuanced understanding of this moment with Anna. While I don't want to jump to a predetermined motivational schema, I also don't want to have to "reinvent the wheel" in the session. That is, I don't want to feel (or pretend to feel) that I enter having no beliefs about human behavior in general, and about my own and Anna's patterns in particular. I want a theory that helps me move toward greater understanding of the clinical moment, not one that starts with a predetermined explanation, nor one that leaves me groping in the dark.

Drive theories can be misused to substantiate a paranoia-like certainty about the meaning of the patient's behavior. Paranoid people think they can completely explain their experience with a predetermined overriding assumption, for example, "They are after me because I am Jesus." All too similarly, analysts can use drive theory to fit a complex human being into one of only a few predetermined Procrustean beds.

In the spirit of Hoffman's dialectic seesaw between ritual and spontaneity (1998) the analyst needs to be able to move back and forth, between the present clinical moment and a *complex and flexible* theory of human motivation. Human beings have certain inherent fundamental emotions, but our life experience patterns them differently in each of us. You and I are both capable of shame. But maybe very intense early taunting has tinged your shame with rage. My shame comes with a different history, perhaps bringing more anxiety than rage in its wake. Of course these would be relative, not absolute, differences.

This slant allows cognition equal recognition along with the emotions. How we think and how we feel so mutually interconnect that sorting them out can occupy analysts and patients for much of their time together. Is Anna so agitated because of the intensity of her loneliness? Her hostility? Her shame and its attendant anxiety? Her jealousy, bolstered by the *thought* that I probably had a better weekend than she did? Is her agitation based mainly on her early experiences with a father who accused her of the "betrayal" of siding with her mother against him? Or does her agitation mainly stem from much earlier experiences of having, then losing, a mother's loving gaze? Memory, thought, emotion infinitely vary as they combine in the life experience of a human being.

As an analyst, I believe I am best prepared to deal with Anna if I enter our session with loosely held notions about how loneliness "smells," the "taste" of fear, the "texture" of intense shame. These are leads that can help me orient, but not certainties that prematurely close down my intuitive understanding. They allow me to honor the tremendous variety of individual emotional life experience and its impact on who we each become.

Assumption 2: Fundamentally, emotions are adaptive.

> Emotions have motivational functions that give them critical adaptive qualities; for example, interest gives focus and selectivity to perception; fear and anticipatory shame protect from physical and psychological harm; guilt motivates moral reasoning, empathy, and reparation of damaged relationships; and joy works as an antidote for stress and a stimulus to social interaction and creative thinking. (Izard, 2001, p. 253)

Understanding the emotions as fundamentally adaptive has broad clinical implications. It shapes our notions of treatment's goals, methods, and the meaning of progress. This view of emotionality affects how we define normality and pathology, and affects our focus in sessions. What we see as important, worthy of therapeutic attention, memorable, and so on, depends on our basic stance toward human emotionality. Henry Krystal (1975) has been critical of what he calls "riddance" theories that assume a goal of treatment is to diminish emotionality. In teaching I have referred to the implicit "pus theory of emotions" that I believe many clinicians (and nonclinicians) hold. It was especially popular in the 1970s to believe that if we could express (rather than suppress) anger in treatment we would be cured of our troublesome emotions. To me, this reflects a schizoid cast inherent in some clinical theories. It is as though "less is more." Less intense feeling, fewer emotions, affective control are considered the ideal state. The clinical implications of this position are far reaching. A patient describes her continuing grief about her mother's death. What assumptions about "normal" grieving do we bring to the session? Do we assume grief should be time limited, or limited in intensity, or in its expression? Without hearing more, do we assume the grief is serving positive functions, or do we begin to think in terms of pathological processes? What makes a person's grief, or rage, or jealousy excessive?

Subsequent sections of this book more fully address the clinical significance of how we each define emotional health, pathology, and ideal functioning. Briefly, I believe that no analyst can be entirely neutral about these issues, and no matter how much we try to follow the patient's lead our own conceptions of healthy emotionality affect what we focus on, remember, and respond to. While I am aware of the destructive potential in emotionality I believe that an orientation that starts with the assumption that emotions are fundamentally adaptive helps us look for what that adaptive function might be. For example, with Anna, it certainly would be easy to see her agitation as troublesome, and its reduction as a treatment goal. In a way, it is. But just as an infant's cry is its language, Anna's agitation is, right now, her only means of expressing a significant unformulated (Stern, 1997) aspect of who she is. If I entered the session with Anna believing (consciously or unconsciously) that expressing her agitation *so as to reduce it* should be the first order of business I could lose a precious opportunity to know her better. But if I believe the emotions are fundamentally adaptive I am more likely to look for the (intrapersonal and interpersonal) functions of the agitation.

Along with the concept that the emotions are fundamentally adaptive, I also believe that every emotion has an optimal range of intensity. Too little, even of painful agitation, is as much of a problem as too much. We would probably be as concerned if an infant never cried as we would be if crying took up its whole waking life.

Anna's agitation tells me there is something she badly wants to express (although I'm not sure yet what it is). But I don't assume my aim should be to cure her of her intense feelings although, eventually, we may try to help her be better able to modulate them. I begin with a relatively unformulated sense that her agitation is her current (rather ineffective) emotional language.

The belief that emotions are fundamentally adaptive has especially important implications for how we define treatment's goals and, more generally, ideal health in human beings. For example, many behavioral and cognitive approaches would see Anna's agitation as a symptom and something to cure. This pits one aspect of the patient (bolstered by the therapist) against another aspect of the patient. If I am working to cure Anna of her agitation *I am working to cure Anna of a part of Anna.* Bromberg (1998) has been especially clear about how such a position can become problematic. Referring to Freud's treatment of Emmy von N., Bromberg says:

> Even though she welcomed his trying to "cure" her, she didn't want him to "cure" her of being herself. She was "unruly" because she needed to get all of her selves into a human relationship and was afraid Freud was going to lose patience because she was insisting, through her symptoms, on her right to have him accept that her "crazy" (unruly) reactions to his therapeutic efforts had to do with him as well as her. (p. 235)

Anna's agitation forces me to pay attention to her as she communicates to me the intensity of her need for something she is not getting. Those coal black eyes pierce as well as disconcert me. She would be easier without them, but she wouldn't be Anna.

Searles (1986) and Sherby (1989) each bemoaned their loss when their "borderline" patients were "cured" of their intensity. I do believe that most patients eventually mellow emotionally, including those who initially rumble with agitation. I would like to see Anna calmer, feeling more joy, and less locked in a continuous snit. But I prefer her snit to her depressive, shut down silence.

Anna will, I feel, be better off when her emotions speak in softer and more varied tongues. Right now they know only a few dialects. Hopefully, in her treatment, we will multiply (*not* subtract from) her means of expression.

Assumption 3: Social competence requires the ability to communicate emotions and read them sufficiently accurately when they are expressed by others.

A wealth of data (e.g., Magai and McFadden, 1995; Tronick, 1989) support the view that very young infants are capable of discerning different facial expressions of emotions, and no one can argue with the notion that emotionality is our first language. But clinically, we certainly can differ about how much the ability to read faces can or should be taught, either to children or to adults (for a very positive view about teaching adults to read emotional expressions, see Ekman, 2003). Once again, this touches on issues of "normal" and "ideal" emotional perception and expression. These questions reverberate throughout the subsequent chapters.

Briefly, I believe Anna will be better off when she is more in tune with her own feelings and her emotional impact on others. She will feel less alienated from herself and others, and more competent as a social partner. But I don't think it would be therapeutically useful for me to simply teach her what a smiley face looks like.

I come to being a psychoanalyst with the assumption that human beings naturally learn about the interpersonal impact of our emotions as we develop, so something must have blocked this process in Anna. Our work together should (among many other things) explore this block. I think Anna really doesn't understand what it is like, as Bollas (1987) might say, to be her object. Or, we could consider

Anna's difficulty a failure in affective mentalization, in Fonagy's (2001) terms. However we describe it, this issue is likely to take up considerable time and space in the treatment.

What can augment or limit my own capacity for reading Anna's emotions and relating to them therapeutically? While all analytic perspectives rely on the analyst's empathic ability, some techniques center on this strength more than others. Clarifying the emotional "right stuff" to be an analyst is an issue at the heart of this book. What does it take to help Anna know her agitation and, at times, modulate it? What must I nurture in myself to be able to help her meet this challenge?

Assumption 4

> Each of the fundamental emotions has unique motivational properties of crucial importance to the individual and the species, and each adds its own special quality to consciousness as it mobilizes energy for physical or cognitive adventure. An intense emotion may be considered as a special state of consciousness experienced as highly desirable or highly undesirable. (Izard, 1977, p. 83)

The viewpoint that there are fundamental emotions that are separate or discrete, rather than merely different in intensity or some other aspect, is derived from Charles Darwin's fascinating contribution in *The Expression of the Emotions in Man and Animals* (1872). So, for example, rather than seeing fear as on a continuum with surprise, with fear as a reaction to a greater degree of novelty, the fundamental or discrete emotions perspective sees fear and surprise as *two separate emotions*, discernible by their differing facial expressions, that create different states of mind.

I believe that the clinical implications of this point of view are enormous. This means that, for example, my lifelong periodic experience of myself angry is a building block of my identity, a crucial part of who I am to myself, and a *separable self-state* from my experience of myself afraid. Additionally, this point of view envisions each fundamental emotion as having *characteristic effects on consciousness itself*, so that, for example, when we are angry our focus is narrower and less freewheeling than when we are less angry, or when we are predominantly curious. Of course, this is as true for analysts as it is for everyone else. I believe it would be hard to overestimate the clinical significance of the *emotions as self states*. This has enormous implications for our understanding of transference and counter-transference phenomena.

So, if each emotion is a discernibly different self state, so that we accumulate a history (conscious and unconscious) of how we have felt when angry, for example, we bring this memory bank to every new day, just as we also bring memories of what it is like for us to feel fear or joy, and how we each tend to experience sadness. These (formulated and unformulated) emotional profiles are a significant aspect of who we are to ourselves.

When I meet new patients I want to know how their angry self state feels to them. I assume it is somewhat like my own, but not exactly the same, because it is partially shaped by a different set of life experiences. I also assume that intense anger and intense fear have some experiential similarities for my new patient, as well as significant differences.

Thus the transference–countertransference interchange becomes for me, at least in part, an encounter between two people whose predominant emotional self states (and their genetic, historical, experiential roots) may be quite similar or differ very greatly. There are regularities in how this plays out between patient and analyst so that, for example, with a particular patient I am often in a state of much more curiosity than he or she is. I bring my own history of being in a highly curious self state to each of our sessions. When the patient notes my state of curiosity, he or she understands it from the vantage point of his or her own history of being in the state of curiosity. Of course this is all greatly oversimplified, as no one is ever in a pure state of any one emotion. But, as human beings, I believe we all have *some* experience of being curious, so we can recognize that state in others. This is a significant aspect of our capacity for empathy. But it also accounts for some of our frequently occurring empathic failures, because my curious state is somewhat different from yours. As is elaborated in Chapter 2, empathic capacity is partially based on a skillful projection. Just as I can only know my own experience of the color "red," and I have to assume that is largely what you see when you say you see "red," so it is with my experience of sadness, loneliness, and other emotional self states.

Applying this to my encounter with Anna, I assume I bring my history of emotional self states to work with me in the morning, as well as a rich personal history of being with people who are in varying emotional self states. This leads me to ask, for Anna and for myself, about the impact our predominant emotions are having on conscious awareness. If Anna feels desperately lonely (with me, in the session, and with her husband, in the experiences she is reporting) she will bring her history of loneliness to this moment in our work. Meanwhile, I will respond emotionally to the loneliness in the content of the material and in the process between us. How do our personal histories of being lonely affect *what we each can register* about the other person? Is loneliness so anxiety provoking for Anna that she can't focus on my responses enough to read them? Is something similar happening to me?

Who we each are, in heightened loneliness, is enacted in this clinical moment. While the experience of loneliness has some commonalities for all human beings (Buechler, 1998) our personal life experience will affect the other emotions loneliness recruits. In loneliness Anna's agitation rises, while my calm intensifies. For Anna loneliness brings profound cognitive shifts. She enters a self state in which the surround becomes de-realized. In her early life her extensive isolation carried the threat of losing the capacity to connect with others, with herself, and with reality. Her loneliest states had a psychotic quality. Maybe we have all known such loneliness at some point, but Anna's experience of it took up a great deal of her infancy and early childhood. In contrast, my experience of loneliness had a different flavor. At least some of the time it brought on fertile impulses to write. Thus, for me, loneliness carries a connotation of changed, but not inevitably impaired, cognition. I may have been dreamy, but, generally, I did not feel dangerously unmoored. Perhaps most importantly, it did not feel permanent and it was, to some extent, sought rather than imposed by others. Given these differences between me and Anna how much can I accompany her to the flat landscape of her loneliness? How much can I understand a loneliness so bereft of recognizable features that it easily morphs into a Kafka nightmare? Anna's agitation is, at least in part, her way of saying, "Please don't leave me in this death state. I have already been there, and I know what it is like. There is no time, nothing solid to differentiate real from unreal. There is limitless terror. Who are you (husband, friend, analyst) if you can do this to me?"

I believe things are considerably different when both analyst and patient are in a mainly curious self state. For each, this state of mind is especially conducive to analytic inquiry. This is what I understand Roy Schafer's (1983) "analytic attitude" to mean, but I would suggest that the patient and the analyst benefit equally from it. In both, freely roving curiosity widens what can enter conscious awareness. A thought is like a toy that can be tossed around and looked at from various angles for the sheer joy of it. Even if there are no immediate "results," curiosity asks, "I wonder what would happen if …" or "what would it mean if instead of x I felt y?"

The wide angle lens of a curious self state sees and remembers at the peripheries of consciousness. Thus it can expand what enters awareness. Also, it brings with it a personal history of experiences in similar self states, times when curiosity reigned. For most of us, curiosity cannot predominate in intense emergencies. If we believe we are dying of starvation we are too focused on our need to wonder much. Relative freedom from pressing need is a prerequisite for entering the state of curiosity. Schachtel (1959) put it memorably:

> Curiosity, the desire for knowledge, the wish to orient oneself in the world one lives in—and finally the posing of man's eternal questions, "Who am I?" "What can I hope for?" "What shall I do?"—all these do not develop under the pressure of relentless need or of fear for one's life. They develop when man can pause to think, when the child is free to wonder and explore. (p. 274)

Assumption 5: The emotions form a system, with a change in one emotion affecting the experience of all the others.

This assumption, too, has tremendous clinical implications. It means, for example, that when a patient comes into treatment hoping to diminish his depression his analyst could just as well focus on his (relative) absence of curiosity as on the presence of intense depression. *Any change in any emotion will affect the whole system of emotions.* This can be very helpful, because patients can enter treatment obsessively fixated on depression. If their analysts join them in this exclusive focus they may both fail to notice crucial aspects of the patients' emotional and interpersonal life. In addition, if the patients bring an expectation that treatment will make their depression vanish instantaneously, they may be impatient with the process. We can all be tempted by the hope that emotions will operate like a thermostat, and that we can learn to raise or lower them with a magical technique.

Sometimes waving a wand does work, as it seems to do in the following snapshot. I have just enjoyed the first bite of my appetizer at a fairly upscale New York restaurant when, at a nearby table, a baby begins to wail. The parents look a bit frantic, glancing around to see whether their fellow diners are taking it in stride. The mother reaches into her voluminous bag, takes out a brightly colored rattle, and waves it in front of the child's face. The baby stops crying.

This is a common event. It seems unlikely that the mother studied emotion theory, latched on to the idea that one emotion modulates another, decided to side with those emotion theorists who consider curiosity an emotion, and chose her action hoping her child's curiosity would trump his distress. My bet would be that had I asked her why she reached for the rattle, she would have said something like, "To distract him."

For many years I have thought about how this works, why it works, and what it can teach clinicians. Other everyday situations come to mind, in which the presence of one emotion modulates another. The child who is fearful about going to the dentist confines himself to a few thin whimpers as he sits in the dentist's chair. Dad's talk, last night, about being a "good soldier" left him still frightened, but also proud to be, at last, a big boy.

Love transforms what could otherwise be tedious, as we recognize every time cousin Louise brings out the 10th photo of her adorable Jeremy. In grief, the world looks dark and ominous, while joy lights everything in sight. Emotions color other feelings, sometimes just modifying their intensity, but often changing them profoundly. The parent whose child has died doesn't need to know any theory to realize how deeply an emotion can diminish or enhance all other feelings.

Hopefully, when we become clinicians, we do not forget all that our lives have taught us. We still know the power of emotions to transform human experience. And they have that power in the clinical situation just as much as they do in every other walk of life. Emotions affect other emotions in sessions in every possible way. A patient, terrified of potential intimacy, hides behind his well-honed contempt. Not only does he *show* no tenderness toward his distraught girlfriend. He actually no longer *feels* warmth for her. Talking about her in the session, his voice is devoid of feeling, as though fear and contempt canceled out his love.

The assumption that the emotions form a system can affect our understanding of treatment's therapeutic action and goals. An elderly woman patient has recently lost both parents and her husband. She is, understandably, quite sad. She asks me what treatment could possibly do for her. My belief that the emotions form a system (along with many other values and assumptions, as I have previously elaborated, Buechler, 2004) will deeply affect my answer. I certainly would not try to "treat" her sadness, which I see as an inevitable human response to her situation. But her response to her situation includes other emotions besides sadness, and these might be usefully explored. Since the *presence or absence of any emotion can be expected to have an impact on the quality of experience of all the others*, if the patient's surprise, or curiosity, or loneliness can be reached, it will have some effect on her sadness.

This raises the particularly thorny question of whether emotions should be "prescribed." Analysts have struggled with this issue since the inception of our field. To put it in the present context, if I believe the emotions form a system, is it my job as a clinician to find a way to augment Anna's curiosity, if I think that would improve the overall balance of her emotions?

I suggest that analytic orientations form a continuum on this issue. At one extreme is the (now derided) "corrective emotional experience." In Alexander's (1961) words:

> The fundamental therapeutic factor consists in *transference experiences* which are suitable to undo the pathogenic experiences of the past. In order to give these new experiences a corrective value, they must take place under certain highly specific conditions. ... The basic model emphasized the patient's emotional insight into the *similarity* between transference reactions and the original infantile patterns. We add now the emphasis on experiencing emotionally the discrepancy between transference reactions and the analyst's actual behavior and personality. (p. 328, italics in original)

Alexander indicates that, while Freud emphasized the similarities between the situation with the parents and the transference, he was focusing on the therapeutic impact of the two situations' being *different*, due to the analyst's responses. Alexander experimented with the idea that the analyst might speed up the corrective experience by deliberately adopting an attitude exactly opposite to that of the parents. But deviations from the usual procedures, he suggests, are only possible after the analyst has a thorough understanding of the patient's problems. Until then, he advises, it is much better to follow the usual rules. Looking back at his work, Alexander believed his greatest change, over time, was an increase in his emphasis upon "the overwhelming significance of the emotional experiences which the patient undergoes during psychoanalytic treatment, and which outweigh the effects of cognitive insight" (1961, p. xviii). He saw the corrective emotional experience in the treatment as the factor that allows the patient to alter the legacy of the traumatic experiences he suffered in his earlier life.

Alexander's concept of the corrective emotional experience fell into disrepute for many years, perhaps because he had taken it too far by suggesting that the analyst might deliberately "stage" having very different responses from those of the patient's parents. I wonder whether cultural shifts toward valuing authenticity made such staging unacceptable to post-1960s analysts.

More recently, in the concept of "enactment," I believe we are reviving Alexander's idea and giving it renewed legitimacy. I will not attempt a summary of the history of the concept of enactment and its conceptual predecessors, in Ferenczi's active technique and the interpersonalists' evolving uses of the countertransference. The literature on the concept of enactment, as introduced by Theodore Jacobs in 1986 is, by now, voluminous. For the purpose of comparing one contemporary use of the concept of enactment with Alexander's corrective emotional experience, I quote Steckler's (2003,) description. Like Alexander, Steckler sees the analyst's participation as deliberate and consciously chosen for its potentially therapeutic impact:

> The therapist does not enter into the patient's expected paradigm for the repetition compulsion. Through that rejection of the ritualized repetition, he destabilizes that long-held pattern. He instead establishes the specificity of interactional patterns characteristic of healthy parent–child relationships and thus provides a safe and secure context within which the destabilization may be tolerated. (p. 722)

Later, Steckler goes on to suggest that, "There may be times when a therapist may wish, deliberately, to destabilize the patient's affective organization" (p. 724). So, by not entering the patient's expected paradigm we are, once again, differing from the patients, as Alexander recommended. By deliberately providing a "safe and secure context," and "destabilizing the patient's affective organization," we are *engineering* our effect on the patient, as Alexander dared to suggest.

Probably most analysts today would be more comfortable viewing their participation in enactments as less consciously formulated than Steckler's statement implies. I believe that these concepts are potentially dangerous enough to deserve our reticence. We can't write a script, based on our conception of what we think patients need to feel, and then enact it to entice them into playing out their role. Whatever might be the initial effect of such a performance, we would condemn ourselves to being fakes, from that point on, *pretending to spontaneously react, but really enacting a preordained attitude.* This entirely undermines the integrity that is so essential to the analytic relationship (Buechler, 2004). But aside from this issue, experientially, sessions feel more like improvisations than scripted performances. Most of the time we don't set out to have a particular impact. Our enactments can be formulated only in retrospect.

What can we take from the resurrection of Alexander's idea? I think the concept of corrective emotional experience has so many lives partially because it honors the powerful role of the emotions in the change process. Patients do need to have different emotional experiences from any they have had before. But the analyst's integrity is a vital prerequisite for any healing to occur. So, without a script, how do we ensure that a sufficiently significant emotional experience happens?

Taking a different position, analysts might attend to the information implicit in their countertransference without any preformulated idea of what patients need to experience. In other words, we should not prescribe, or even want to prescribe, at all. No particular outcome of the session is preordained as desirable. This stance seems to me to be implicit in many clinical presentations at conferences.

Personally, I would like to find a place between the extremes of this continuum. With Anna I don't want to prescribe a dose of curiosity, joy, love, hope, or any other feeling, as an antidote to her agitation. Besides the fact that we would then lose the chance to mine the information in her agitation, that would make treatment inauthentic, more like a scripted puppet show than a real encounter. But I very much appreciate the need (particularly in less experienced clinicians) to have an idea of where treatment might profitably go and some sense of what relative emotional health looks like.

What would a stance between the extremes suggest in my work with Anna? I feel I know curiosity would help her, but it wouldn't be appropriate for me to try to force her to become more curious. Were I to attempt that, I would lose all spontaneity as well as all the advantages neutrality confers (Greenberg, 1991). I can't make Anna more curious about herself, but I can bring to the session my belief that curiosity opens minds and lifts spirits. This belief will have an impact on my mind and spirit and how I operate in the session. In some way that is hard for me to articulate I think it will help Anna, too.

Just believing in a multiplicity of motivational states and a complex interconnected system of emotions gives me the feeling that there are endless possibilities. I will not deliberately try to induce Anna to be hopeful, curious, joyous, or more loving. But I know these feelings exist; I believe them to be a potential for Anna, and I trust that they could have the power to take the edge off her agitation.

Lately, "positive" psychologists are busy trying to understand resiliency, or human adaptability. Jeremy Safran (1999; Safran & Muran 2000), for example, asks how faith and will can facilitate coping and enhance therapeutic outcomes. Fredrickson (2001) has developed a "broaden and build" theory of why some people seem better able to bear the slings and arrows of outrageous fortune. As I understand it, her research measures the capacity to contextualize—that is, to take in life's pain against a background of more positive experience. Hardships are not visited upon us in a vacuum. We have lived through them before. Furthermore, we can focus on aspects of our current lives that are separate from the hardship. The tenor of this philosophy seems to me to be consonant with the idea that the emotions exist in a system. Difficulties occur in an emotional and interpersonal context that profoundly affects how I experience them. If I can keep positive feeling states alive and vivid, they will modulate my experience of hardship, and I will be more capable of bearing it and moving on. While I would not try to teach this to Anna, as though treatment were a graduate course, I think that everything about who I am, including my understanding of emotionality in human beings, has an impact on the clinical exchange. My ideas about human emotions go with me, as I remember some things Anna said last week and forget others, as I listen to her and respond.

More broadly, I believe that we each have a "theory" (parts of which may or may not be consciously formulated) about what emotionally fortifies us to cope with the human condition. How much do we each rely on will power to pull ourselves through crises? What do we each count on to enable us to bear the potential losses, indignities, medical and emotional hardships of aging? Some of us look to religion, work, or human connections for strength, and for the sense that our lives are meaningful. But all we each have is a personal theory about what can give us the strength we will need.

Perhaps it is equally important to look at what can delimit our emotional strength to cope with life. I think certain defensive patterns cut us off from potential emotional fortification. The severely paranoid person won't fully know curiosity's delight. The profoundly obsessive person will cling to routine too much to fully enjoy life's surprises. The chronically depressed won't be lifted up by joy. The intensely schizoid person won't feel the healing warmth of love. When we cut ourselves off from significant emotional experiences we delimit our own resources for coping with our lives.

My faith in the system of emotions and its power to modulate intense feelings will have a (consciously unscripted) impact on how I live my personal life, as well as how I work. As a woman pours out her anger at her boss I will be (inwardly) partially entering into her emotional state (see Chapter 2 on the interpersonal nature of this process). But, because I am always me, I will also be internally moving toward my own emotional balance, as naturally as a photosynthesizing plant inclines toward the sun. This is not a script, but an essential part of who I am. It is inherent in me to strive toward integrity, that is, the wholeness of consistency between what I intellectually believe about emotional balance and what I am currently feeling with my angry patient. Thus I will incline toward my own emotional balance, not to serve as an example for the patient, but because I need to do this, in order to be myself. However, if I am open about the process of struggling with the emotions that the patient and I evoke in me, I will, hopefully, naturally demonstrate something about regaining emotional balance. Because this is not a deliberate strategy, game plan, chess move, but comes out of a genuine need on my part, it will be possible for the patient to identify with it. In other words, as patients watch, I struggle to regain emotional balance as I contain my countertransference to them. What they witness in me is related to what they feel, but not the same, since it is passed through the prism of who I am. But to the extent that it is similar, they get to see a person who arches toward balance while being impinged on by the patients' anger. In that my process is related to theirs I will resemble their old objects (Racker, 1968) in some way. But I am also a new experience in many ways, including my ongoing effort to reclaim emotional balance.

Assumption 6: What we each feel about our own emotionality depends on the interpersonal "socialization of emotions." (Tomkins, 1963)

Everyone has a history of how others have reacted to our expressions of each of the fundamental emotions, and this history is a significant aspect of our identity. Clinically, therefore, it is meaningful to understand, for example, a person's reputation for being angry. Was the patient as a child known to have violent tantrums? In first grade was he or she handled like a time bomb? This has enormous impact on the people they became in their own eyes. A "rageful" little boy is likely to grow up to be a rageful big boy, partially on the basis of inborn temperament, but also because of how others have responded to him, and how he has come to think of himself. "Studies have found that even in infancy, emotion expression styles have considerable stability over time, and that toddlers' expression styles predict behavioral outcomes in later years" (Izard, 2001, p. 251).

I think of this emotional identity as a very significant aspect of who we each are to ourselves. No less for analysts than for anyone else, this emotional profile can contribute or detract from self confidence, self esteem, and expectations from interpersonal life. In a sense, we each develop a certain "reputation" with each other and with ourselves, which can become an inflexible prejudice. Do I see myself as unable to change how I act when I am angry (or anxious, sad, ashamed, and so on)? Do I see my teenager or spouse as hopelessly unable to maintain emotional equilibrium when provoked?

In my clinical experience, it can be particularly troublesome when we develop hardened stereotypes about the emotional capacities of those we are closest to. It is so easy to fall into "he always blows up," or "she is always too emotional." Thinking we know each other well has its advantages and disadvantages.

What do I think I know of Anna's style of being agitated, and my style when confronted with someone's agitation? We are probably each aware of only a portion of our assumptions about each other. As analysts I think we have a special obligation to become increasingly aware of our unformulated beliefs about human emotionality in general, as well as any rigid stereotypes we carry about our own and our patients' emotional natures.

Assumption 7: The relationship between emotion and cognition is not unidirectional.

Sometimes emotions shape cognitions, and sometimes cognitions are primary. A voluminous literature passionately advocates various conceptions of the relationship between cognition and emotion. Some authors provocatively advance notions that deny importance to one or the other, but most are more balanced in their appreciation of the importance of cognition and emotion in human experience. An important tenet of Izard's differential emotions theory (1971, 1977, 1989, 2001) is that "... emotions do not always depend on knowledge or cognitive mediation, (that) emotions make independent contributions to individual and social functioning ..." (2001, p. 250).

Psychoanalytic theories have taken a variety of positions on the question of how cognition and emotion interact, and the related issue of the existence of unconscious emotions (Rapaport, 1967). What does it mean to say an emotion exists, but is not cognitively recognized or, in Stern's term, formulated (Stern, 1997)? To believe most in the power of the cognitive, consciously verbalized insight to modify emotion is very different from a fundamental belief that it is mainly felt emotions that have the power to modulate intense feelings. Our analytic literature often takes for granted that cognitive insight most persuasively alters experience. But, in practice, analysts increasingly turn toward "enactment," or actual felt experience, to evoke emotions that facilitate change (see, for example, D. B. Stern, 2005; Stoeri, 2005). The topic of the roles of cognition, emotion, conscious formulation, and enactment in the therapeutic action of analysis is, of course, complex, and I will not attempt to summarize it. But I do suggest that it is consonant with discrete emotions theory to view insight as most often following, rather than creating, emotional and behavioral change, in treatment and other walks of life. Discrete emotion theorists would not be surprised by the idea that the most powerful aspect of the analytic engagement can be an emotional experience that is never verbalized or even formulated. Thus, through the concept of enactment, some analysts are coming to a belief about therapeutic action that is consonant with emotion theory's reliance on the power of unformulated, lived-out, emotional experience.

Because I believe unformulated emotions are often primary in treatment (that is, shaping cognition more than the reverse) I trust them to do much of the work. Thus, with Anna, I believe my calm is, itself, a significant interpretation, whether she consciously registers it or either of us names it. Her felt experience of my calm will contrast with her felt experience of her own agitation. This will tell her there is more than one way to live at this moment. My calm *experientially points out* her agitation; it does not merely modulate it. Does it tell her more, or does it tell her less, if we verbalize the contrast? Can unformulated emotional experience be more powerful than verbalized and formulated insight? What do we gain, versus what do we lose, if we use words to interpret the interaction between her agitation and my calm? I am not trying to glorify emotionality or the unformulated, or minimize the significant role of cognitive formulations and verbal interpretation in analysis. But I would argue that once I have begun to formulate what is going on between me and Anna I have decreased the emotional contrast between us. *That is, once I start to put our interchange into words she is likely to be less lost in her agitation.* The sharp contrast between her agitation and my calm will be less palpable. I suggest that something extremely useful may be gained by the increased clarity, but something highly significant therapeutically may be lost. My point is that conscious verbal formulation inevitably alters the emotional exchange. The change in the emotional climate that formulation brings may mainly facilitate *or* diminish therapeutic effectiveness.

As will be discussed in Chapter 2, this does *not* mean I deliberately, consciously choose to be calm because I think this is what Anna needs from me. I am calm mainly out of my own needs. I have felt some of Anna's agitation but resisted it, using my way of creating emotional boundaries, which naturally differs some from Anna's. Thus, manifesting my personal emotional signature can, itself, be an interpretation. It says there is more than one way to be a human being. Neither my way nor Anna's is *the* way to be human, but each is *a* way to be human. For any of us, knowing there are other ways facilitates mentalizing (Fonagy, 2001). That is, contrast teaches us each something about ourselves we might not have otherwise realized. Levenson has often remarked on the clinical usefulness of the saying, "The last one to know about water is a fish." Without an experience of contrast we can't be aware of the "water" that is all we have ever known. To know myself I first have to experience the contrast between you and me.

Emotion theory gives us a way of understanding how unformulated interpersonal emotional experience can facilitate change. The patient gets an opportunity to know what it is like to metabolize life differently. *This gives him or her a chance to become more familiar with how he or she usually metabolizes emotional experience. I emphasize that the message to the patient should not be "here is how you should be," but, rather, "there is more than one way to be."*

An analogy might be useful. As children gain exposure to friends' families they learn that other families operate differently from their own in some ways. This increases their awareness of their family's particular characteristics. Similarly, in group therapy, patients often have the chance to see new ways of interacting, live and up close, and thereby to understand more about their own interpersonal style. Contrast is inherently freeing because it says, implicitly, there is more than one way to be human. It is inherently educative because it allows us to register what has been too consistently present to be consciously noticed.

Thus, the analyst's enacted contrasting emotional style is, itself, an interpretation of the patient's style. My calm told Anna how agitated she was, more convincingly, I believe, than any verbal interpretation possibly could. I suggest that at some *later* point, discussion of the interchange might be very useful, to underline and clarify the meaning of the contrast.

Assumption 8: Emotion theory and interpersonal psychoanalysis have both posited that our emotions inform us about ourselves, in addition to communicating our experience to others.

Thus, for example, it can make a difference that I think of Anna's agitation as, in part, a message from Anna to Anna. If she begins to hear it that way, too, she will appreciate one of its values. The ability to remain in touch with one's feelings has been seen (Spiegel, 1980) as vital to remaining free from an alienated depression. One goal of treatment can be improving the patient's ability to recognize nuances of different emotional experiences in herself. Promoting this requires the analyst to be highly attuned to nonverbal expressions of these nuances, in himself and the patient (Buechler, 1997).

I believe in the clinical utility of these assumptions about the motivating functions of the emotions, their operation as a system, and their relationship to cognition and to formulated experience in treatment. While no theory will ever tell the clinician the best focus in a session with a patient, these ideas can provide guideposts. Taken together they point to the significant role of unformulated interpersonal emotional experience in opening the patient to an increased awareness of who he or she is.

But what can help the patient get beyond increased self-awareness? In other words, what can make a difference in how a life is lived and how it feels to live out that life? Here is where insight is often simply not powerful enough, as legions of clinicians have discovered.

The emotional sources of the capacity to effect change are the same for the clinician as they are for the teacher, theologian, or political leader. In thinking about this I am guided by my own experience and my faith in the motivating power of human emotions. But I think I do not differ from many others in my belief that to be transformed in any meaningful way we need to be inspired by an emotional experience.

The moment of inspiration and transformation has been a favorite subject for visual artists. Whether we look at Michelangelo's miraculous Sistine Chapel or countless portrayals of the Annunciation, we see a magical transition. Spiritual passion inspires a life and it changes course, because it is *touched* (whether symbolically or in actuality).

God's finger touches Adam's in order to transform him. I think the human truth these artists tap is that we need to be touched (emotionally) in order to be moved (emotionally). The story of someone making a real difference is as old as humankind and, to my mind, it is essentially a story about love.

2

Empathic Recovery of Emotional Balance

In that special way we intimately know some few people I know Arlene, who walked into my office just about 1 year after the termination of her treatment. There is no need to create a sense of "us." It is there as soon as she enters, for I have known her in her earlier youthful struggles with relationships and professional possibilities, and I have wondered, with her, whether she could overcome psychological and medical obstacles and conceive a child. Within the peculiar confines of an analytic relationship, she and I celebrated her daughter's birth. But, even before that, I was the absent member of her wedding party, the one missing from the pictures, but, in other senses, in them all. Like the invisible playmate some young children imaginatively create, I have been a constant unseen companion. Perhaps, at times, I am now in the way. Have I outlived my usefulness? Might Arlene's husband wish I wasn't in the bedroom as he hopefully gathers her into his arms?

Today I need to let go of this worry, to be with her. Her face is lined, tired, grayer than I remember. It looks flattened. Even before I hear what has happened since we last met, I feel sad about what life does to us all. For a brief moment I remember a film I saw recently. Interviews of aged movie stars interspersed with clips of their youthful performances on stage, their fresh, exuberant faces so moist compared with how they look today. Life has dried them and, like flowers pressed between pages, they are near to disintegrating. Time's dehydration of us all seems so unfair as I look at the familiar face of my patient.

Tears immediately break over Arlene's face, as though a face could know it needed moisture. I wait, because it might be kinder than pushing to understand everything at once.

As I will discuss shortly, some might call empathy "feeling into" what she feels. But for me that is only the first step of empathy. I do feel weariness, but I am not content to dwell in it. Perhaps I should linger there longer, but it is in my nature to keep moving. Thus, I momentarily feel something like *her* weariness, but it quickly becomes *my* weariness, which I respond to in *my* "signature" way.

I am listening as Arlene tries to pin down her unhappiness, to collect and identify it, like a butterfly specimen. I try, too, to name her misery, as though we could soften it by knowing what to call it.

It is as automatic for me to register what I am feeling as it is to breathe. Usually I don't have to focus on either one. It is only at the most dire moments that it becomes necessary to remind myself to breathe, or to register my feelings. Both seem a bit unnatural when they follow a direct command, but they do inevitably obey.

This time, as I feel her face with my eyes, I focus on the missing joy. Other things are missing, too, but joy is most conspicuously absent.

I look for it. Assuming it might be found is one way I can contribute to our work. When she is ready to wonder what is wrong, when her question seems clear enough, I will have my own question to offer her. Somewhere, in the midst of a considered and considerate life, she has lost all the joy. I believe that depression, like so much else people come to treatment for, does not change until the way life is lived changes. It may sound simplistic but I believe the fabric of a life—the routines that make up the daily grind—have to change before how life feels can be different.

What have I done so far? I felt her face. Her tiredness registered and called out my version of it. Once I was feeling *my* tiredness it evoked what tiredness tends to evoke in me. I crawled out of it, in some way that is characteristic of me.

In another example, a patient enters her session tense, wound up tight. I recognize a state I have seen many times before. Nerves jangled, words tumble out at a fast clip, in a high-pitched voice. There is no pause, no rest. Statements have question marks, and questions have exclamation points.

The room has gotten smaller before I realize it. I am unusually aware of my stomach and I lean forward. I notice the way I am gripping my pen.

And then I find myself talking slowly, steadily, as I resist being drawn into her maelstrom, in my way of resisting maelstroms. Am I being empathic?

Clinically, this question seems moot, since I know how hard it would be for me to stay inside this affect storm. If I don't seek some kind of cover I will resent "her" disorder too much. I will be too anxious to escape her, along with escaping "her" affect.

Rescue can take the form of simply wondering what happened. How did I get swept up in this so quickly? Why? Curiosity somewhat saves me, as it slows me down. Thinking makes a difference. The room is no longer pressing, oppressing, because I am partially outside it, looking in at two women talking. Why are they so charged up?

With each question I ask myself, my breathing gets steadier. I believe the empathy in this is not "feeling with" or "feeling *into*" but, rather, "*feeling out of.*" It is true that I had to get caught up in the tension in order to long to escape it. I believe it quickly became my personal brand of tension, which called out my personal longing for escape. That longing was important, because it moved me to access my emotional resources for dealing with maelstroms. This prepared me to be able to offer something potentially possibly useful to the patient if she, too, wants to escape her maelstrom. Of course she might feel differently about maelstroms, and might not long for escape. If this is true, she will probably experience my behavior as non-empathic. But it still might be the only viable option for me.

Getting to Know the Elephant

Most of us heard, as children, that a group of blind men couldn't agree about elephants because each one touched a different part and extrapolated, thinking he knew all there was to know about elephants, when he was acquainted with only a select portion. In this chapter I argue that a similar confusion reigns in our understanding of "empathy." To me it seems that empathy with anxiety is a very different creature from empathy with sorrow. Yet they are usually collapsed in a concept that is supposed to describe both. Authors explore the nature of "empathy" as though it does not matter whether one is empathizing with someone's anxiety, sorrow, shame, or hope. No wonder empathy is so hard to pin down. In this brief historic "tour" I list some of the ways we have thought of empathy. (For a more extensive discussion, see Blechner, 1988 or Sharma, 1993.) In what follows, I name what I find most notable in each author's perspective.

It seems appropriate to begin with Aristotle, since the word *empatheia* appears in his *Rhetoric* (Rhys translation, 1924). It came to be used to connote the quality that allows us to appreciate art.

What do we make of this root for the word that describes a process so central to analysis? I am reminded of Rilke's warning to prospective art critics, "With nothing can one approach a work of art so little as with critical words: they always come down to more or less happy misunderstandings (1934, p. 17)." It seems to me that what is relevant is that the spirit of artistic "empatheia" is an uncritical "taking in."

References to this idea reflect a commingling of the disciplines of philosophy, aesthetics, and psychology, which seems fitting. In her extensive review of the concept of empathy Sharma (1993) outlines its German roots in Theodor Lipps' (1903) use of the word *einfuhlung*, which describes how we identify with a work of art and develop an internalized representation of it. In the same decade, Titchener (1910, in Sharma, p. 3) was using the English word empathy to mean "feeling oneself into."

Freud's (1921) perspective on empathy (in *Group Psychology and the Analysis of the Ego*) was that it allows us to understand what is most foreign to us about other people. But it was Ferenczi and the interpersonalists who developed the notion that when we empathize, our own subjectivity colors what we perceive. Ferenczi (1928, p. 96) suggested that, in treatment, the analyst's mind moves back and forth between self observation and empathic perception of the other.

It seems to me that much of this literature focuses on the boundary between self and other, asking just what happens in that region during an empathic moment. Sullivan, with his usual originality, dramatically departed from previous perspectives on what happens at the borders. Sullivan's understanding differentiates one emotion—anxiety—from all others. He believes that the process of early transmission of anxiety differs from the process of transmission of any other emotion. To my knowledge, Sullivan was the first analyst to emphasize a difference between how a particular emotion is communicated vs. how others get across the "border" between people.

From Sullivan's (1953) perspective, early anxiety in the infant is experienced through contagion:

> The tension of anxiety, when present in the mothering one, induces anxiety in the infant. The rationale of this induction—that is, how anxiety in the mother induces anxiety in the infant—is thoroughly obscure. ... I bridge the gap simply by referring to it as a manifestation of an indefinite—that is, not yet defined—interpersonal process to which I apply the term empathy ... although empathy may sound mysterious, remember that there is much that sounds mysterious in the universe, only you have to get used to it; and perhaps you will get used to empathy. (pp. 41–42)

What is most relevant to the present discussion is that Sullivan singled anxiety out, privileging it compared with any other emotion, in both its mode of transmission and its tremendous impact on other aspects of human experience. Sullivan's view of anxiety differs from his view of other emotions in that:

1. Infants develop anxiety during the process of socialization. In other words, it comes from experiences with others. It is, from that standpoint, the ultimate interpersonal emotion, in that it is literally a product of an interpersonal process.

2. Most often, since it is the anxious parent who evokes the child's anxiety, that parent is not, at that moment, capable of doing anything to ameliorate it. This can lead to an escalating of the anxiety, with it snowballing as it passes from parent to child, back to the increasingly anxious parent, and so on. (1953, p. 53)

3. Unlike other negative feelings, anxiety cannot be effectively modulated by another emotion such as curiosity. Anxiety interferes in cognitive abilities, so distraction does not bring relief, as it might with other painful feelings. More generally, anxiety clashes, in a sense, with all the other emotions, rendering them incapable of their usual modulating influence. Sullivan (1948) expresses this in a rather schematic style:

> … anxiety combines with other tensions only in opposition. In vector terms the tension of anxiety is always at 180 degrees to any other tension with which it coincides. Moreover, other tensions cannot suppress or defer activity resulting from anxiety. (p. 4)

4. Anxiety affects consciousness in such a way as to preclude clear representation of it in awareness. Thus, anxiety is hard to manage, both interpersonally (as has already been noted) and intrapersonally. Sullivan (1953) puts this succinctly when he says "There is in the infant no capacity for action toward the relief of anxiety." (p. 42)

Sullivan is differentiating anxiety from other emotions, in its induction, impact, and in its status, in a sense, outside the usual possibilities for relief. I would suggest that this thinking has much in common with the assumptions derived from emotion theory in the first chapter of the present book. Like an emotion theorist, Sullivan does not assume all feelings operate similarly, and, aside from the special case of anxiety, he expects emotions to have the strength to modulate each other.

Sullivan insisted that the empathic connection between infant and caregiver is the channel through which anxiety, a potentially highly disruptive experience, is communicated. This emphasizes both the interpersonal nature of anxiety and the importance of viewing each emotion as a separate phenomenon. My own view is that we should expand these ideas, to look at:

1. How different emotions are communicated differently. I suggest it is not just anxiety that has its own way of jumping the gap between one person and another. In subsequent chapters I explore this notion more fully.

2. The emotions as separable self states in human experience. Each emotion has a history in the individual, and affects consciousness in its own unique way. Thus, for example, one way I can think about myself is to explore what anger has been like for me throughout my life. What kind of angry child, adolescent, and adult have I been?

3. How each emotion affects cognitive functioning, including the limits of conscious awareness.

4. The interpersonal aspect of empathy with each emotion. Empathy with a patient in sorrow may pose a different clinical challenge from empathy with someone experiencing tremendous rage. Studying how empathy differs with each discrete emotion may help us understand some of the difficulties we face clinically. For example, if a man is feeling strong anger *and* fear, what does it take for his analyst to empathize with *both*? Is that possible to do? While it seems likely that what is possible depends on the individual analyst and his or her empathic capacities, there may also be some emotional combinations that are frequently especially challenging. Just as Sullivan saw empathically ameliorating anxiety in the infant as extremely difficult, so might we find that the presence of certain combinations of emotions (in either participant) often threatens the survival of the treatment relationship.

The Empathic Power of Modulating Countertransferential Emotions

To the idea of empathy as an interpersonal process that differs depending on the emotion most intensely involved, I would like to add an emphasis on active modulating empathy as opposed to what I will call passive mirroring empathy. The sense of empathy as merely reflecting emotions back was the original conception of it, as has already been suggested. "Feeling into," or entering the patient's emotional state can, of course, be a very significant element in a therapeutic response. But I suggest it is often not enough. I cite many situations throughout this book where the analyst's empathy had to manifest as an active process, helping the patient balance his or her emotions, not through any directly educative behavior on the part of the analyst, but, at first, via the analyst's self care of his or her own emotional state. Just as, on an airplane, we are told to make sure we have a supply of oxygen for ourselves before we try to help anyone else in an emergency, so do we need to attend to our own emotional experience in a session in order to help the patient.

The history of a conception of empathy as an active treatment method goes back at least as far as Ferenczi (1928). So many analysts, including Josephs (1988); Mendelson (1988); Schwaber (1983); Szalita (1955, 1976, 1981, 1988) and a multitude of others have contributed to this literature. I cannot summarize it here, but would refer the reader to Sharma's (1993) excellent synopsis. Blechner, (1988) reviewing various analytic uses of the term, asks "… is empathy just to feel what another person feels? Is it also to understand and conceptualize that feeling? Is it also to find a way to respond to the other person based on that experience?" (p. 303).

Blechner cites Arlow's definition of empathy as an active process. In Arlow's understanding, registering the emotion felt by the other is only the first step. For example, if a mother senses her child's anxiety, and then experiences that anxiety herself, this should be only a transient identification. Her anxious feeling should alert her to the need to act helpfully so as to alleviate her child's distress.

Blechner believes that bundling the therapeutic action into our notion of empathy blurs and confuses the concept. I think that is true, yet once we think we have an understanding of what the patient feels, action is often extremely tempting. For example, when Ferenczi understands the child's identification with his sexually abusing parent he immediately suggests, "If we can help the child, the patient or the pupil to give up the reaction of identification, and to ward off the over-burdening transference, then we may be said to have reached the goal of raising the personality to a higher level" (Ferenczi, 1933, reprinted 1988, p. 204).

One of the tremendous difficulties in the process of analytic training is our lack of clarity about how much it is or is not "proper" analytic technique to try to be immediately helpful to the patient. I will wager that many candidates, reading Ferenczi's words, have breathed a sigh of relief that such a respected forebear so directly advised us to take action to help patients shed their unwarranted guilt. Perhaps, in line with Blechner's suggestion, we should have a name other than empathy for our efforts to help patients achieve emotional balance. But whatever we call this effort, I suggest that it often initially involves better balancing of the *analyst's* more intense emotions. This self-help may take seconds, may be accomplished on an unconscious level, may involve, for example, a lightning-fast identification with our own analyst, or a teacher, or supervisor. It may involve access to our own deep curiosity about human beings, which can tilt us toward an "analytic attitude" (Schafer, 1983). We may, in an instant, draw strength from what I have elsewhere (Buechler, 1998, 2004) termed the analyst's "internal chorus," that is, the mentors whose therapeutically wise counsel we have internalized. But I believe that, without necessarily formulating it, we intuitively call upon whatever can inspire us in order to maintain sufficient clinical responsiveness. I think it is sometimes possible to learn something important from *how* (at this moment, with this patient) we recover our analytic capacity. What I need right now to regain emotional balance may tell me something meaningful about the patient (as well as about myself).

I am proposing that what we can learn from our own process of emotional recalibration is often useful clinically and can form the basis of a type of active empathy. Each time I recover countertransferentially I can learn something about myself, my patients, and their interpersonal lives. I know that my recovery is not entirely like any other interaction in their lives or mine. But, in some important ways, it is not entirely different.

A patient of mine protests whatever she finds unacceptable in an aggressive display of escalating tension. This woman feels tremendous guilt after she argues with her husband, so her anger is directed inward *and* outward. I have always believed this is one of the hardest things to treat. In a sense there is nowhere safe for the patient. Danger lurks in the world and the self. Vibrating rage is everywhere.

The patient moans that she is horrible to her husband and begs me to change her, but also believes this is something she will never allow to happen. She and I are a team, pitted against the part of her that charges blindly, demolishing everyone in her path with her sharp, critical tongue. She knows she will not have many people in her life if this does not change. She has used her verbal dexterity profitably in the business world, but it has been devastating to her personal relationships. The precociously competent only daughter of a successful entrepreneur and his socially climbing wife, she has always been a high achiever. She has piled up ruined relationships like gutted carcasses. She came to me about to add significantly to the pile. She asked me to stop her, since she had finally found a kind, loving partner whose only sins seemed to be forgivable weaknesses. Her plaintive cry, repeated endlessly was, "How can he stand me?"

After a while it seemed like a reasonable question to me, too. What is empathy, in this situation? If it is experiencing what she feels, which "she" do we mean? The "she" that destroys, or the "she" that desperately watches and calls for my help?

I can imagine presenting this material at a solemn case conference. Some colleagues would gently suggest I am not doing analysis. I am pitifully eager to facilitate behavioral change. The poor, benighted analyst, cowed into trying to satisfy a talented bully. What would be likely to follow, I believe, would parallel the presenting problem, but this time *I* would be at the tender mercy of my colleagues, instead of the patient's being verbally violated, (in her childhood, by her mother) or verbally violating (her husband and me).

Of course, my colleagues would be raising a very significant point. Is this emotional interchange analysis? Does my focus on the outcome invalidate it as analytic? After all, neutrality has been understood as evenly hovering attention to id, ego, and superego (A. Freud, 1936). If I align firmly with one aspect, how can I claim neutrality? Put another way, am I not doing psychotherapy, rather than psychoanalysis, if I concentrate on "fixing" the patient? If what I provide centers on behavioral change so much, doesn't that disqualify it as analysis? One of my most fundamental beliefs about treatment is that insight most often follows change, rather than preceding it. Only after we alter how we operate can we begin to understand why we behaved as we did. Therefore, to facilitate insight, *I first have to help the patient change her behavior.* Behavioral change is a prerequisite for profound insight. I must focus, first, on helping this patient change *how* she treats people, so she can ultimately understand *why* she treated people that way.

I return to the question of what constitutes empathy with this badgering patient. I believe there are several steps in the process:

1. First, I feel battered, in *my way* of experiencing this, with my own history and my set of associations to being treated this way. I may "feel into" her experience, to some degree, but I still retain my history, my associations, and my core ways of being a person.

2. Next, I internally react to being in this position, in one of the ways I have available to me, given my limitations as a particular human being.

3. Then, given who and where I am, I fight for awareness of what is going on, using my particular personal and professional tools. I struggle to find a way to bear, and eventually use, what I am feeling. My first task is to return to being what I would call a "going concern." That is, I have to recover from the battering enough to go on with the work. Eventually, exactly how I recovered may teach me something about myself, and, perhaps, something about the patient, but that may not happen right away.

4. As I become more self-aware, my emotional balance changes, first of all because I need that for myself, but gradually, because I am trying to find a way to use this experience to help the patient. For example I become curious. How did the patient and I get here? Other feelings begin to change. I take some pride in what I am doing. I feel some pleasure in the sheer effort, and in the eventual accomplishment of greater self-understanding. At the same time I become less anxious, because I am more focused on my own response (something I can, potentially, control) than on the patient's attack (something I cannot control).

5. Self-reflection prepares me to communicate what I have experienced to my patient. She has already probably intuited much of my process. She knows she threw me off balance, and she knows I recovered. She may not know as much about how I recovered, though, as I think she can with my help. Our question has to eventually become, "What just happened? Why did we go through this? What does it say about each of us?"

I have a visual way of understanding the analyst's active process of empathic self-recovery. Some birds chew up food before giving it to their young in a form they can swallow. I believe I am doing something equivalent. I am working over my emotional experience, first for my own benefit, but soon, to change it into a form my patient may eventually incorporate. This is the form of empathy I most trust.

I am emphasizing that an important aspect of this empathy is its reliance on righting my own emotional balance. When I can emotionally recover from my patient's verbal assault, I will be able to use *how* I recovered as information about us both.

It is not mere semantics to say that I define empathy as including this whole process of regaining emotional balance. If I tilt off balance physically I will instinctively try to right myself. The "off balance" moment contains in it information about my natural inclination toward balance. Similarly, my experience of being off kilter with my patient contains information about her impact on others, and, probably information about how she was verbally thrown earlier in her life. But it also speaks about who I am. It would not feel as it does if I were not built, as a human being, as I am. It is, in a very real sense, a product of an interpersonal interaction. Both being thrown and recovering contain, in how I live them, information about me and information about my patient. *The whole process of being thrown and recovering is my way to empathically know my patient.*

It is fundamental to my interpersonal belief system that I can feel only my version of the patient's feelings colored with my history of relationships and life experiences. I don't believe the patient can "project into me" her experience, without its reshaping, in me, to fit into the context of my emotional vocabulary. In me, her experience is in a different affective milieu. This creates a therapeutic opportunity. It allows me to chew it up differently and re-present it to her. While this way of perceiving the analyst's role is not unusual, my emphasis is on countertransference as a system of emotions that can be modulated through a change at any point in the system. *How* I regain a workable balance potentially tells me something vital about how the patient and I operate.

Hopefully, the words I find for my experience elicit further thoughts. When I tell her what I did to come back to her she may remember something, or realize something that helps us recover the origins and the meanings of her verbal bombardments. We may then pursue understanding of their place in her current life. How her own objectives can be better served will usually occur to her at some point, without my having to say anything.

Mattering

But why would a patient care about what I am experiencing? This raises the question of how the analyst gets his or her way of coping emotionally to be of enough interest to be noticed. We have to become salient enough for patients to be observing us closely, just as we observe them. Just by being our patients, they stimulate us to notice how they function, but how do we get the same attention for ourselves? In other words, how do we get *the patient* to have an "analytic attitude" *toward us*?

It is difficult to describe how one human being becomes important to another. What do we have to do to matter enough to be watched? I think one way is to be emotionally open, transparent, readable so that patients become interested in what they can learn from how we tick. When patients really feel, in Sullivan's (1953) terms, that they can "expect to derive benefit" from knowing me, I have gotten their attention.

Perhaps a simpler way to describe this is to say that patients have to feel that they will learn something from watching how an analyst lives with them. They want to pay close attention because they are curious about me, or feel they can learn from me, or both.

Returning to my battering patient, I think that, for her, being all wound up is a safer way to be angry than screaming. I think of this as halfway to depression. If depression is, in one sense, a kind of anger directed at the self, then this spiky tension, this electrified charge, is anger that is (partially) pointed toward the self, but still has the feel of active anger, rather than the deadened look of depression (subsequent chapters spell this out further). The direction is depressive, but the atmosphere is alive with anger. Personally, I would rather have a patient revved up than inert. I think there is more of a feeling of hope.

I remember a time I could not bear another patient's tension, and I told her she had to be quiet for a while. It was hard for both of us, I think mainly because it inevitably felt like I was treating her like a child. What softened the impact of this, I think, was that she knew I was desperate. I had borne her tension many times before, so it was clear I really couldn't this time.

I think for this person, as for me, this affective state is difficult, but preferable to a dead depression. Her extreme childhood isolation and bleak depression left her willing to accept any alternative, as long as she didn't have to feel dead again. Whenever she feels slighted, disregarded, unappreciated, her tempo quickens. I feel the fit coming on, and I tend to take cover by moving a few inches away from her emotionally, watching her and waiting for her to observe what I am doing. Sooner or later she comments on her observations of me, because she cares enough about having me in her life that she is afraid of alienating me, and because she thinks I might discover something potentially useful to her in the way I live with her tension.

Once we have found a way to matter enough to be closely observed, how can we recover emotional balance vividly enough for the process to be informative?

Settling for Hate Rather Than Indifference

An almost comical example of the struggle between an intensely emotional woman and her longsuffering analyst is reported by Bollas (1987), in his work with "Jane." Few tales can reveal treatment's humorous as well as agonizing potentials as clearly as the saga of this patient's determination to get a rise out of him, no matter what it took. In a particularly pointed interchange, Jane complains "don't you think it would be nice if you could just be a teensy bit warmer (a gushing effusive laugh follows this). I mean, I wonder if you could just be a teensy bit warmer. Not much warmer. Just an insie bit. It's just that you are so cold" (pp. 227–228).

We could view Bollas and his patient as having an argument about normal emotionality and its expression. Each is trying (verbally and behaviorally) to convince the other to change. Each is saying to the other, in effect, be more like me, and we will have a better relationship. From Bollas' point of view his patient's emotionality is a symptom and a resistance. In his own (hardly classically analytic) words to Jane, he tells her "it's my view that if you could convince yourself to stop being so goddamned traumatic, then I could be quite a bit more at ease with you...." (p. 228).

But what is Jane's view? Perhaps it is that Bollas is cold to her, not because she traumatizes him with her affect, but because he sees her affect as pathology, its control as progress, and whatever makes him uncomfortable as an attack.

A dialogue about healthy emotionality is a time-honored spat between analysts and their patients. Most commonly, male analysts have tried to convince their female patients to tone down their emotionality, while female patients have argued for more affect from their analysts. The patients see the analysts as withholding affect. The analysts see the patients as suffering from a pathological excess of affect. Like certain marital battles, this argument seems to have a robust life of its own.

What would our conceptions of health, defense, resistance, analytic attitude, therapeutic action, and the goals of analysis be, if we really believed in the power of emotions to modulate other emotions? How would our thinking about treatment change if we first concentrated on our own emotional balance before we focused on our (often unarticulated) goal of muting the patient's emotionality?

I am suggesting that one concept that would be affected by this shift in thinking would be our understanding of the role of empathy in treatment. Let us take the aforementioned Bollas and Jane as an example. While I know I am conjecturing, it does not seem to me far fetched to imagine Jane as filled with hate toward an analyst she experiences as cold and unyielding. Is empathy the act of feeling Jane's hatred for Bollas along with her? Momentarily, perhaps, but certainly, for the health of the treatment (as well as both participants) the process should not stop there. I suggest the analyst's empathic response would have to include:

1. Momentarily feeling Jane's hate, so as to register it.
2. Experiencing the hate in one's *own* way of feeling this emotion. That is, when I experience hate it is within the context of my emotional life. I hate in my way of hating. No one can "project into me" their way of hating (at least, not for long). Hate, like every other interpersonal experience, is different when it is embedded in a particular context. I have a personal history of hating that I bring wherever I go. I can only hate in my way of hating. And when I hate, whatever I associate with hating will be part of my internal reaction. If hating makes me anxious, I will get anxious. If it makes me ashamed, I will feel shame. If it evokes guilt because of aspects of my interpersonal history, I will feel guilt.
3. *Now I will begin to struggle toward balance* in a way that has been shaped by my interpersonal life history. Let us say, for example, that hating easily makes me feel guilt, since it violates essential aspects of who I feel I should be, and how I feel I should conduct myself. But because I am struggling to refind balance (and I believe that is absolutely essential to my life's work) instead of feeling escalating hatred and guilt, I might begin moving toward a kind of transitional emotional space; an "as if hating" and "as if guilty" state.
4. Probably, by this point, I would be comfortable enough to become curious about what just happened, and why. I would think about this, which would be likely to further change my own emotional

balance. Now hate has been modulated by guilt, "as if hate," "as if guilt," and curiosity in me.

5. Making this whole experience available to patients in some way is the greatest therapeutic challenge. It may not always be helpful simply to talk about it. Sometimes, particularly if patients have developed a strong "analytic attitude," and are vigilant observers of me, talking about what just happened would be most effective and useful to them. But I think that much of the time my immediately verbalized, undigested self-reflection may either do the patients no good or, perhaps, distract them from themselves in an unhelpful way. I believe that the vogue for the analyst's self-disclosure can have the appearance of great honesty, directness, and equality, but its overall impact on patients can be negative, at times. Patients may feel so indebted to the self-revealing analyst, and so flattered by his or her confidences, that they can't formulate how focusing on the analyst's experience has rendered them unable to concentrate on their own problems, or worried that the analyst is too self-preoccupied and vulnerable to hear them.

6. My notion of active empathy is embedded in the next step. My experience of struggling to regain emotional balance is likely to prime me to *hear* the subsequent material differently. What it took to recover my capacity to work analytically will bring some aspects of the material into the foreground. Formulating this is, for me, at the heart of the process of therapeutic empathy. *Thus, in my view, therapeutic empathy requires the analyst to experience a change in his or her countertransferential emotional balance, retain (or regain) the ability to be curious and work analytically, selectively attend to material that resonates with this emotional sequence, and eventually formulate the meaning of the entire chain of events, often with the patient's help.*

There is no recipe for this aspect of the work (fortunately, I would say). In the example of Bollas and Jane, having just recovered (in his *own* way of recovering) from his version of Jane's hate, Bollas might be unusually responsive to themes of hate and expiation in the material that followed. If I were in Bollas' shoes, given who I am, my experience of just having recuperated from the danger of overwhelming guilt about hate would prime me for dealing with guilt issues, and it would be unusually easy for me to hear them in the patient's material. This would definitely not be a preprogrammed strategic response. I think, as such, it would not be therapeutically effective. I am not planning to create a hate-and-guilt exercise, but I am, now, unusually ready to deal with those emotions as they occur in the process. Empathy, to me, is most often initially expressed by the analyst's recovering enough from the countertransference to selectively hear themes that are resonant with his or her recovery process in the patient's material. Analysts may not, at this point, be aware of this selectivity in their focus. But their ongoing self-reflection should, at some point, make them aware of it. As they become able to formulate their experience, the question of what to share with the patient becomes salient. This is a clinical judgment that, in Hoffman's (1998) terms, requires spontaneity rather than any ritual or predetermined technique.

The Many Sides of the Moon

In what I find an extremely moving account, Mitchell (1993, pp. 215–221) provides us with an example of the complexity of responding empathically when more than one intense emotion is evoked in both patient and analyst. He tells the story of his work with his patient Sarah, a dancer in her 30s and the daughter of a very prominent, and very controlling performing artist. Sarah and her father conducted their relationship, in part, via his harsh criticism of her dancing. Mitchell portrays a tyrant whose narcissism seems to allow him limitless license. His sadism was supposed to be taken as constructive, his selfishness as necessary to the realization of his genius.

We enter this triangle just as Sarah has a chance for an artistic accomplishment of her own. She is about to audition for a celebrated dance company. Sarah and her analyst use this situation to explore their roles with each other. Briefly, one question becomes whose agenda should shape the last session before the audition.

In this context, Mitchell is so wary of enacting the role of the dominant father that he tries to avoid being any kind of father to Sarah:

> Sarah longed for a more benign but still powerful and dominant paternal figure. Her project—finding a better father—was something I saw as part of the problem, not part of the solution. A central part of my problem and challenge in the countertransference was to find a way to be with her that was neither malignantly nor benignly paternal. (p. 215)

Later, Mitchell admits

> ... I found her extremely appealing as a patient/daughter. She made
> it very easy for me to feel fatherly in a way I found quite pleasing and
> reassuring, and she had many qualities that I could only hope my own
> much younger daughters might have when they reached her age. There
> was something very compelling and enticing about the opportunity she
> offered me to play out the role of a kindly and very helpful father to a very
> special daughter. (p. 216)

It is with profound sadness that, reading these lines now, I realize
his early death robbed him of the chance to be a father to his own
daughters in their adulthood. The loss for him, for them, for his colleagues and friends, and all who knew him, is immeasurable.

I mention this because I think that, ironically, mourning for a lost
father is extremely relevant in understanding the clinical vignette.
I believe that trying so hard not to be Sarah's father may have precluded Mitchell from a full awareness of the mourning experience
that was an important part of the therapeutic task with her. For me,
this illustrates one of the central challenges of the empathic process.
When we feel strong empathy for a patient, can we recognize that
what we are feeling may privilege one emotion over others that may
be equally salient to allow the patient's treatment to be fully effective? Mitchell felt Sarah's angry need for freedom and psychological
space. But because of the intensity of this emotion I think he was
not able to *also* empathize enough with her sorrow. It may be especially difficult for us to empathically actively respond to certain pairs
of emotions, such as the coincidence of anger and mourning that I
believe occurred for Sarah.

Sarah was unable to free herself from a larger-than-life father. She
was so busy being him or not being him artistically that she couldn't
find her self. It seems that her need for legitimized separate space
was relatively easy for Mitchell to empathize with. But I think she
also needed her analyst to be unafraid of occasionally fathering her,
so that his style could help her *mourn the loss of the perfect father* she
could never have in reality. Mourning may be even harder to understand when it involves someone still alive. But I believe part of the
reason Sarah came to treatment was to mourn the better father she
was just beginning to see she would never have, and to mourn the
aspects of her father she had to renounce, to find room for herself.
But mourning a renounced father can require exquisite emotional

balancing of sadness alongside the other emotions that can complicate grief.

Here is where I believe Mitchell came in. Could he be a father
who would facilitate this delicate process of mourning? What kind of
father was needed for this difficult task? Of course my view can only
be speculative. But looking at this case material allows me to explore
how the clinical situation can be understood differently, with the
importance of actively empathizing with *each* of the patient's intense
emotions in mind.

I would suggest that Mitchell was avoiding the gratification of
letting himself fully inhabit a paternal role with Sarah because it
seemed counter to his sense of what was appropriate for him as her
analyst. His tremendous zeal to free Sarah made it difficult for him
to see her other needs. It made it hard for Mitchell to empathize
with Sarah's grief as much as he empathized with her yearning for
freedom. I imagine Mitchell would enjoy looking at the case now as
an example of the incredible complexity built into our role as analysts. From my point of view, he had to feel the pull to parent her, the
pull to refrain from parenting her, the pull to save her, and the pull
to help her mourn. After recognizing his countertransferential tilt
toward protecting her from all the fathers that might impose their
agendas on her, he needed to realize that his focus on the material
reflected his way of dealing with his countertransference. Becoming Sarah's protector from overbearing fathers allowed Mitchell
enough of a feeling of emotional balance to continue their work, but
it cost him part of his empathic vision. His personal resolution of his
countertransferential slant allowed him to know about her needs for
space more than her need for fathering, and her yearning for freedom rather than her choked off mourning.

How could the empathic understanding resulting from a fuller
recovery from the countertransference have played out clinically?
First, I would say it might have led the analyst to push harder for
more frequent sessions. In the vignette he tells us that in order not
to be the bad father he "… chose to accept the frequency she was
comfortable with as the lesser of two evils, knowing in my bones
that it was, even if arguably the lesser, still an evil with consequences
we would have to discover and contend with" (p.216). I think if he
had forcefully advocated at least two sessions a week Sarah would
have had to deal with his imperfection as an accommodating father
and the difference in their agendas for the treatment. This would

encourage her to define herself, partially through contrast. It might also further her knowledge of the absence of the perfect father and her need to mourn him.

In short, I think Mitchell didn't want to be too good a father to Sarah because that felt inappropriately gratifying to him, but he also didn't want to be another harsh, unyielding, selfish father, because that felt too hurtful. He was left with no acceptable alternative—tied in knots, in a sense. In his own words:

> There seemed to be no way for me to help her maintain her agenda that did not feel like a demand that she submit to mine. In my efforts to figure out how to help her avoid getting churned up, I was getting very churned up indeed. The position I felt boxed into was making me angry at her, and I felt there was no way to interpret what was happening without using interpretation as a retaliatory act. (p. 218)

I suggest that Mitchell got caught up in the issue of her anger and need for freedom from submission to her father. The emotional freight of this countertransference rendered him *unable to fully empathize with the sorrow* of her loss. I feel this to be a very common problem. Countertransferential empathy with one strong emotion makes it very difficult to simultaneously empathize with other feelings that may be equally important to the treatment. Changing our view of empathy so that it reflects an understanding of discrete emotions may enable us to think about this more clearly. I would suggest that empathy with anger moves us in an entirely different way from empathy with sorrow. When we empathize with a patient's angry need to assert we are mobilized for action, and we often feel centered, coalesced, and purposeful. When we empathize with sorrow we are likely to be in a very different emotional state (subsequent chapters will deal with these differences more fully). Each of us, bringing our own emotional history and proclivities, might privilege one of these feeling states over the other. But unless we are alerted to the idea that empathic availability with each emotion is a very different process, and that the task for the analyst sometimes includes holding contradictory positions at the same time, we may not catch that, in our powerful emotional reaction we have recognized only one part of the empathic challenge. Could Mitchell have felt Sarah's angry need for freedom from submission and her sorrow at the same time, even though feeling these two emotions at once is inherently difficult for a human being? In recognizing the selective focus that resulted from his particular way of dealing with his countertransference, could he have come to a fuller empathic understanding of the many sides of Sarah?

One of the phrases I remember Mitchell using often was, "There is no way to interpret outside the transference." The truth of this is apparent, I believe, in this vignette. Mitchell really had no choice about being a father figure to this patient, and, inevitably, he would at some point become authoritarian in her experience just by being a separate person. Her recognition that this father, too, was not perfect, that no father ever would be, that the perfect father had to be mourned (that is, let go of *and* retained as an inner object) that in differing with him she might find herself, all were aspects, I would say, of the work ahead of them. Does it matter if Mitchell and his patient did the work of assertion first and the work of mourning later? I would say that it does, in that part of what I think Sarah needed to experience is how a human being both asserts and sorrows at the same time, since that tremendously wrenching simultaneity is an aspect of the human condition that she was struggling with on her own. So, from my point of view, empathy with Sarah requires struggling with many countertransferential pulls, learning how they shape how we hear the material, and, eventually, collaboratively with the patient, formulating enough to make it possible to learn something new about the interpersonal "signatures" of both participants.

It is always risky to interpret the dreams of someone we don't know personally, but this dream of Sarah's seems so apt, to me, that I feel I should include it here:

> There is a hazy early part of the dream which I do not remember, but has something to do with a man who has gone. Then I am walking at night, turn a corner, and become suddenly aware that something terrible and frightening has happened with the moon. The illumination of the moon has somehow become separated from the moon itself. The light has become detached from the dark sphere of the moon, which is only very dimly visible. (pp. 220–221)

Of course this dream could be understood in many ways. I focus on the man who is gone, that is, the man she has lost. Mitchell sees the moon in the dream as representing the patient, who has never been treated as generating her own light (glory). To me it seems that the dream is the story of losing a man. She has to turn a corner, only to face a sudden, frightening, terrible awareness. The terror is in the inevitable detaching, splitting off. Just by starting out she has lost him. There is no way to take this journey without a sudden jolt. In a good sense, turning the corner means she is on the road that leads toward seeing. But what she will see is inherently sad. Our story is always one of loss, separation, bifurcation, a man who has gone, from whom we have to walk away, alone, into the dark. What can make the journey bearable? Love, connection, joy, wonder, the fathers we find and refashion along the way, and the deepened awareness of our own separate vision that, however dim, is all we ever have to guide us.

Mitchell clearly felt deeply for Sarah's angry assertion against her father's tyranny. Trying to protect her from any hint of tyranny, Mitchell couldn't simultaneously experience the mourning that was also, I believe, at the heart of this treatment. I suggest that ideally he would have "felt into" Sarah's mourning for the good father, inevitably experiencing this loss in his subjective way. Then, he would have to (partially) recover his emotional balance, again, in his particular way of recovering. Frequently, I would say, the most empathic use of this whole experience would take the form of a heightened sensitivity to the issue of mourning in the material. Not as a game plan but as a natural inclination, he might, for example, center on the "man who has gone" in the dream Sarah reported. The analyst's empathy could initially express itself in an (unformulated) selective focus on this man as representing the idealized father who "has gone."

Thus, for me, empathy with Sarah would include: (1) "feeling into" her sorrow, as well as her anger, but really (2) feeling sorrow and anger subjectively tinged by the *analyst's* emotional history, and then (3) recovering, some, in the analyst's personal style of recovery, and (4) emerging with unusual readiness to hear material about anger and about mourning as they occur in the patient's material, and, eventually, (5) talking about this sequence, if not immediately, then at some later point.

This empathy frees the patient to be fully herself. She impinges on the analyst, and they both learn from this experience. She can count on him to respond to her impact in what he privileges as he hears her. Most importantly, she can count on his ongoing capacity to be emotionally affected and yet always remain himself.

On Being Unable To Empathize

By way of summary, I will recount a clinical experience of my own. It occurred on a Friday. I had almost completed an especially draining week. As the last patient of the day headed toward the couch I was momentarily distracted by a sinking sensation. A familiar image came to mind—the baseball pitcher, left in the game for one too many innings, wearily lobs the ball way outside the strike zone. Where is the coach who should have taken him out of the game before this happened? Where is the relief pitcher who could take over, fresh from enough rest to do the job right?

My weariness was partially the result of the number of hours I spent in proximity to the sorrows of the human condition. Our literature makes much of the vicarious traumatization clinicians often feel from hearing accounts of their patients' abuse. This is, at times, tremendously painful. But what of vicarious yearning? What of our exposure to all the other ways life brings grief, terror, impotent rage, and, perhaps worst of all, unremitting resignation?

Living through so many kinds of sorrow did not, I reflected, prepare me well for this last session. Even though it was Friday I was still in the grip of Monday's news that a very aggressive cancer had resurfaced in a patient who had had hope for a few more good years. I had shared, and even helped nurture those hopes. I had wanted her to believe in them for her sake, for my sake, for our sake.

The week had given me many chances to test out my theory that the analyst's empathic process includes learning from her own recoveries. On Wednesday I heard about how a beloved parent, sinking into Alzheimer's disease, no longer recognized his grown daughter. And yet he still looked a lot like her daddy, the big gentle bear of a man, who could often be cajoled into singing, or reading a story.

But now it is late on Friday, and someone is lying on a couch in my office and talking about how difficult it is, nowadays, to get stores to take back imperfect merchandise. What happened to the era when they would stand behind their products? The patient wonders whether this pisses me off, sometimes, too.

It doesn't take her long to exchange that inquiry for another. How come her analyst is so very quiet today?

Let me be clear that I am not advocating any particular response to this patient. I am not expecting myself to commiserate, agree, or feel any specific emotion. I do, however, expect myself to be an analyst. To me this means I expect myself to struggle toward a fundamentally curious emotional state. There will be many times I cannot achieve this stance. But I believe I can struggle toward it and learn something about myself and the patient in that process. As I struggle

I will hear the material selectively, with aspects that resonate more strongly than others. Eventually, with the patient's help, I hope to formulate what happened, and what it means about each of us. To me the empathic process includes all of these steps, and what we can learn from them.

My version of empathy with my complaining patient includes:

1. Entering, rather than backing away from, my sense that her problem sounds trivial to me, at least on its concrete surface.

2. Beginning to wonder why I am so ready to hear only the level of her communication I can so easily trivialize. Perhaps I would rather feel contempt for her, or anger at her, than stay with the sorrow that has been this week's overriding feeling. Do I want to use her as a diversion? Am I looking for a way to feel stronger? Might a distancing emotion, like anger or contempt seem to offer me relief, or at least greater cohesion?

3. Retaining, as backdrop, all my previous thoughts, including the range of human sorrows as I experience them. But also beginning to think about other potential meanings of this patient's words. What could her complaint mean, in the concrete situation as she describes it, but also in other contexts, and at other symbolic levels? Perhaps things really aren't the way they used to be *between us*. Maybe she can't find a complaint department that will give her restitution for a damaged analysis or a damaged life. Perhaps the world, or, at least, her world, has changed in ways she finds unacceptable. Maybe she wants to know if it has changed for me, too. Maybe she feels she needs to know what *I* do when I am given something irreparable, and expected to accept it. Might saying any of these thoughts be helpful to her?

4. Relevant to the topic of empathy is my belief that I can learn something about myself and something about my patient from what it takes to move toward a fundamentally curious stance with her. In this case, recovering required me to recognize my countertransferential angry contempt, and ask why it was so unaccompanied by other feelings. Since I believe that the emotions exist in a system, how was my angry contempt affecting my other potential feelings? And how was the week's grief still impacting me? In other words, what was the overall balance of my emotions, which usually available feelings were missing, and what would it take to regain enough of a curious stance to use the moment in the service of the treatment? How was my struggle with my countertransference shaping what I could hear, and what I selectively inattended in the material?

I hope I have made it clear that I am not expecting or wanting myself to ignore the difference between a broken lamp and a broken father. Nor do I wish to regard all injuries as equal or dodge negative transference/countertransference feelings by focusing on them at a removed, symbolic level. What I do want to do is emphasize that in my role as an analyst I believe I am always losing my emotional balance, to greater or lesser degrees, and in ways that privilege some parts of the material over others. Every alteration in my emotional balance is a potential opportunity to learn something new about myself and my patient. Formulating this ongoing process is part of what can make it maximally useful as a learning experience for us both, although I do believe that it can be therapeutically helpful even before it has been fully formulated.

I would also like to highlight that I differ from those who would see my feelings in terms of projective identification. I don't think anyone can "put" their emotions or early experiences into me, as though I were a receptacle or blank canvas. When I feel angry contempt, for example, it is my version of angry contempt, no one else's. It may have been (partially) triggered by the patient, but the way I feel it is a product of my history as a human being and the other emotions I am feeling (or not feeling) at the time. I have my own history of feeling contempt, of times it surfaced, of other peoples' reactions to it, of other emotions it tends to recruit in me. I bring that history with me everywhere I go, including the chair behind the couch in my office. I am always me, being contemptuous in my way of being contemptuous (if that is the predominant feeling I am having, at that moment). If, in my life experience, being contemptuous became something deeply shameful I would bring that to the session with the patient who was complaining about the imperfect lamp. I have been myself for many years. She can't insert into me a new history of what it is like for me to be contemptuous. If, until today, contempt has easily recruited my shame it is likely to do so again in our session. Of course, the patient has a great deal to do with what I feel. Of all the potential Sandra Buechlers, she brings out some more than others. Each one that she brings out influences which others are also likely to be elicited, as well as which are unlikely to make an appearance today. But she can only bring out, in me, an analyst with *my* history of angry experiences, joyous experiences, and all the other emotions I have known.

Making a Difference

How does our recovery process make a difference in the patient's life? With Arlene, the patient whose entrance into my office began this chapter, I felt sad (in *my* way of feeling it) and struggled (in *my* way of struggling with sadness). My understanding of the interpersonal aspect of my position is that I see my response as *occasioned* by my contact with this patient, but *shaped* by *my* personal history of experience with sadness. No one "puts" their sadness into me, as though I were an empty receptacle. My lifetime of emotional experience comes with me to the office in the morning. I never leave it home and come to work blank.

Even though the only sad I can know is a Sandra Buechler-shaped sadness, it has much in common with other peoples' sadness. Similarly, my profile is unique *and* similar, in some ways, to other peoples' profiles. Thus, when my eyes feel Arlene's withered and weary face, they immediately recognize her sorrow. For I, too, have known how sorrow can exhaust us, and how tears can, ironically, dry us out.

So far I have merely registered a feeling, in my way of experiencing it. Felt by me, in my heart, it is Buechlerish sadness, but it is still sadness. There are probably many parallels to this. One person's perception of a color is near enough another's for us to use the word "blue," but there are also differences. Some blues immediately remind me of those delicate shades Fra Angelico used when he painted angels. Seen by me, in my eyes, this blue is a Fra Angelico blue. I can see blue only with *my* eyes, and feel sadness with *my* heart.

As I mentioned at the beginning of this chapter, struggling with the sadness Arlene occasioned in me, I felt an absence of any joy and wondered about it. For many reasons, this is a very Buechlerish way of being sad. It reflects my bred-in-the-bone-belief in a system of emotions (as discussed in Chapter 1). It is also active, looking for what is absent at the same time as it senses what is present. And it is curious. One might say it is a very alive way to be deadened. I think it is shaped by my defenses, my character style, the way I cope with being human.

This empathic process will eventually make a difference for Arlene because, in some way that cannot be predicted, scripted, or prescribed, it will affect how I am with her. Perhaps I will be unusually ready to sense the missing joy in her next dream. Or, my language may contain references to sadness and joy embedded in discussions of other matters. Or, I may focus on my own sadness and joy, perhaps without any (consciously formulated) clear understanding of why. I am inwardly prepared for an interchange about this topic, which is likely to affect my focus in the session. I will (unconsciously) seek chances to talk about sadness and joy, and, when they occur, I will respond to them.

Thus, in the analyst, *the active empathic process of recovery from an emotional imbalance creates an inclination toward noticing related material.* I want to emphasize that this is usually outside the awareness of the analyst; unnoticed and unformulated.

So now I am poised to respond to sadness that is present and joy that is missing. How will this make a difference in Arlene's life? First, to the extent that the patient and I differ in how we respond to an emotional imbalance, the contrast can teach us about ourselves and each other. This does not have to assume that my response is in any way better or healthier, but only that it is different. Any difference from usual can let the "fish" know that he has always unknowingly relied on the availability of "water." That is, by empathically experiencing and recovering (to some degree) the analyst changes the atmosphere, *which points out how things were.* The analyst's style of empathically experiencing may not be any more effective than the patient's, but it will differ in some way, and by differing it will provide contrast. This has some chance of clarifying the patient's style of coping. But, perhaps equally importantly, it implies that there is more than one way to be. Thus, my patient may intuitively apprehend my search for the joy that is missing. For her this may be an unfamiliar response to sadness, so it may help her feel some hope that change is possible.

But, even if Arlene becomes clearer about how she usually responds to sadness and feels some change is possible for her, this may not make a significant difference in her life. What does have the power to make that kind of difference? Winnicott's (1971) concept of the capacity to be alone tells us that our aloneness is colored by who we are alone with, when we are alone. That is, if we have internalized the presence of others we are better emotionally equipped to deal with life's inevitable challenges. When my patient watches me struggling to regain my emotional balance with her, she is has a chance to internalize an aspect of me. I may not regain balance in a particularly effective way, but I will struggle in a characteristically Buechlerian way. From that point on, in a sense, *her* struggle with sadness becomes *our* struggle with sadness. This is a qualitative change that has the potential to make a difference in how this moment, and, more broadly, how the rest of her life feels to her.

Arlene and I have had a long history with each other, as I suggested in this chapter's first pages. I have had many chances to matter to her enough for her to take aspects of me inside her. I believe that my presence in her inner world *has* made her less painfully lonely, so it has made some difference, but, obviously, not enough. I would wager that my inner presence has helped keep her from self-persecution at this moment. Before our years of treatment she would have attacked herself for her sadness, blaming herself for being unsatisfied with a life that, outwardly, has many privileges. In our previous work together, I entered her inner world enough to soften that response. This time she took her sadness as a signal to come back to treatment, not as a sign of pain that must be suffered alone.

And yet, despite our many years together, despite her personal and professional achievements, despite knowing real joy, something has not changed enough. What more can my empathy do for her? As we go through emotional experiences together, Arlene will have more chances to sense how I recover when I am with her, or to ask me about it. Because she cares about me, and about having me in her life, my recovery process will matter to her. Of all the things she could focus on, it will probably command her attention often. She will bring me her sadness; I will feel it in my way, and try to feel my way out of it and recover my emotional balance. We will watch me do this, and learn about ourselves and each other. More importantly, we will both have a greater motivation to learn than we would each have on our own. I will *want* to recover and learn something from it, for my own and for Arlene's sake. Arlene will *want* to become better at coping for me and for her self. Just as a child takes her first steps into a parent's arms we all grow, partly, to make someone else beam.

I believe there are two basic ways we make a real difference in peoples' lives. First, if we can become important enough to the person to be internalized, our presence in their inner world can change how it feels to be them. They are never again as alone as they once were. And, hopefully, the best of our intentions toward them bring out their capacity to care for themselves. Ferenczi (1929) noted that we are not born knowing how to take care of ourselves, but we learn how by internalizing parental caretaking (if we are lucky enough to experience it). I think patients can internalize how the analyst takes care of the patient, as well as how the analyst takes care of herself. This internalization can both decrease the feeling of being alone in the world and increase the capacity to take care of ourselves.

The second way we make a difference is by becoming someone worth growing for. The poet Rilke put it beautifully when he argued against relationships' being occasions for merging (1934). On the contrary, he said, they are "a high inducement to the individual to ripen, to become something in himself, to become world, to become world for himself for another's sake ..." (p. 54). Whatever Arlene becomes, I think much of her growth will be for herself. But I believe some part of it will be for me.

3

Empathic Responses to Shame

For countless single women the years of feminist literature have not had much impact on the proclivity to be ashamed that they are not in a relationship with a man. Shame shadows some of these women, becoming their constant companions. It goes with them to the movies on lonely Sundays. For some, Sunday is the only day they can allow themselves the public disclosure of going to the movies alone. It counts as less of a pronouncement of defeat than the same solitary trip on a Friday or Saturday night.

But even on Sunday their state of manlessness defines them. They enter the darkened theater and look around, less for the ideal place to view the film than for the ideal seat to be inconspicuous. They are careful to buy a moderate snack, to prevent anyone from concluding they are nursing their aloneness with a binge. Popcorn without butter says they still have hope, while a huge chocolate bar would signal that their search is over, and they have settled for sugar's lonely consolations.

Before the movie begins they look around, hoping to recognize no one. With luck, the film can, at least, provide a 2-hour respite from shameful desperation. Of course, this assumes they have chosen carefully, avoiding movies with moments romantic enough to miss the casual warmth of a draped arm, or the easy familiarity of holding hands. A mistake in the movie they select can leave them sobbing at all the wrong moments, crying for themselves while the heroine celebrates her romantic adventure.

Clinically, we know these feelings are not exclusively the province of women, but we meet them more frequently in our female patients. Many women who can muse philosophically on most aspects of the human condition are reduced to early adolescence alone in public on a Saturday night.

Privately, the pain can be exquisite. The joys of a richer life seem just beyond their reach, so tantalizingly close, and yet so far.

In treatment there is only one topic: WHAT AM I DOING WRONG? That there is some fatal tactical error is not merely a hypothesis. It is an unquestionable, fervently held dogma. Without this assumption there is no hope. If the problem is something in her approach to meeting men, that can be changed. But if the problem is not what she does, but who she is, there is no sense trying. Or if the suspicion that the game is rigged is the truth, and there just are no more good men available, there is, at least, the cold comfort of victimhood. Most therapists have learned the potentially high price of questioning this premise.

With such a patient my modest inconspicuous wedding band can feel gaudy and weigh heavily on my finger. I have had the fantasy of removing it before the session out of decency. Of course, I don't. Generally no mention is made of its presence, but once in a while it evokes resentful comparisons. I have occasionally felt a strange, illogical combination of reactions from the patient. It is as though she feels our merit has been assessed and I cheated somehow and won unfairly. Or, the tone can be more depressive, self-blaming. Unlike the patient, I am thin enough, successful enough, smart enough, emotionally healthy enough to be desirable. Sometimes shame, anger, and envy or jealousy combine. The patient is fixated on comparing my (fantasized) life to her own, with my life coming out ahead in every category.

This backdrop can frame a treatment ostensibly focused on the patient's quality of life. She speaks of wondering what is going on behind her married neighbors' closed door. She describes the heightened tension of a family event (when she can bring herself to attend one). For her, all eyes seem to stare at the chair next to hers. Why is it occupied by her cousin, and not by a man who believes her good enough to be his life's companion and partner? She has been summed and found wanting, in more than one sense.

To point out the patient's shame is to exacerbate it. Shame is, to my knowledge, the only negative emotion that invariably heightens when given attention. We may or may not become more angry talking about our anger, or more fearful talking about our fear, but we inevitably redden talking about shame, because the self-consciousness of shame increases in the spotlight.

Because analysis requires patients to verbally expose their feelings, shame is potentially a substantial aspect of the work. But shame is a significant aspect of human experience, and not just the province of the unmarried female psychotherapy patient.

I believe that, while shame often announces itself with easily recognizable signs, it just as often appears in disguise. Is the child who balks at going to graduation suffering from shame or rebelling against authority? Is the quiet child expressing a normal variation of temperament or frozen in fear of being shamed by saying something others deem foolish? How much is shame the central problem of the depressed adolescent? For analytic patients (and their analysts) when is the couch preferred for its technical advantages, and when is it a convenient way to avoid literally and figuratively facing shame?

Shame's role in treatment, and, more generally, in all human experience, has been the subject of many articles and books, particularly since Kohut's (1971) and Helen Block Lewis's (1971) ground breaking contributions. Many books (e.g. Lansky and Morrison, 1997) have been devoted to summarizing its part in the treatment dialogue. No comprehensive survey will be attempted here. My first goal is to describe my clinical experience with three forms of shame: shame profoundly connected to anxiety; shame embedded in the context of anger; and guilty, regretful shame. This will illustrate how some emotions modify each other. My second, more technical objective is to suggest some ways of working psychoanalytically with shame that take advantage of treatment's dialogic opportunities. Briefly, these include:

1. Treatment can provide a dialogue about shame that makes clear the differences among shame, shame about shame, fear of shame, shame and guilt, shame and anxiety, shame and envy, and other distinctions.
2. The analyst often has a chance to spare the patient shame by taking it on herself or at least by sharing it.
3. The analyst can sometimes reframe shame by being unafraid of it.
4. The meaning of shame can be altered if other feelings that are being experienced can change. For example, I have found clinically that one of the most effective "antidotes" to shame is pride. Being proud of the courage to face oneself can balance shame about what one has to confront.

The concept developed here is that shame, like other emotions, is profoundly affected by the company it keeps. Shame in an "atmosphere" of curiosity is not the same as shame surrounded by rage or accompanied by fear. Rather than ask, for example, whether the fundamental sources of shame are Oedipal or pre-Oedipal, I focus on shame that recruits anxiety separately from shame that evokes anger or shame that is closely aligned with guilt. Like a primary color, shame is a range of experiences. While central to it is a feeling of insufficiency there is a vast difference between shame or anxiety that evokes dissociation and angry, raging shame or self-reflective, guilty shame. In general, I suggest that emotions, like coping styles, seldom occur in isolation. No one is purely paranoid, as paranoid coping easily recruits schizoid withdrawal in some, while in others (perhaps due to natural endowments and interpersonal experiences) it recruits obsessive tendencies. Thus, the "flavor" of your paranoia differs some from mine. We each have some degree of capacity for paranoid functioning, though that degree may greatly differ. Just as we each have some potential for paranoid, schizoid, hysteric, obsessive, depressive, and narcissistic coping, we each can experience the profound shame or anxiety that acts like a circuit breaker, shutting off input to prevent further flooding. But each of us also knows other "flavors" of shame, though to varying degrees. I may rarely have moments of shame/rage or shame/anger, in which feeling insufficient immediately recruits a furious response. But, perhaps, I often have another kind of insufficiency experience, a self-reflective state in which many negative evaluations of myself blend. In these states I feel shame/insufficiency, but also a kind of guilt (that I have failed myself and others) and, perhaps, regret. This "brand" of shame may be characteristic of me, but not of you. Of course, human experience is too complex to be adequately pigeonholed by two-word descriptors, but I think shame/anxiety, shame/rage, and shame/guilt give a sense of these emotional states more accurately than when shame alone is discussed. Thus, instead of the question of whether the source of shame is Oedipal or pre-Oedipal, I focus on whether the shame is anxiety ridden, angry, or guilty/regretful.

We have not always adequately recognized shame's inherently interpersonal nature, and how it differs from other closely related emotions. Nor have we consistently acknowledged shame's adaptive functions and how it is modified by other feeling states (see Chapters 1 and 2 for a general discussion of how the emotions operate inter- and intrapersonally). After considering shame's role in the family of emotions, I look more specifically at the clinical situation and what the analyst does that may intensify or delimit the patient's shame as well as her own.

Generally, shame is an interpersonal comparison (Morrison and Stolorow, 1997). The self is being unfavorably compared with a more ideal other. In addition to shame, this comparison can evoke anger, anxiety, envy, fear, curiosity, and jealousy. My point about this is that an alteration in any of these emotions in either treatment participant affects all the emotions in both. My shame affects your anger, and your anxiety will impact on my curiosity. The clinically useful corollary of this is that we can have an effect on any emotion by addressing any other emotion (Buechler, 2004). We are not necessarily stuck trying to diminish the patient's shame by addressing it. This is similar to the situation when we try to treat depression. If we focus on the depression itself we can become obsessively fixated on it and hopelessly lost in failing attempts to change it.

While shame takes many shapes its most dramatic form, in my experience it is accompanied by anxiety. Though shame and anxiety may seem to blend, I think it can be crucial clinically to tease them apart and examine the sources of each. As opposed to a classical Freudian, Kleinian, Ego Psychological, or Kohutian approach (Lansky and Morrison, 1997; Michels, 1997; Bacal, 1997) I assume that the sources of an individual's shame and anxiety can *not* be predicted by *any* predetermined theory, but must be discovered via the psychoanalytic process. Each of us has known inadequacy, but which human predicaments have most vividly elicited this feeling differs according to our personal histories. Shame/anxiety is, I suggest, the earliest form of shame, and expresses the helplessness inherent in the human condition. In these moments we feel we *must* be able to do something that we cannot do. But this could be most deeply attached to hunger for some of us, and for others, connected to a confusion of love for an unavailable parent. Still others may have known their deepest shame/anxiety in the face of an opaque, unreadable parent. The analytic process uncovers the tributaries of the individual's shame/anxiety, as well as the wellsprings of her rageful shame, and her guilty/regretful shame. Thus, for me, Schafer's (2003) distinction between Oedipal and pre-Oedipal assumptions about the primary sources of shameful feelings has limited clinical application, because, for each person, *different human situations* may have provided their most profound experiences of anxiety-ridden shame. In general, it seems to me that where drive theorists saw conflicts between instincts and society, the interpersonalist can focus on such recurring human dilemmas as the "impossible/necessary," that, although played out differently in each person's history, often recruit certain combinations of emotions such as anxious shame (for a thorough review of analytic and other revisions of drive theory, see Safran and Muran, 2000).

Traumatic Shame: Shame and Anxiety

The session is unremarkable so far. A middle-aged man is recounting his unpleasant feelings of difference and insecurity with his colleagues. The topic is familiar to both of us, because he has raised it often in our decade of analytic work together.

It is near the end of the hour and I decide to comment. As I frequently do at this point, I make a summarizing remark, inviting the patient to step back with me and look at an overall pattern. The patient has been describing his preoccupation with a recent observation that some of his team mates at work show signs of being as unsure of their popularity as he is. At the same time, though, he bemoans his ongoing inability to take a stand on the issues the team is confronting. They are a group of educators, trying to find common ground in shaping next year's curriculum. As often happens, this task evokes considerable controversy. In the heated discussion two camps are forming, allegiances are solidifying, and my patient will have no voice in the decisions that will be made if he does not speak up now.

My remark connects his last two points. I say that, first, while it is relieving for the patient to realize he is not the only insecure person on the team, he remains concerned about his social position. Second, worrying about how others will assess and feel about his input keeps him from focusing on his beliefs and formulating a personally meaningful position.

Perhaps because this material does not seem particularly new or challenging to me, I am especially startled when the patient then says, "I couldn't hear you." I ask what he means. He says that he heard my first point, about his relief, and he knows that I made another point, but he couldn't hear it and would like me to repeat it.

Suddenly I am more intensely engaged. I express my curiosity about why he didn't hear my last point. Did something else preoccupy him at that moment? Was he aware of the approach of the end of the hour and did that take up his attention, or did something else occur to him?

We end the session, but come back to this interchange the next time we meet. He again asks me what I had said and I repeat it, wondering why he could hear the first point and not the second. He suggests that the first point makes him feel good about himself, while the second makes him feel bad. Seeing insecurity as a common human feeling makes him seem like everyone else—"normal." But realizing that, unlike many others, his insecurity keeps him from formulating an opinion on a significant issue makes him feel ashamed.

By now I am aware that:

1. It might be very useful to understand *how* the patient didn't hear me. That is, just what were the patient's cognitive and emotional experiences during the moments he was "not hearing" me? I believe his mounting shame quickly recruited anxiety, which, as Sullivan suggested (1953) acts like a blow on the head, that is, has a predictably dramatic effect on cognition.

2. The patient's reaction seems to me very much like a response to trauma. He can't (or won't) hear. It is as though his psyche drew a "line in the sand," and refused to take in anything that could further his shame/anxiety.

3. *We are enacting the content in the process.* That is, the patient is focused on my response to him as I interpret his preoccupation with how he is perceived.

Work with this patient and others has led me to believe that shame, accompanied by anxiety, operates very much like a micro-trauma, eliciting momentary dissociation. A significant part of the experience is lost to memory. Thus, it doesn't get processed in any potentially corrective, productive ways. Furthermore, because talking about shame can elicit more shame, the "trauma" and the dissociating response often repeats in the session.

In this example the patient is an extremely observant person who is very familiar with analytic process. He was aware that he had missed part of my comment, and interested enough to point this out. When I said that his insecurity kept him from formulating an opinion, he felt ashamed of this limitation *and* of being seen and described this way by me. The process enacted the content in that he is ashamed (1) that his insecurity keeps him from formulating an opinion, and (2) that I see him as someone who has this handicap and am describing him this way in the session.

Of course, it is quite possible that my description evoked feelings other than shame/anxiety for this narcissistic injury—such as anger at me. Many aspects of this interchange are interesting to me, but for now I am centered on the "not hearing" as a trauma response. Much like Freud's definition of the traumatic as anything that overwhelms the ego, my comment was too much for him to take in. He avoided being flooded (and, perhaps, enraged at me) by not hearing me. We could see his not hearing as a form of rage, rather than as a way to cope with potentially engulfing shame/anxiety. Or, as is so often true with clinical material, many emotions may be present. But in any case, I believe snowballing shame and anxiety were part of his experience, and "not hearing" was a way to delimit potentially traumatizing affect.

My reaction to the interchange included a moment of sharp anger. Why? I think this is not just because of the time wasted (see below for more extensive exploration of this countertransference to the patient's self esteem protection). I think my response was partially shaped by how intense the patient's response appears to me. Shame's impact on cognition can be so severe as to seem unbelievable. How could the patient "not hear" me? It feels too extreme not to be willful consciously intended resistance. In other words, my own self esteem has been wounded. How dare the patient choose not to hear my point! His self-protective shame avoidance seems like a powerful, primitive enemy, capable of halting our progress and estranging us. As though the treatment suffered a sudden stroke, we have lost our capacity to communicate.

The cognitive cost of experiencing the combination of acute shame and anxiety could suggest that human beings would be better off if we could eliminate shame from our emotional vocabulary. And yet, in many ways, it can be a tremendous ally in treatment and other interpersonal contexts (for a discussion of clinical uses of an understanding of shame, see Nathanson, 1992, 1994, 1997).

The Social Value of Shame

The social value of shame has been documented, as well as its value to the individual (Lansky and Morrison, 1997). Hanson, (1997, p. 173) for example, called shame "social glue." I would like to add to the testaments to shame's contributions to interpersonal connectedness.

Adam and Eve have been portrayed in ways that I think illustrate the pain and the potential for connection in self exposure. In Giotto's painting of them in the Arena chapel in Padua, Italy, Adam shields his face while Eve covers her genitals. Each attempts to delimit a different kind of exposure. Perhaps this expresses the exposure that hurts each most. Whether we understand their shame as stemming from their curiosity, their desire, or their daring, they paid for eating of the Tree of Knowledge of Good and Evil by being forever burdened by an acute awareness of human life's limitations. Dust to dust. Giotto pictures the differences in their embodied shame as they set off on their shared exile.

From some points of view this is a cautionary tale about guilt, but from others it may be read as our first lesson in finding salvation in human connection. While Adam and Eve are condemned to leave paradise, *they are bound together* to share their plight and their shame.

Do we see shame as a natural response to exposed intense curiosity, much like the classical analytic view of the child's shame about his sexual curiosity? How much is shame about greatly heightened curiosity a learned, socially induced response? This is a very complex question, because curiosity expresses a need, and the expression of any (potentially unfulfilled) need can bring shame. I am not sure we can know to what degree it is possible for human beings to feel no shame over our needful, dependent state. Being powerless to get what we deeply need is an aspect of being human that may inherently create shame and anxiety, given the universal experience of some unmet need in infancy. We all (in some sense) remember being *not enough* to get what we painfully needed. As was articulated in the previous section, I am suggesting that one reason shame is universal is the universality of our interpersonal experience as helpless infants. Here I focus on helplessness more than the "dirtiness" Schafer (2003) emphasized. I refer to situations that call out acute feelings of insufficiency as instances of the "impossible/necessary." In these moments something beyond our capabilities is nevertheless absolutely vital. Our personal experience of infantile utter helplessness is revisited.

Like mourning, shame can bring us together out of a heightened appreciation of the shared human condition. No one is a stranger to shame. Just as we feel for loss in others because we, too, have known losses, we can identify with shame in other human beings and grow in compassion. Someone's profound struggles to overcome shame-induced inhibitions can evoke our tenderness. Thus, I believe clinicians are often especially responsive to patients who rarely ask for help. It can be moving to see them brave shame to make a request.

It is interesting to think about our attitudes toward humility and how they reflect our feelings about shame. In so many religious texts humility is considered a virtue and a road toward freedom. I think the glorification of humility expresses an idealization of freedom from the need for status. The humble person is, presumably, immune to the shame of failing to achieve an exalted position (for a similar view in a discussion of Nietzsche, see Wurmser, 1997).

Anticipating shame (and other feelings) often warns us not to behave in ways we wouldn't like. Reminding ourselves to consider how our actions will reverberate can help us modulate impulses. Out of an effort not to create bad memories for myself I may make wiser, more considered choices. A woman who struggles with the urge to drink can sometimes withstand the impulse when she thinks about the shame she will feel if she drinks to excess again. A man is able to continue abstaining from smoking because he knows he will be ashamed of himself if he gives in to the impulse to smoke. A mother walks out of the room rather than slap her child, knowing the shame and guilt she would feel later. These are among the many examples of how anticipating shame can strengthen our resolve.

I have often tried to harness the power of this anticipation. I believe that lowered self-esteem is largely a product of how we feel about our *current* ways of living, and not only a legacy from the past. While much shame can accompany memories from childhood, often the more debilitating shame is a judgment against ourselves in the present. We believe we are not measuring up *now*. While the current source of shame may well evoke painful memories, it is, I think, this current iteration that causes the most vivid shame. Clinically, this focuses me more in the present, exploring with the patient how shame is being created now. My emphasis on the present is not a denial of the importance of the genetic roots of shame, but rather the expression of the belief that these roots cannot be predicted by any theory but must be discovered for each person and can often most easily be discovered through a thorough exploration of *current* shame experiences. Fully elaborating current shameful moments and then comparing them with thematically related situations in early life leads to insight about the nature of each individual's ongoing experience of shame. Thus, clinically, an initial focus on the present has the advantage that it may delimit the patient's *creation* of new shame *and* may more efficiently lead to an understanding of shame's genetic roots in that particular individual.

I believe that when shame is not accompanied by fear of shame it can be a very powerful medium for interpersonal connection. For example, years of working with couples taught me to recognize that the treatment often depended on the development of an atmosphere where shame is not feared. One person had to "hand ammunition" to the other for the treatment to succeed. That is, the husband, let's say, had to volunteer to tell about something that the wife could use to prove her favorite case against him. He had to trust that she would not use the moment to cause him shame or guilt. If he withheld everything that could be used to shame him, the treatment probably would go nowhere. Of course, the same is true for the wife. Vigilance about self-esteem can be greatly inhibiting. Material vital to working out the relationship can be lost if either partner is overly concerned about how he or she looks in the session.

On the other hand, moments where one person lets go and reveals something that could be used to shame, condemn, or hurt him or her are often moving. A woman spent long hours in a volunteer job that her partner resented. The partner felt she was privileging the job over their relationship. The woman resisted this idea, but, in a session, revealed that she felt she was becoming obsessed with the job. I think both her partner and I felt respect and gratitude that she trusted us not to use this revelation as an opportunity to say, "I told you so." She did not let a fear of shame stop her from asking for our help. I am sure this elicited deeper compassion in us than we might otherwise have felt.

I suspect that fear of shame is a problem more often than shame itself. Like much of what we fear, the anticipation is worse than the actuality. When we fear shame less we can have the experiences that might actually help us feel greater self-esteem. A woman spent many years exiting potential relationships, fearing they would, in one way or another, make her look like a "loser." Fearing shame kept her from having experiences that might have garnered her increased self-respect as well as joy and satisfaction with her life. As I believe is true for many emotion combinations, fear and shame can be much harder to bear than shame alone.

Shame's Companions

The companions shame keeps shape its impact. Thus, shame laced with regret and guilt is a much more potent brew. On the other hand, shame modulated by positive emotions can, I believe, be much more bearable. In treatment I have often worked hard to help people feel pride in *how they live their situation*, rather than shame about the situation itself. More than anything else, pride seems to me to have the power to delimit shame. But curiosity and other positive emotional experiences can also help. Wondering, in a truly open frame of mind, can counteract some pain. I have often tried to distinguish the question "Why am I in this position?" from "Why the hell am I in this position?" When "why" is truly a question, not a pseudo question, it can evoke genuine curious exploration. Thus I am suggesting that, in contrast to the usual relationship between curiosity and shame, in which heightened curiosity (e.g., about sex) evokes shame, heightened curiosity can *delimit* painful shame. Sources of joy, love, and hope also can help, in that they frame shame differently.

I believe that many negative emotional experiences can be borne if they are not accompanied by other strong negative emotions. That is, for example, shame may be bearable if it is not joined by intense anger about feeling the shame. Similarly, shame is easier to deal with if it is not intensely feared. What happens when intense negative emotions combine? This is the question I would most like to see addressed in a wide variety of clinically informed research efforts. Many fascinating possibilities seem likely to me. Are human beings unable to process some emotion combinations neurologically, psychologically, or both? Are individual differences in this ability greater than similarities? Does this depend mainly on inborn variations or experiences? Do some people get "flooded" more easily with all intense emotions or only with certain emotions in combination? Do intense negative emotions always occur in combinations or are there, for example, "pure" sad, angry, or fearful moments? Do some people feel many negative emotions in "purer" form than other people do? Why? PET scanning studies have shown that people prone to panic attacks exhibit overactivity in the right para-hippocampal regions of the brain, the areas where cognitive information enters emotional networks (Panksepp, 1998, pp. 95–96). More generally, what individual differences in brain activity characterize people who differ in how their emotions tend to combine?

I think it would be important to look at combinations of negative and positive emotions, intra- and interpersonally, neurologically, and psychologically. Do some people find it easier to modulate
negative emotions with positive ones? Why? I believe some people
can alter their angry feelings more easily by becoming curious about
them. Is this entirely learned, or are some people *born* with a greater
capacity for this kind of learning?

Clinically, I often find it most useful to focus on the emotion that
is just outside the patient's awareness. I will wonder, for example,
what the visibly angry person *also* feels. Is he ashamed of his anger,
anxious about its impact, or feeling guilty? It is easy to get stuck,
along with the patient, focusing on the anger itself. People come in to
treatment asking something like, "Why do I frequently get so angry?"
While this may be a useful question I think it can often save a lot of
time to wonder what else these patients feel when they are angry.
Of course, emotions are complicated, and cannot be described fully
with a simple one-word label. But finding words for each nuance can
often lead to greater awareness and a clearer sense of an individual's
recurring emotional patterns (among many others Krystal, 1975,
and Spiegel, 1980, have written extensively about the value of differentiating and naming emotions in treatment).

As clinicians, we would probably all like to think we help our
patients articulate and modulate painful shame. This, of course, is
often far from the case. My own clinical experience is much less
than sanguine. In fact, I often find my efforts increasing, rather than
diminishing the patient's shame.

Countertransferential Lust for Life and the Patient's Angry Shame

When I start thinking about a certain collection of poetry by Adri-
enne Rich during a session with a patient, I know I am in the throes
of a fierce countertransference reaction. The collection is titled *A
Wild Patience Has Taken Me This Far*. This brings me to the topic of
shame modulated by anger, rather than fear or anxiety.

My sessions with one patient were very often bracketed by jokes.
Entering or leaving, he would weave the joke so smoothly into the
material that I did a frequent double take. We came to call it the
"transitional joke," because, like a Winnicottian stuffed animal, it
soothed him in the space between inside (the session) and outside.

In between jokes, though, much was far from funny. Almost any interchange with another person could become an occasion for jousting for position. Who was "on top"? Who got "dissed"? Although the characters shifted, to me the plots seemed remarkably alike. Whether the interchange took place at work or in a social or familial context there would be a conflict of some kind, with the patient experiencing his budding adversary as failing to pay him sufficient regard. Things would find a way to heat up, an issue would coalesce, the battle would be on. For a period of time nothing mattered, other than teaching this adversary an unforgettable lesson.

I am in the wings, watching the latest fight. Just an observer now, I know my time will come. I will be drawn into the ring sooner or later. But for now, I watch from the sidelines. I wonder about my role. Have I been cast as the admiring fan? What happens if I don't stick to the script?

One of the more difficult aspects of this situation, at least for me, is that it feels as if it takes up a great deal of time. Here is where thoughts about "wild patience" often occur to me. I begin to want more than I am getting. I want a bigger part than my role in the audience of the "jokes and jousting" hour. I get more and more impatient. I know I am particularly sensitive to the issue of life wasted, but I feel that nothing is changing.

I become more uncomfortable. I intuit that no matter what I do it will be wrong, in some sense. If I adopt a mirroring, Kohutian stance I feel inauthentic. It would seem to me like I am playacting, only feigning an accepting attitude. If I confront, I feel I am electing to step into a central role in the drama. I am exchanging my part as loyal fan for a leading role as adversary de jour.

As has been noted by others (Levenson, 1983), it is often easier to see an enactment in the treatment when we are supervising the work than when we are engaged in it ourselves. When I supervise clinicians facing the challenge of working with narcissistically injured patients I can generally suggest an approach that allows the participants to talk about what is going on between them. But with my own patients this can be much more difficult.

I think one reason for this is the anger in me about life "wasted." Sometimes I find this so upsetting that I treat the patient's character structure as though it were an obstacle to our work, rather than the work itself. I am, in a sense, narcissistically invested in the patient's dropping his narcissistic concerns. But my anger is not only about my own narcissism. My greed for life itself also feeds this anger. I always want more, for myself, and for those I care about. I wanted my "joking and jousting" patient to "cut it out," stop playing around and get down to the real business of life (as I see it). I am aware of the many dangers of defining the "real business of life" for another person. I have written about the inevitability of the impact of the analyst's values on the treatment (Buechler, 2004). I think our values have an especially strong effect on what we choose to focus on, respond to, ignore, and remember. The inevitability of the influence of our values does not mean we should become blasé about their impact. I believe it is important that we make every effort to be aware of how our values about life are playing a role in our work.

This is a tremendously important issue, and cannot be thoroughly examined here. For further discussion of the inevitability of the impact of the analyst's values, see Greenberg, 1991 and Buechler, 1999.

My anger in this situation often narcissistically wounds the patient. Thus, I *do* shame him. I actually *become* the adversary through my own reactions, and not just his casting me in that role. I believe that with this particular patient, in this particular hour, my anger is, partially, a reaction to my own *other* emotions and his. Like distant music I am aware of a vague foreboding that, unpredictably, life's chances end. I am angry he is (in my view) squandering life, wasting precious time evening scores that exist only in his head. As I stare at my own anger it melts into sorrow for those I have known whose chance to be foolish (by wasting time) has suddenly ended. I feel as though my anger is really a plea, begging him not to waste today, because it could be all we will have.

I am aware of a self-righteous quality in my plaintive decrying of "wasted" time. How can I decide that life spent pursuing pride is a waste? My impatience with his score-settling really expresses my fear we will both look back at this moment with regret. I believe that at its most self-righteous my illusion is that I am representing those who can no longer speak for themselves. Indignant for them, I am saying to my patient, "How dare you waste time in this meaningless nonsense, when life can be so arbitrarily, so painfully cut short?"

So, hearing yet another story of my patient's fierce determination to show the latest antagonist who is boss, I grow impatient. My feeling may be expressed directly, in annoyance, or more indirectly, in failing to join his effort. How I focus is a sure indication of what I judge to be worthy and unworthy uses of time. It seems likely to me that my weary response narcissistically injures my patient. I am telling him that what matters to him should not matter so much. My silent rebuke is like the stinginess of each of King Lear's elder daughters, who indicate Lear should know better than to "need" a big retinue. In an eloquent defense of prideful need, Lear replies:

> O reason not the need! Our basest beggars
> Are in the poorest thing superfluous;
> Allow not nature more than nature needs,
> Man's life is cheap as beast's. Thou art a lady;
> If only to go warm were gorgeous,
> Why, nature needs nor what thou gorgeous wear'st,
> Which scarcely keeps thee warm.
> (*King Lear*, Act II, scene ii, pp. 255–256)

Lear so beautifully reminds us how often our yearnings are not about what we, strictly speaking "need," but about what we *want*, in order to service our pride. Like Lear, my patient is asking me to "reason not the need," that is, to understand that the hunger for pride can be as profound as any other human striving.

Why do I sometimes most resemble Lear's eldest daughters, in my failure to take shame adequately into account? Sometimes I think I act out of loneliness, without being aware of it. Wanting the patient to have some kind of shared vision with me I focus a spotlight on the interaction between us in the present moment and cause the patient *unnecessary* shame.

I think that the patient's shame can be different if she feels it could have been avoided, as opposed to when she feels she has to bear it in the interest of her treatment's progress.

Gratuitous shame often evokes a potent brew of shame and anger that we frequently label "narcissistic injury." The intensity of this feeling can come just as much from the anger as from the shame. In her anger, the patient may be expressing something like, "You didn't have to make me feel this. It was not necessary to our work. You chose to shame me, when you could have chosen otherwise. Maybe you like to see me squirm. Maybe you enjoy feeling superior to me, or reveling in the power to shame me."

I think it is important to realize that the patient is likely to be interpreting our motives just as vigilantly as we may be examining his. As an example, a male patient of my supervisee said he did not feel ready to examine what was happening between them at that moment, so he found it overwhelming when the analyst nevertheless directed their attention to the here-and-now interaction. The patient reacted with discomfort that the analyst took as confirmation of his (Oedipal) interpretation. The analyst thought something like, "I was right. My patient experienced me as his shaming father because I asked him to reveal himself to me." This, in a sense, is true, but what it leaves out is that the similarity in the patient's experience of his father and his analyst stems more from his anger at their deliberately, perhaps unnecessarily, causing him pain, rather than from his shame at being exposed. It is often extremely difficult to distinguish shame from anger at having been gratuitously, willfully exposed, but I think making this distinction can be clinically useful.

Patients are often reading our behavior for what it can tell them about our motives, just as we read their behavior. There are times that I feel it is a priority for patients to be able to trust that, generally, I wish them well and I am trying to preserve their self esteem as much as I can without sacrificing the treatment's effectiveness. I think that, often, the only way patients can engage in a process that deconstructs their defenses is if they believe I care about my impact on their feelings about themselves. Inevitably, treatment evokes some shame, but if it is palpably not my aim to hurt them unnecessarily it does not create the anger/shame combination that, I think, can stalemate the work and heighten the patients' defensiveness *iatrogenically*.

Of course, there are times when the analyst actually does become deliberately hurtful. For example, one male patient is extremely sensitive to perceived rejections. In the past he has reacted with contemptuous behavior, including incidents that have brought him into conflict with the law. His analyst (who is my supervisee) has shown tremendous sensitivity and caring toward him. The analyst has been extremely flexible with the frame, gentle with interpretations, genuinely concerned about the patient's welfare. As is so often the case, the patient finally takes entitlement one step too far, and his analyst becomes intensely annoyed, as if having saved up resentment from the many times he has bent over backward to be accommodating. In this case the patient barrages his analyst with telephone calls between sessions. The analyst feels rage and does not return any of the calls, uncharacteristically ignoring even those that would usually evoke a ready response from him. But then the analyst is preoccupied with worry. What if the patient acts out on this "rejection"?

I suggest that the analyst is paying the patient back for, among other things, narcissistic injury due to the analyst's own overly accommodating stance. The analyst is also vengeful because he feels emotionally blackmailed. He hates the position of being afraid he might set off the patient's dangerous aggression. He is in a rage that this patient's aggression has intimidated him. What, at the time, felt to the analyst like therapeutic empathy on his part, now feels like masochistic surrender. The analyst feels strong wishes never to see the patient again.

This sequence is probably familiar to most clinicians. Many of us have found that the more we expect ourselves to be nurturing to all patients, the more likely we are to run out of the capacity to deal with some narcissistic patients (for a discussion of analytic stances and burnout, see Cooper, 1985). In our attempts to be "empathic," in our concern not to narcissistically injure, we go into overload. In the patient's experience we have suddenly, dramatically changed from loving understanding to hateful rejection. Usually, in truth, our negative feelings have actually built gradually, but this may have been outside our own awareness, as well as the patient's. In any case, we are tempted to act out our rageful countertransference at this point.

Whatever love we had for the patient seems to have vanished. Sometimes patients feel seduced (by our previous positive responsiveness) and then abandoned (by our exasperation). They may have loosened their grip on defensive behaviors, trusting us to look out for their sense of self. Perhaps this mirrors earlier experiences the patients had with others. Reinforced in the patients is the feeling that they eventually drive everyone away, drain everyone of positive feelings toward them (for an elegant discussion of the history of negative responses to "narcissistic" self interest see Zweig, 1968).

Here, I feel, is the moment when our own relationship with shame can make a big difference. If we are not too afraid of shame and guilt we can sort this situation out with the patient. We can look at how we played a part in creating a treatment frame that was, ultimately, not viable. I would suggest that our greatest impact may come from how we deal with our own shortcomings. If it is palpable that we are affected but not destroyed, we both may benefit from the exchange. That is, if becoming aware of our participation does not elicit too intense shame, guilt, regret, or narcissistic rage, our behavior may say to the patient that facing limitations is part of being human and can be borne.

What can enable us to modulate our own shame, guilt, and regret when we see that we have unwittingly acted something out that threatens the life of the treatment? I am suggesting that I know of nothing other than love that is strong enough to propel us forward in such a moment. I am including love for the patient, love for ourselves, and love for analysis in this statement. Our love for ourselves enables us to forgive whatever we now regret of our participation. Our love for analysis helps us find purpose in continuing the inquiry, even when it hurts, and maintaining an "analytic attitude" toward our own behavior, as well as the patient's. Our love for the patient motivates our willingness to do whatever it takes to keep the treatment viable (for examples of the maintenance of analytic concern in approaches to narcissism, see Bromberg, 1986, and, of course, the work of Kohut, 1971, 1977, 1984, among many others).

Sometimes this can move us to try to avoid causing shame by prioritizing this over other goals. For example, a patient makes a slip of the tongue that I hear, but decide not to point out. Silently noting is probably the most frequent form shame avoidance takes.

At times, I think if I am reluctant to cause shame it says to patients that I care most about how they feel. The love expressed in this reluctance may mitigate their *fear of shame*. It is often hard to separate fear of shame from actual shame, but it can be useful to do so. Fear of the spotlight is, I believe, most often a fear of shame. A female patient, a highly experienced supervisor with strong opinions about how her profession should be conducted, nevertheless passed many meetings in silence. After much inquiry her fear of shame became apparent and its self-fulfilling aspect clarified. Because she spoke up so infrequently she felt that any comment she did make had to be brilliant. Exploring actual moments of shame was not as pertinent as studying her fear of shame. It is not that this person had been so traumatized by actual shame experiences, although she had suffered many. While she had felt painful shame, it is not just the legacy of these moments that accentuated her fear, but, rather, her adult inability to modulate shame. She couldn't say to herself that it would be over, that the feeling would pass, that she was still herself, that others would still remember her many accomplishments. Her fear was based on what shame could do to her, as well as on what it had already done. Her greatest fear was a fear of the *next* shame experience, not, solely, based on shameful memories, but also based on a reading of her current capacity to modulate shame. This, once again, demonstrates that no theory can predict "universal" sources of shame in predetermined, early stages of development (for a thorough discussion of shame in early development, see Broucek, 1997).

The Couch, the Telephone, and E-Mail

In mid-20th century technology was hailed for its work-saving possibilities. Now, I believe, it can be hailed for its face-saving opportunities. We have so many ways to communicate without facing each other. In treatment, as elsewhere, this gives us new ways to avoid causing shame. I think we more often conduct treatment (and supervision) by telephone and accept this as appropriate. This, of course, expands our geographic reach. It also expands what we can say without evoking immobilizing shame. It can be easier to say and to hear something potentially shaming without facial exposure. We can cover up a blush, or cry silent tears. We don't have to look into someone's eyes as he or she shames us. Just as the couch allowed an unparalleled freedom for both participants to focus without undue concern for each other, so these other mediums of exchange give us the power to feel unseen as we communicate.

But there are more old-fashioned ways to avoid causing shame or the fear of shame.

The Power of Love To Mitigate Various Forms of Shame

I believe the fear of shame and various forms of shame can be modulated by love. It is not only the analyst's love that mitigates the patient's fear of shame, but also the patient's self-love. Of course the analyst's fear of shame can be similarly modulated. Love is like a parallel track running alongside shame. It suggests that shame will not be the only recognizable feeling. It delimits the fear of shame because love says shame will not have absolute power over the sense of self. Love makes a promise to stay, no matter what happens, and mix with any shame that may occur. It decreases the fear of shame by offering to serve as a counterweight. I wonder whether it is some form of love that most often mitigates angry shame, since love suggests that whatever shame is felt was probably not deliberately or gratuitously inflicted. Additionally, love often has the power to counter and modulate shame, since if we feel loved we can believe we are "enough," at least in someone's eyes.

I have found that when I am able to notice them, clinical hours abound in choices between concern for pride vs. the health of the treatment for *each* of the participants. If I expect patients to "free associate," I am, in effect, asking them to abandon caring about how they look to me and to themselves. I am suggesting they check their pride at the door. To say whatever comes to mind is to relinquish the carefully coddled defenses against shameful self-exposure we have all developed. Interestingly, children at around 4 years of age often fail to differentiate when they are silently thinking from when they are talking aloud. They will say things that adults have learned to censor. We are asking patients to return to a similarly uncensored behavior. Another analogy suggests that, in a psychological sense, we are asking them to verbally "undress" while we remain relatively clothed, examine and analyze. This difference in exposure seems likely to elicit some form of shame.

Is it reasonable to ask this of adults who have been acculturated in our society? I think it is improbable that they will be able to drop censoring unless we join them in some way. I am not suggesting that the analyst should free-associate, but that we sometimes share a thought before we fully know where it is going. This is, I think, similar in spirit to Bollas' (1987) technical suggestions. A thought becomes like a ball being passed back and forth between analyst and patient, with neither knowing, in advance, precisely where it will land. To be willing to engage in this process is an act of love because it prioritizes the treatment over one's own pride. It says, "I care more about helping you than I care about how I look." It demonstrates the priority of love over pride.

At these moments our impact depends on who we are. There is no way to fake this love. Saying the right words will not have the same effect. I believe that patients can generally tell when we really care about them and their treatment. They sense which opportunities we pick up on, which risks we are willing to take, which moments we let pass with a silence that speaks volumes about our priorities.

Our love for patients is expressed in many ways besides our willingness to express thoughts before they are fully formulated (Stern, 1997). In a paradoxical sense, I think there are forms of neutrality that, as actions, are acts of love. How often does one person accord another the freedom to be, say, or feel anything? In effect, we say to patients, "I don't need you to express something that supports my pride, view of my self, sense of my role. Say whatever comes to mind, regardless of how it sounds, how it reflects on you and on me." Perhaps like the injunction to abandon hope that is said to crown the gates of hell, we ask our patients to abandon serving their pride, as well as our own, when they enter our offices. We ask them to take a chance on love. We suggest that they trust us to take adequate care of their egos for them, so they need not bother with the censorship that has long protected them from shame. As was suggested above, it seems daring of us to expect relative strangers to have such faith in us. How can they know we will adequately protect them from disintegrating insecurity?

Like the group therapy exercise, where a patient leans backward and trusts others to hold him or her, in any analytically oriented treatment we demand that patients relinquish some of their carefully hewn defensive strategies. Give up repression, we say, and make the unconscious conscious. Bring the dissociated into awareness. Connect split off thoughts. Counter denial. Replace obsessive indirectness with forthrightness. We assure patients that these defenses are unnecessary, at least with us, and that the defenses tend to obfuscate. We invite patients to open themselves to us. Implicitly, I think we promise to catch them as they fall. Do we fulfill that promise?

Out on a Limb: Mitigating Shame by Sharing It

I would suggest that one way we try to fulfill the promise is by making of ourselves a "fool for love," that is, by volunteering to be the one who looks foolish. In different ways our willingness to risk showing our own inadequacies has the potential to mitigate each of the three forms of shame I am discussing: anxious shame, angry shame, and guilty shame.

Should I go out with him again? Do you think my child needs a tutor? Am I taking too much abuse in this relationship? Should I tell my mother how she hurt me? Is it wrong to have this affair? Should I get a second opinion, or go through with what my doctor recommends? Is this what everyone sometimes feels in a relationship, or does it mean this is not the right person for me? How sexually attracted must we be for it to work? Was my father really inappropriate with me? How involved should I be in my son's homework? Was the argument we had last night worth having, or should I have kept quiet? Do you think I should protest that grade?

Any clinician can probably come up with an endless series of questions like these, which very frequently permeate sessions. Some patients will ask these questions directly and demand solutions, insisting the analyst knows the answer. Other patients meekly suggest it would be nice to know what we think. Still others don't verbalize the question, but subtly lead us to formulate it. According to the traditional classical technique, answering these questions was clearly contraindicated. It departs from neutrality and abstinence. I think many analysts would still like to believe we can avoid answering these questions and certainly should try to do so. We do not have the answers and, even if we did, it would be inappropriate for us to presume to make these choices for our patients.

I agree that honoring these limits shows sensible, reasonable humility. The problem, as many have noted (Poland, 1984; Jacobs, 1986; Ehrenberg, 1992; Buechler, 1999) is that we can't entirely avoid "answering." As I have already suggested, even with our best, most humble intentions we still selectively focus on the material, and some patients will read our focus as an implicit answer to their questions. A man asks if he should go out with a woman he met at his place of work. Whatever I say, or don't say, is an answer, in some sense. Do I focus on how they met, which department she is in, what he feels about her? Do I say nothing but hold my body stiffly? When I next speak does my voice sound tense? There are infinite ways we "answer," whether we are willing to know it or not.

This is definitely not meant to imply that it is, therefore, fine to tell patients how to live. An "answer" subtly embedded in the quality of our voices is not the same as an outright judgment. I truly do not know how much help people should provide to their teenagers who have difficult homework assignments. The uncertainty in my tone of voice is, in a sense, a more truthful response than any outright "answer" would be.

But I also believe that sometimes there is good reason to go out on a limb and venture further toward an "answer." The patient who suffers from excessive shame might benefit from a close encounter with my own uncertainty. Of course I still don't know how much help a parent should offer when a teenager is having trouble with homework, and I wouldn't pretend to have "the" answer. But being willing to say what I would probably do, under the patient's circumstances, suggests "an" answer, rather than "the" answer. I am taking a chance since I could look foolish (or, perhaps, impulsive) if my "answer" ends up working badly. I have ventured out of an easy safety and into the nebulous world of palpable uncertainty. I have taken a position, at the expense of my own (at least momentary) security. I suggest this may be worth the risks if it allows the patient to be less alone in the shame of her own uncertainty as a parent. I hope it is clear that I would not suggest to the patient that I am sure my answer is the right one, but only that it makes some sense to me. This might facilitate the patient's ability to come to her own answer, by "bouncing" off mine, just as many of us, during adolescence, defined ourselves partially by contrasting with our parents.

Specifically, in the presence of a patient's sense of inadequacy,

1. I believe that I modify the patient's "shameful" insecurity by, in a sense, sharing it. My behavior (not just my words) says, in effect, we all have to make judgment calls in the midst of our uncertainty. Just as you make these calls with your child (and others) I make them with you (and others). It is part of the human condition not to know what to do, but to have to make choices anyway. I am enacting my personal acceptance of this in the *process* of telling you my answer, as well as in the content of my answer.
2. Thus the patient is not the only one bearing the shame of having to make choices without "knowing" what to do. The shame of this "inadequacy" may then be more bearable because it is not accompanied by loneliness (and, perhaps, anxiety, anger, or guilt, the three negative accompaniments to shame highlighted in this chapter).
3. The patient's shame is also modified by the (new) interpersonal situation. Interpersonally, a "team" is facing the homework question now, not an individual.
4. Shame has been differentiated from fear of shame. That is, I may not know how to answer the (homework) question but my behavior says that I am not afraid to show my limitations.
5. To me it seems likely that if, initially, a mother felt shame about perceived insufficiency as a parent, envy of what she imagined was my advantages, guilt that she was not figuring out how to help her child, and lonely anger at my "withholding," she might now *only* feel shame. Shame alone, without these other emotions, might be bearable.

More specifically, I believe that my willingness to take an extra helping of shame can sometimes decrease the patient's *fear* of shame. Elsewhere (Buechler, 2004) I have described how I believe much of the literature on analysts' disclosures can be read as an exercise in willingness to be a "fool for love," that is, to lead the way in courageous self-exposure. By disclosing, the analyst is saying, in effect, "I have foibles too, and I am not afraid to reveal them to you. Nothing terrible will happen."

But self disclosure is only one form that being a fool for love can take. Less notably, but more frequently, I believe that I offer to spare patients shame by taking chances for them. They can't remember something from a previous session, and I try to remember, volunteering to be the one who may be wrong. In effect, I place myself between the patients and shame.

A pioneer in volunteering to take the shame "bullet" for patients was Melanie Klein's daughter Melitta Schmideberg. Perhaps Melitta's experience of being written up as a child therapy "case" contributed to her care for her patients' self esteem. Her inner life had been displayed to strangers at an early age. This could have developed her sensitivity to the pain of shame. At any rate, in her clinical work she clearly strove to avoid shaming her patients. A brief clinical example will have to suffice, but many others could be quoted. Schmideberg believed that patients need to see our limitations in order to be able to bear their own. She had no misgivings about showing hers, "I do not want to impress the patient either with my omniscience or with any other virtue. One day I arrived late for a patient who was herself habitually late. I was rather apologetic about the fact that she had to wait outside in the cold, but she beamed all over her face. Recently I had an accident and several patients saw me when I was in pain. This had a very good effect on all of them, bringing home the fact that I am human after all" (Schmideberg, 1947, in Stone, 1986, p. 99).

Guilty Shame

Aside from anxious shame (in response to the "impossible/necessary") and angry shame (in response to the gratuitous) the third form I want to highlight is guilty, regretful shame.

I have sometimes had patients identify me with someone from their past who served as an idealized parent. If patients can see me as this aunt, or nanny, or friend's parent who made a positive contribution to their development, they may then be able to increase their self-esteem by identifying with me. This seems to contradict

Schmideberg's notion that the analyst helps by being palpably limited, (as described above). But it makes sense to me, in that it is another way we can have a positive impact on the patients' sense of self. Some people were unable, as children, to identify with this positive figure, at least in part because it would have evoked guilty shame in relation to the actual parents. Treatment can offer them another opportunity. Of course this would be stilted and inauthentic if it were planned as a deliberate technique. All we can do if it does happen is allow it to happen, taking care not to interfere.

The idealized non-parent is someone who either actually existed or lived in the patient's fantasies. This person came to exemplify a significant quality that (in the child's experience) was missing from the parents. For example, the immigrant boy may idealize a teacher who seems able to navigate in his new culture better than his parents can. A patient idealized a family friend who was more cultured and educated than her working class parents. Another saw a nanny as the ideal, warm, accepting person that she felt both of her biological parents could not be.

The patient's attitude toward this figure often combines fierce loyalty, admiration, and yearning to be with and to become like him or her. But the identification with this person can be fraught with guilt, since it clearly contains negative feelings toward the actual parents. The wish to be like the idealized figure may be accompanied by a fear that one is condemned to be more like the actual parent. A woman patient of mine is constantly proving to herself that she is warm, and more like her accepting nanny than like her cold and distant mother. Another woman yearns to be an intellectual like her family's more educated friend, but never feels her taste, intelligence, knowledge, or creativity are adequate. She is condemned to being working class, like her parents, no matter what professional achievements she attains. There is an angry edge to this feeling of inadequacy. It is as though she feels kept down by her parents, as though they won't let her ascend to a higher professional, educational and social level than they occupy. This might be seen as a product of her own guilt about her contempt for them. Perhaps she sees them as vengefully delighting in her feelings of inadequacy. She may be projecting her own envy of the family friend onto her parents.

This situation can create a powerful but complicated countertransference. Personally, I have found myself *less* aware than usual of my own striving to be this figure. It has sometimes taken me a long time to realize how much I am trying to be that warmer nanny or that cultured family friend.

A patient often expresses fear that his "limited intelligence" will be unmasked. This man, well into his 50s, is truly afraid he will be seen as too limited intellectually to be befriended, even though there is much evidence of his professional gifts. His history includes acute shame about the status of his family in their community. They were the poorer neighbors in an upper middle class environment. The patient's mother struggled to afford a home in an area that allowed him to attend fine public schools. His mother had to work in a field that could be seen as blue- or as white-collar, depending on your point of view.

Through her work, the mother made the acquaintance of a highly cultured public figure who took the patient under her wing and introduced him to the finer things. He was extremely appreciative, but always felt out of his depth, worried he would unintentionally expose his ignorance.

As a middle-aged adult, the patient glowingly recalls his cultural initiation. He still feels profoundly grateful for his patron's attentions, but feels largely undeserving, haunted by lingering yearnings to measure up, somehow, to being intelligent enough for her rarified circles. So, many years later, social occasions still quickly become intelligence tests for him. Any misstep costs many points. Reviewing his performance in our session, he cringes with shame. Once again he has misquoted the *New York Times*, or used the wrong fork to eat his salad. Self-recriminations lead to a period of avoiding socializing for a while, until an unavoidable obligation forces him to repeat the cycle.

I am a reluctant bystander as he recounts these occasions. I feel my impatience growing as I hear how the appetizers were cleared away, and how the patient felt compelled to break the silence with amusing chit-chat. My mind gallops ahead to the inevitable review, which will rate the chit-chat as yet another social and intellectual failure.

I have had many opportunities to respond to material like this in the years of our work together. Sometimes I find myself more empathic than impatient, but often it is the reverse.

I have wondered what response the patient hopes I will have. Does he wish I would say something like, "You are unnecessarily worried. I find you great company, very intelligent and desirable." By now, I am sure he knows I will not say anything like that, but it is as though

he needs to present me with endless opportunities to judge his intellectual and social adequacy.

The countertransference reaction I find most interesting is my
own internal dialogue with his "patron." I am often tempted to play
a role that, upon reflection, I see as similar to hers. I want to open the
gates to the "higher" circles and the "finer" things. I feel a strong urge
to share my love of art, theater, books, poetry, etc. I want to explain
why I think Ingres a great painter. I don't usually experience this in
treatment sessions.

Of course my reaction is personal, and reflects many aspects of
my character. I am focusing on just one, my tendency to identify
with the patron. Aside from reflecting my own narcissistic needs and
intellectual strivings, I think this urge speaks to guilty shame as a
subtext of this treatment.

I experience myself as wanting to be the person who generously
"shares" rather than "hoards" culture. But, perhaps more importantly, I want to be the sophisticated, knowledgeable patron, rather
than the "dumb," but earnest hardworking mother.

Aside from speaking to my personal intellectual and cultural
ambitions, I think this reaction is also about hope. I want to say to
the patient that the aesthetic "pearly gates" are open to us. We are
just as good as anyone else, just as welcome at the museum, and I
will lead the way. My impulse to talk about art with this patient is,
I believe, a product of many aspects of who I am, but most especially, I think, it is an urge to limit guilty shame (his and my own)
by modulating it with generosity, hope, curiosity, and joy. I want
to believe that nothing has to preclude our finding a "place at the
table," so to speak. I have a hope that in front of dazzling beauty his
sense of inadequacy (and my own) will yield to joy. In the presence
of the incomparable, differences fade. When any two people stare at
a Rembrandt portrait they are more simply human than otherwise,
because they are both humbled by its perfection. In other words, I
feel if I can only bring us there, in that exalted company, shame will
be dispelled. I imagine this is what the patient's patron hoped, too,
in a way. She believed that this child could forget shame, lose a sense
of limitedness, in front of blinding beauty. His mother's "menial"
job wouldn't matter. Curiosity and joy would act as equalizers, the
ultimate democracy. Anyone can get lost in beauty. Difference melts,
and shame, which is fashioned from comparisons, also should disappear. The patient will no longer feel guilty shame for his preference

of the patron over his parent, and I will no longer feel guilty shame for hoarding advantages.

While I don't actually talk about Ingres in sessions with this patient, or any other patient, what interests me is the impulse that, I believe, is an instinctive attempt to modulate shame. It is as though shame were the "dragon" that I secretly believe can be slain by participation in the limitless. If hope can be stirred, if a kind of "ascension" seems possible, if joy is felt, if fascination is evoked, shame will melt like the wicked witch in *The Wizard of Oz*.

I am aware that this is unrealistic, since the patient's shame did not melt with the magic touch of his patron, and, in fact, probably deepened. Also, of course, my role as his analyst differs markedly, and meaningfully, from this patron fantasy. But its presence in me speaks, I believe, to my wish to rescue us both from shame. Although modulating shame is more complicated than my wish would suggest, the roles of other emotions, such as hope, curiosity and joy, remain vital issues in my view. Patients who become deeply curious about themselves can gather self esteem from the courage it takes to look at oneself, regardless of what they see when they look. An analyst who feels joy when profoundly swept up in the process can withstand its inevitable narcissistic injuries. There can be joy in being carried along in the powerful grip of a process that has taken off, that has achieved a life of its own.

Remaining Me

Discussions of countertransference are inherently limited. I am reporting my own reactions to working with shame in the hope it can stimulate others to identify similarities and differences in their responses. Over my years of doing clinical work I feel my reactions to this kind of material have softened. I am less prone to the agitated impatience that marked my earlier years. While I still believe that concern about shame can block development in general, and psychological treatment in particular, I no longer experience it as an "enemy" to the work (or to myself) but as an aspect of the work. Fear of shame, in particular, can inhibit the self-examination and self-revelation that treatment depends on. But it is a profoundly significant element of who a person is, rather than an obstacle to getting to who that person is.

I could look at this change in my countertransference as a modulation of anger. I think that would be an accurate description, but not an explanation. What changed? As I have said elsewhere (Buechler, 1999) I believe that the analyst's personal growth entails becoming less *narcissistically* invested in one's work, but *not* less invested in it. I think changing feeling as though patients' fear of shame represented a personal obstacle has helped me. But this is only part of what changed. The whole balance of my feelings working with anxious, angry, and guilty shame has shifted. How can I understand this?

Other emotions present themselves as candidates for understanding my countertransference change. Am I less prone to shame myself and therefore less in need of eradicating it in others? Perhaps. Am I less anxious about the outcome of the treatments I conduct? More curious about why the patient feels so committed to avoiding shame? More swept along in the process itself, enjoying that it seems to have a life of its own? Am I better able to bear the sadness and regret of life's limitations as well as my own? I feel sure that each of these is correct, in some sense. Over all, the balance of my emotions has shifted, and every change in an individual feeling affects all the others.

When I think of patients who have struggled mightily with shame, and my attitude toward them over the years, my central experience is that I have developed greater strength to remain myself with them. That is, I think I can better remain a self that is easily recognizable to me. This is probably akin to Sullivan's (1953) "me," as opposed to his "bad me," or "not me." More reliably remaining "me" enables me to be less agitated about patients' shame, fear of shame, shame about shame, resistances to shame, and so on.

I believe this is much more complicated than it may sound. All psychological growth involves an expansion of what can be known about the self (making the unconscious conscious, in a sense). So, at least theoretically, "me" should be more and more inclusive. What, then, would the injunction to countertransferentially remain myself mean?

My work with one particular patient comes to mind. I would call it a generally useful, analytically oriented psychotherapy, a bit longer than 5 years in duration. The patient is a middle-aged man, self-employed, professionally successful, recently married.

What has characterized his life, I feel, is a vendetta against shame. He will not allow it near him, though, of course, it dogs him. His life seems to me to be a series of close encounters with shame. It threatens, he mounts an offense; it subsides, he escalates his campaign; it fades away, he momentarily relaxes his vigilance; it threatens, and so on. Life is a series of shadow-boxing matches with shame. It is his longest running adversary and companion. People come and go, but the relationship to shame endures.

What has been my role in this context? Perhaps, if he has been shadow boxing with shame, I have been the coach. Early on, I hoped he could land a knockout punch. But I don't think this has ever been *his* goal. He merely wants to win every match. He doesn't entertain the possibility of leaving the ring altogether. I am not sure he can imagine life outside the ring.

When I say I am more recognizable to myself, I am not just reporting diminished countertransference anger at his narcissism. It is not merely a matter of anger or any single emotion. I am more myself in my purposes, relationship to my work, and emotional balance.

I once asked a male gynecologist how he keeps from being distracted by sexual thoughts during his work day. He said, "I don't see women. I see tissues." This may sound cold, distancing, literally and figuratively disembodied. But I think there is an important truth in it. After a while we focus on the psychological challenge at hand more than anything else. With my patient when my own vendetta against his shame aversion subsided, when I became less of a prophet, I could concentrate on the meaning of the dialogue between us. In a sense, I could feel that his shame aversion was costing *me* less of my own sense of self.

I am not suggesting that my former prophetic behavior was entirely unfamiliar to me. But, at least as a countertransference, it interfered with my being fully recognizable to myself. When I enter my office I expect myself to think and feel some things relatively consistently. I tend to leaven difficult moments with humor, for example. I am rather intensely emotional, but also drawn toward logical arguments. It is hard for me to recognize myself without these ongoing qualities.

I would say I retain them more often now in my sessions with this patient. He still tells me the play-by-play of his "matches" with shame. While I don't think his aversion to shame has changed much, what seems different is the overall flavor of the session. He still wants to win but each encounter is woven into the fabric of his life. It feels less knock-down-drag-out-decisive. Perhaps we have both accepted that he will always rise up against potential shame, and the outcome will always feel important to him, but no one battle will end the war for good. For both of us, this is a war that cannot, really, be won or lost. As can be the case in the outer world, peace is only an interlude in his inner life. When I felt my job was to help him achieve a lasting peace I experienced his shame aversion as our most significant obstacle. Now it is so closely aligned with who he is to me, that "curing" him of it is as unthinkable as "curing" him of being himself. He will always deeply want to avoid shame. In a sense, the good news and the bad news is the same for us both. We can relax more. For him the "ongoingness" of his shame avoidance contextualizes each "round." For me, it spares me substantial loss of who I usually am.

I realize that it is possible to see us both as settling, in a negative sense. Our goals have diminished and the lowered bar is easier to reach, hence less frustrating and anger inducing. I think this is a part of the truth, but does not take into account the greater access to a sense of overall integrity in us both. I believe we are clearer about how his shame aversion is a profound aspect of who he is as a human being, no more possible to "excise" than his unconscious. With less at stake I can still see the humor in some moments, still feel a range of emotions intensely, still appreciate his genius at logic. I am fighting less and wondering more, in both the curious and awestruck senses of the word "wonder." With my wonder and other qualities more intact, I experience the patient's shame aversion as costing me less of myself. My responses vary more. They less frequently resemble an impassioned quest and more often have the feel of an ordinary fragment of interpersonal life.

Emotional Coloring

An analogy to color theory makes clearer the approach to emotions suggested here. Briefly, the artist-teacher Josef Albers (1963) developed a way of understanding the interaction of colors. Albers, a member of the Bauhaus group in Germany in the 1920s, came to the United States and taught at Yale until his death in 1976. He studied how our perception of a color changes, depending on its background. In Albers' (1963) words, "Because of the after-image (the simultaneous contrast) colors influence and change each other forth and back. They continuously interact in our perception" (p. 73). So, for example, yellow against a white background looks different from yellow against black. In this chapter I have suggested that, analogously, shame is a different experience, depending on its emotional context.

I have especially emphasized differences in shame in the context of anxiety, shame connected to anger, and guilty, regretful shame.

Applying this to the single women whose shame introduced the chapter, most treatment efforts would aim to change the shame response itself, either through a cognitive shift, or, perhaps, a more traditionally analytic understanding of its roots. As the clinician focuses on what the solitary state means, the patient gets a message that says something like, "You should not be ashamed of this," or "You are ashamed of this because it reminds you of when no one wanted to sit near you in the third grade lunch room," or, "This brings you back to your father's preference for your mother, rather than you. You feel that the other woman is valued and you are not." For the sake of brevity I am using shorthand and caricaturing these approaches, just to approximate their messages.

What I am suggesting is that the patient's shame is, indeed, a feeling of inadequacy and unworthiness. Of course it is shaped, in part, by previous experiences. And the patient would feel shame about not having a partner even if she were not in treatment. But her shame in a session is also deeply affected by its interpersonal, emotional context in several senses. First, the other emotions she simultaneously feels color her shame. If she is also enraged, feeling she is at an unwarranted, unfair disadvantage in the race of life, her shame will have a different cast from the shame of someone who does not primarily feel rage, but, perhaps, regret for having passed up chances for relationships. Obviously, no one feels zero rage, or solely regret, or any feeling in isolation. But emotions can predominate and lend a particular coloring to the person's overall state.

The interpersonal emotional context with the analyst further complicates the situation. If, for example, the patient's analyst feels guilt for having failed to help the patient handle social situations more adroitly, the analyst's guilt will affect the patient's shame. Similarly, if the analyst feels mainly curious about the situation, this will have a different impact on the patient's shame. Again, I am oversimplifying, naming a few emotions when in reality there would always be a more complex array.

Like yellow against white vs. yellow against black, I am suggesting that the patient's shame is different when it occurs against these different backdrops. I know that we cannot deliberately vary our own emotions or the patient's the way we can consciously choose colors. But I believe that it makes a difference to enter a session with the attitude that what will probably help the patient most is *focus on her shame's emotional context* and its accompaniments "in" the patient and her interpersonal surround. I am suggesting that the word "in" is an approximation, since emotional experience is a product of multiple interactions at the borders of self and other. The patient's shame in the session is shaped by her history, (including her history of shame experiences) her culture and its attitudes toward single women, her other emotions, her analyst's feelings, and so on.

The clinically useful implication of this is that it is generally more effective to first sort out the other emotions accompanying shame, rather than the shame itself, to have an impact on the shame experience. People are often obsessively involved in an emotion they wish were less intense. They frequently enter treatment hoping to modulate their sadness, fear, anger, shame, guilt, and so on. They approach emotions as though they operated like a thermostat that can be deliberately regulated.

Because of this obsessive quality, the predominant emotion is very often the least amenable to change, at least at first, and, therefore, I believe it should not be the treatment's initial focus. Thus, patients who come to therapy because of their "depression" or their "anxiety," for example, often are too preoccupied with these emotions to usefully address them early in the work (see Chapter 1 for a fuller discussion of this issue).

Looked at from another angle, the "analytic attitude" (Schafer, 1983) advocated for the analyst is an important state of mind to be cultivated in the patient. Curiosity about oneself will probably positively affect overall emotional balance as much as anything else.

I find this perspective hopeful because it suggests that there are many approaches to impact emotions. As an analyst, my work on my countertransference, for example, may affect the emotional climate in the treatment, and, hence, may change the patient's experience of shame. Or, we might work on her curiosity about herself or her self-respect for how she is living her life situation, or her anxiety about aging, or countless other emotion-laden aspects of the situation. The shame, itself, is probably the least rewarding treatment focus initially.

Anxious urgency is the mood that comes to my mind when I think of the clinical encounter with one particular single woman patient. The urgency agitates us both, making it hard to settle into any dialogue. Each potential topic fails the implicit test of whether it is "going somewhere" that could change the problematic, concrete, shaming position she is in as an unattached, middle-aged woman. Because of this agitation we don't have conversations that could, at least theoretically, leaven the shame. A dialogue that could spark empathy in me, or curiosity in her, or love in us both, is less likely. Like yellow against black our senses of inadequacy stand out against this background of agitation. No other more vibrant color fights for center stage. I believe that to transcend this state we need to look toward the rest of our feelings. For example, I could ask myself why my own curiosity isn't more prominent. I could wonder again, and be more fully me.

To relate this to one of this book's central themes, I see regaining my more usual self as an example of active empathy. My own recovery could potentially have a positive impact on both of us. By having experienced the agitation and then pulling away from it I got to know it, but probably won't resent her as I might if I couldn't regain my own equilibrium. I felt (my version of) her agitation, found my way of regaining emotional balance, and now would be ready to use this experience in the service of the treatment. Additionally, her perception of my process might provide a useful contrast, enabling her to experience (probably in a somewhat unformulated way) that her ongoing agitation is only one of many possibilities. Although it is possible that none of this would be consciously formulated by either of us, I think the experience would affect our focus on the subsequent material. We might, for example, become readier to seize opportunities to work on the part urgent agitation plays in the patient's emotional life. I believe that this emotional experience and recovery would "prime" me for making good use of whatever material follows.

At the Nexus

As a subject, shame occupies several nexuses. It lies at the crossroads of psychology and religion in that humility has been considered a virtue in religious tracts for centuries. In our more scientific era do we still admire freedom from concern about how we look, and thus negatively regard shame? If humility is a virtue, is shame a sin?

While humility has been a respected topic in religious circles for centuries, shame is relatively newly respected in analytic discussions.

We have moved it up in status, from a devalued "footnote" to a subject of great significance (Michels, 1997).

Shame is at the border of self and other. Whose shame is it, anyhow? Can I feel shame, unless you are shaming me? I have often found myself (subtly) advocating that shame-prone people should develop a more internal standard, judging themselves based on their *own* values. But is this desirable, or even possible? Perhaps shame is the ultimate relational emotion, a product, and a sign of our profound enmeshment in an interpersonal surround. Your "yellow" makes a more intense statement against my "black" than it would against someone else's "white." It is not the same yellow. It is the topic of shame, more than any other, that confronts us with what the social constructivists describe as the interpersonal derivation of the sense of "self" (Cushman, 1995).

The topic of shame brings us to the meeting point of culture and the individual. It challenges our notions of individual "self." It gathers up our ideas about there being no such thing as the baby (without the mother as interacting other). In that shame is especially the province of those who narcissistically seek specialness, it reminds us of Sullivan's (1953) privileging the simply human over the uniquely individual.

Shame, I have suggested, takes on a different coloring in the context of profound anxiety in response to the "impossible/necessary." Faced with this conundrum we tend to dissociate, forfeiting cognitive awareness to embrace escape. This has a qualitative difference from the angry shame that is a response to the perception that shame is being gratuitously or unnecessarily elicited. And both anxious shame and angry shame differ from the more self-reflective guilty regretful shame that mournfully reviews what might have been. All three colorings of shame are amalgams, products of interpersonal and interemotional processes. Shame focuses us on the interstices where we live.

4

Facing Painful Regret

My first professional job as a psychologist was in a New York State mental hospital. Every weekday started with a death-defying drive on the Long Island Expressway. This was before speed limits kept the truckers from edging past 70 miles an hour. Their game was to take over all the lanes and drive in tandem, nudging me from behind, alarmingly close.

I usually arrived at the hospital with a few minutes to unwind before the day officially started. But there was Tommy, waiting for me in the parking lot, his huge, soft body and pleading voice repeating his morning greeting over, and over, and over. Tommy's mind had decided to lock in place when he was about 4 years old. I didn't know whether to believe his reputation for sudden violent tantrums. Was this a convenient excuse for the night nurses and aides to beat him in a quiet stairwell when no one else was around?

So here was Tommy, testing my patience once again, and before coffee could hearten me. I learned that if I brushed him off like an annoying fly buzzing in my face, Tommy's eyes wouldn't leave my mind all day. It was much quicker to make comforting greeting sounds, ask how he was today, though knowing the answer. If Tommy was badly beaten the night before he would cry, his confused story tumbling out.

I was very young to be a non-medical team leader in the increasingly politically correct state hospital system. Until that day I had been proud of moving up the ladder so quickly, to become the first state psychologist in charge of a team of psychiatrists, nurses, social workers, and psychiatric aides. My job included running ward meetings, working with the team to create treatment plans for new patients, deciding together which patients could go on leave or be discharged.

My first task on one particular morning was to interview James, a newly admitted patient, and then run a team meeting where we would discuss how to work with him. I remember little of the interview, except that James seemed unresponsive, head down as though fascinated with the floor. Nothing I asked, nothing I could think of, seemed to interest him enough to engage him in the interview. Did I give up too easily?

The team meeting was held in my office, a huge, dingy square room whose only advantage was that it had a door that closed. This gave us all temporary relief from the day room, where televisions blasted and patients kept up a steady stream of invective punctuated by sudden, threatening, unpredictable outbursts. To do my job at all took a well practiced blindness to the revolting smells and heart-rending sobs.

The meeting was going smoothly until a wild-eyed aide called me out, telling me they had found James in the men's bathroom. He had succeeded in hanging himself from the overhead light fixture. He was dead.

I remember being numb, yet grateful there was so much to do. How would I know what I must not leave out? I called the police first, thinking they would tell me. Then I followed the aides, who were going into the bathroom to cut James down. They tried to get me to leave, but I would not, although what they had to do was physically beyond my strength.

Before I called the family I thought about how to tell them. Best to blurt it out right away? "James is dead. Sorry." Maybe it would be better to tell them more slowly, easing them into understanding. "Something bad has happened to James."

What I remember is doing one thing after another, focusing on the details, the reports to be made out, the paperwork of death. At the end of my shift I drove off the hospital grounds. I parked my car without any plan of what I would do next. I walked all night, passing through towns, apparently intent on keeping moving. In the many hours before morning, before going back to the parking lot and Tommy and work, I asked myself what I had missed in the interview with James. There must have been clues to his desperate state of mind. A more experienced clinician would have picked them up and could have prevented the tragedy, somehow—could have persuaded James to hope, or at least put him on surveillance. I shouldn't have this job. I wasn't ready. What did I know? Why hadn't I taken more time, instead of giving up on reaching him? Because it was time for me to run the team meeting? It was time to discuss his care, so there was no more time for me to talk to him?

Reviewing these snapshots of myself on a day many years ago, I recognize a regret so mingled with sadness and guilt it is very hard to tease them apart. My regret was for danger I had not recognized. My sadness was for life spilt. My guilt was for the selfishness of taking a job because I needed it, not because I really felt qualified. I think guilt and regret mingled in my sense of myself hurrying to tick off the day's tasks, so that missing signs of James's desperation reflected, for me, a truth about my character. I was always too much in a hurry to stop long enough to talk to Tommy. I accepted James's unresponsiveness too easily, because it shortened an interview that was keeping me from conducting the next meeting on time. Moving up, moving on, that's me.

Regret in Literature

Regret plays a significant role in many works of philosophy, fiction, and poetry. Some writers emphasize the healing potential of facing regrets like those I feel about James. For example, the poet Maxine Kumin (1974) tells us, "That a man may be free of his ghosts he must return to them like a garden." In the poem "Tears, Idle Tears," Tennyson (1942) expresses a different regret, the kind of longing we can feel when love is gone: "Deep as first love, and wild with all regret; O death in Life, the days that are no more!" A yet more complex regret visits Tolstoy's Ivan Ilych. Like my regret about the patient James, Ivan Ilyich's regret is laced with guilt. In Tolstoy's (1886) great short story, "The Death of Ivan Ilych," he examines the transformative potential of regret, as well as its power to elicit exquisite pain.

Briefly, Ivan Ilych, an examining magistrate in a small town, lived a professional and personal life designed to require little exertion. Petty power struggles and routine official business occupied his mind. The years glided on glacially, until he (literally and figuratively) "stumbled" while arranging some furniture. From that moment on, he lived in a private hell he could neither communicate nor explain. Something was wrong with him. Gradually he understood he would die from it, "And he had to live thus all alone on the brink of an abyss, with no one who understood or pitied him" (p. 255). He struggles, but has to admit the truth to himself:

"Maybe I did not live as I ought to have done," it suddenly occurred to him. "But how could that be, when I did everything properly"? he replied, and immediately dismissed from his mind this, the sole solution of all the riddles of life and death, as something quite impossible. (p. 273)

Ivan Ilych does not want to feel the full measure of his regret, but finally has no choice:

He lay on his back and began to pass his life in review in quite a new way. In the morning when he first saw his footman, then his wife, then his daughter and then the doctor, their every word and movement confirmed to him the awful truth that had been revealed to him during the night. In them he saw himself—all that for which he had lived—and saw clearly that it was not real at all, but a terrible huge deception which had hidden both life and death. This consciousness intensified his physical suffering tenfold. (pp. 276–277)

In a sense, Ilych is dying of regret about failing to live. At the story's moving conclusion he transforms the meaning of fear, pain, and even death by genuinely caring about the better life his wife and son will have once he is gone. He concludes, "… it will be better for them when I die," and, with that, dies in peace (p. 279).

Whose Idea of Health Prevails?

Unlived life was also a source of regret for "Anne," Peter Shabad's patient (2001, pp. 272–277). Anne could not let herself feel the extent of her loss in her early adulthood when her mother died. She became "dumbstruck," and, for more than 2 decades, suffered a kind of inertia. When she entered treatment at 49 there were many "roads not taken" to mourn.

This case is rich with illustrations of how clinicians inevitably enact our views of health and pathology in treatment. In treating Anne, Shabad lived out his ideas about healthy mourning, guilt, responsibility, and independence. In a sense, a whole philosophy of life, of what is important, of what it means to be a fulfilled human being, is reflected in this treatment. I think it is inevitable that we live out our assumptions about life in the therapeutic work we do, which is why it seems to me to be vital that we examine these assumptions as much as we can. They play an important role in shaping how the clinician can imagine making a significant difference in the patient's life.

Briefly, Anne was the third child of what sounds like an over-involved symbiotic mother and an elusive, strange, removed father. When Anne, who wanted to be an artist, was 23, her mother suffered a mild heart attack, then died of the second attack 2 years later. During the 24 years that passed between her mother's death and the beginning of this treatment, Anne went through a series of failed attempts at finding a relationship and having an art-related career.

In this context, it seems to me, Shabad assumed that: (1) Healthy mourning meant feeling sorrow over her mother's death *so as to let go of it*; (2) health meant "moving on" from grieving, and building a life in the present; (3) health could only be achieved through the development of a sense of personal agency. Being responsible for her own life was necessary for Anne to be able to have a richer life.

Here I am reminded of Mitchell's (1993) exploration of the differences that often exist between the hopes of the patient and the analyst's hopes for the patient. Mitchell also emphasized that we should think about why we sometimes see as an irrational wish what the patient experiences as a need. We may then define this "wish" as part of the patient's pathology, to be "treated" or eliminated. This can create a gap between how the patient sees the treatment improving his or her life vs. how the clinician envisions having a constructive impact. When this gulf widens it can seriously threaten the treatment relationship, sometimes leading to premature termination as, I feel, Shabad's case illustrates.

Returning to Shabad's patient, Anne, he reports that:

> She clung to her symptoms tenaciously, continuing to report fatigue, anxiety, and insomnia. She indicated subtly that it was I who seemed most invested in her being symptom-free. ... When I asked her whether she felt I was rushing her to health, she quickly backed down, saying it was she who was frustrated with herself. Anne was not entirely off the mark, of course. I was frustrated with the circularity of what seemed to be two steps forward and two steps backward. And I have no doubt that Anne was sharply attuned to my countertransferential zealousness. (p. 275)

Shabad goes on to say that Anne was fleeing her own sense of regret and guilt about her wasted life. Later, Anne dreams of having a baby, and Shabad interprets this as a wish to give birth to herself. Six weeks later, she terminates the treatment, and Shabad summarizes its limited success: "She never completely mourned the undeveloped time of her life, but she attained sufficient self-acceptance to meet life on its own terms; she has learned to derive small but substantive pleasures from her everyday activities" (p. 276).

Shabad ends Anne's story by reporting that she has worked steadily at a secretarial job and taken figure-drawing classes. It does sound as though this patient derived very considerable benefit from her treatment, but I suggest that Shabad's assumptions about healthy mourning and regret played a very significant role that is crucial to examine carefully. In Shabad's own words, "... mourning is a paradoxical process in which a person must affirm precisely those orphaned desires that are most unrealistic and impossible to fulfill *in order to relinquish the irrational demand for their fulfillment*" (p. 309; italics mine).

I think it is possible to make a different set of assumptions about health for Anne, and, more generally, about what constitutes healthy regret and mourning for lost opportunities:

1. As Gaines (1997) and I (2000; 2004) have suggested previously, mourning can be seen as a process as much involved with *retaining* the object as with letting go of it.
2. While it is certainly plausible to interpret Anne's dream as about giving birth to herself, I might first take it more literally, as about giving birth to a baby. I wonder if my interpretation is colored by my own gender, but my thought is that Anne could be trying to face her childlessness. Unlike the fictional character, Ivan Ilych, who could bear his regrets by finding peace and redemption in loving his wife and son, Anne had no such outlets. Was she trying to assimilate how this absence was affecting her mourning?
3. The termination of the treatment leaves me uneasy. I wonder if some of the differences between Anne's goals for herself and Shabad's goals for her and more general assumptions about psychological health were just too difficult for Anne to formulate and address with him.
4. As with other emotions (see Chapter 1) regret is to be *mined* for information, and *lived fully*. This attitude toward regret reflects a conception of health and pathology very different from a belief that painful feelings are the expression of a neurosis. The attitude that pain is part of being human, and that it can't and shouldn't be avoided, but rather that it can be lived, learned from, and balanced with life's joys, has implications for every aspect of the therapeutic endeavor.

Interestingly, Shabad also refers to Ivan Ilych, but his understanding of what eventually brings him peace is significantly different from my own. Shabad says of Ilych that, "Only in the very end when he confesses his regret does he attain the enlightenment of release...." (p. 285). Shabad sees the "therapeutic action," in this fictional account as a product of *confession and insight*. As I elaborate shortly, I see it as a product of recognizing the significance of his love for his wife and son, and acting on this recognition. Thus, in understanding Tolstoy's story as well as Anne's, I am assuming that what counts most is the *balance* between redemptive love and what is irretrievably lost.

Defining Regret

While dictionary definitions (*American Heritage*, 1969, p. 1096) emphasize the grief in regret, it seems to me that when we use the word we often imply that it is a hybrid of sorrow and guilt. We would say we feel sorrow for a loss, but regret an opportunity squandered in some sense. I think regret implies more of a sense of agency (being the owner of one's actions and decisions) than sorrow. I regret mistakes that have cost me something significant but I grieve the losses life brings me.

This difference is of more than academic significance to me. Regret contains a different set of meanings and different information about ourselves. Whatever I regret spurs me toward *both* mourning and atonement. One without the other will not sufficiently address my regret. Thus, I believe that Ivan Ilych (and "Anne," and me, in relation to James, who committed suicide) needed to face *sorrow and guilt* over lost chances at life and atone for them. By adding to life we might, in a sense, feel more as though we evened the score. Anne's "child" could make up for lost life, just as Ivan Ilych's generous impulse toward his wife and son does. Ilych connects with his deep longing to make them happy, and this becomes what matters most. His greatest need, and his atonement, is to give them what *they* need most. Similarly, I am sure that ever since James's suicide my own work has had the meaning of atonement for me, among its other meanings.

Quintessentially regret, then, seems to me to mingle sorrow and guilt. When we regret significant losses that we could (at least, theoretically) have prevented we sorrow as we would for any other loss. But when the loss seems to us to be caused by our own failure to live up to a personal standard of conduct, then guilt marries sorrow. Together, sorrow and guilt beget the ache of regret. Since the pain of regret joins sorrow and guilt, treatment must address the need to mourn as well as the need to atone.

Atonement

The concept of "atonement" has been understood (Frankel, 2003) as, literally, being "at one," that is, integrating oneself internally, and integrating with others, as a community of selves. Frankel (2003) interprets the Jewish Yom Kippur rites of atonement as symbolizing our return to oneness as a people:

> In order for us to come into our wholeness, all parts of the self must be held together as one. And when we join together as a collective, something greater constellates than the simple sum of individuals. Joined together, we atone for one another, for what one of us may lack another makes up for, and one person's weakness may evoke another's strength. In community, then, we find our wholeness and healing. (p. 162)

Drawing on mystical traditions Frankel (p. 161) describes an incense offering, the *ketoret*, that the high priests performed on Yom Kippur, the holiest day of the year. The *ketoret* was made of 11 different spices, one of which was, by itself, foul smelling. Its inclusion symbolized unity and interconnectedness among people, that we must welcome the vulnerable among us and our own weaknesses so that we do not fragment our inner selves, or ourselves as a people. What we deny or reject becomes an adversarial force, which takes away from our strength. Frankel concludes that, "Despite whatever has been broken or shattered through our own mistakes or fate itself, Yom Kippur, the day of at-one-ment, gives us a chance to heal and be whole once more" (p. 163). Thus, personal atonement is integration of the "foul" in ourselves, and interpersonal atonement is inclusion of the weakest members into the human family.

Healing regret, then, requires the "at-oneness" I believe Ivan Ilych achieved. By identifying so completely with his wife and son he transformed the meaning of his own death. Regret for life wasted was balanced by being so "at-one" with them that their welfare was also his. Similarly, when Anne (Shabad's patient) dreams of having a child I think she is hoping to atone for her regrets by investing in life. How could a therapist help Anne find atonement? Perhaps it would entail helping her *feel her regret fully enough to integrate what it means about her.* We can't help her by hoping she gets past it, or offering her a perspective that takes away its meaningfulness, however much this might be motivated by good intentions. More specifically, Anne needs to mourn missed opportunities for forging loving relationships and developing her artistic potential. Anne can "atone" only by being "at one" with the squandering aspect of herself. If we aim to help Anne get "past" these regrets we may not sufficiently help her *use* them to transform her life (Kleinians might understand this transformation as a move toward the depressive position).

The regret that continues to sap our strength, I would suggest, is the sorrow and guilt that is not balanced by atonement. Its "foulness" comes partly from its nature, but if it were more fully repented, atoned, and integrated it could add, rather than detract, from our strength. Turning to Frankel once more (2003) I find what I think is a wise understanding of the part of the process of atonement that is sometimes referred to as repentance.

Though typically translated as repentance, *teshuvah* actually comes from the Hebrew root *shav*, to return. The implication is that we all have within us a reference point for wholeness to which we can return—a spiritual essence encoded within our souls that enables us to remember who we truly are. *Teshuvah* is not something one does for once and for all; rather, it is a lifelong journey, a journey of spiritual homecoming (p. 129).

Forms of Regret

Regret for the Loss of the Unharmed Self

Clinically, I have found that a special form of regret is the longing abused people sometimes develop for what I call the unharmed self. There can be a kind of psychological attachment with a fantasized version of the self. This healthier "self" is the person the abuse victim feels she could have been had the trauma not occurred. The regret this "double" of oneself does not exist in reality can be exquisitely painful.

This "self" may live an underground existence alongside the patient, not unlike the "doubles" that Otto Rank (1925) studied, which have long populated fiction. One example is the main character of Dostoevsky's short novel *The Double*, who finds that there exists an exact replica of himself. This increasingly threatening facsimile is much more capable than the man himself of advancing his self interests, currying favor, and obtaining a promotion and a successful marriage. One commentator (Harden, 1985, p. xix) has described the story as being about the total disintegration of a human being's self-esteem. That seems apt to me. The heightened contrast between the self as it now exists and the self as it, in some sense, ought to exist, can drive some mad.

One question to consider is how we help people mourn the loss of the self they might have been had they not been abused. Knowing that you could have been freer, happier, loved and trusted more easily, aches the heart. To see, in your mind's eye, the person who would have been more at ease in the world, yet feel you will never be that person, brings exquisite pain. How can we help someone bear this? What does it mean to mourn the self that could have taken some things for granted? Do we aim to bury it, so that someone else might be born? Or, do we try to bring it back and resurrect innocence? In short, what does mourning the self that might have been really mean?

I would suggest that sadness over the loss of the unharmed self is unavoidable. But regret that, to me, implies guilt as well as sadness (see above) is another matter. Sadness is an inherent part of any mourning reaction, and cannot be avoided. But if we focus on the emotions that may accompany the sadness, such as shame, guilt, anger, or loneliness, we might be able to help. The emotions experienced and expressed by the analyst also play a role for the patient, as I discuss shortly.

A sadness that does its work may be more possible to bear. In other publications (2000, 2004) I have discussed the potential sadness has for eliciting empathy and heightening our understanding of the human condition. But I also believe that the balance of emotions always counts—that the quality of sadness depends, partially, on whether we are also feeling shame, anger, fear, loneliness, or guilt, etc. Here is where we may find a very significant part of our work in therapy and an opportunity to make a real difference in the patient's life. I would say that the person mourning the loss of the unharmed self would have to be sad. It is human to be saddened by such a grievous loss. But what other emotions could modulate that loss and make it more bearable, or, perhaps, work the other way and make it unbearable? Is the patient better off if sadness is tinged by rage? Will she or he recover the will to live if it is less mixed with shame? Will it be impossible to bear if it is loaded with guilty regret, with a feeling that one, in some sense, caused or deserved the harm or could have prevented it? Will love for someone strengthen the resolve to heal? Are there emotions that can help us forgive what life does to us? Can they be nurtured, or can they only be found where they already exist?

I believe these questions are vital for the treatment of mourning for the unharmed self. Freud, (1917/1915) in his monumental paper on mourning and melancholia, taught us that sadness tinged with angry ambivalence was more intransigent than other forms of grief. I think we can extend his thought, to consider, first, how anger can be *useful* in sorrow, and second, how emotions other than anger can also complicate sadness. When I see someone in mourning for a self that could have been, that should have been, I often feel that anger may help coalesce determination to survive, but that shame and guilt may weaken the sufferer, and render him or her unable to fight for him or herself. Of course, I know that emotions can not be measured like ingredients added to a cake. But (as I elaborate in Chapter 1) I do believe that thinking about combinations of emotions may help us have a vision of how to help. When people have suffered a tremendous loss, as the loss of an unharmed self surely is, I think we have to accept their sadness. It is inherently sad to lose the better life you could have lived had it not been torn apart by senseless violence. If we ask patients to give up their sadness, (perhaps communicating this in what we choose to focus on or ignore) I feel we do them a disservice. At best, out of concern for us, they may try to comply and gain something, not from this act of compliance but, perhaps, from loving someone enough to make this sacrifice. But I think we do better to focus on other emotions that complicate sadness, such as shame, guilt, and regret, and, most especially, loneliness. If we can hear pain we cannot change, if we are willing to bear the unalterable, if we don't try to make it go away, we render the pain shared. It is different because it is shared, although it is still pain and still hurts. But, as in so many other moments, if someone is willing to listen, and not close his or her eyes to what is raw and unendurable, the loneliness, at least, may lift. Although sadness remains, it may be a less bitter sadness. The self that might have been, the self that could have been lighter and freer, has at least been seen by someone.

A female patient I have seen for about a decade was sexually enticed by her mother, forced to share her mother's bed for many years, until the patient absolutely refused. She has always blamed her father for everything that happened, believing that his emotional withholding drove her mother to behave as she did. The patient feels kinship with her mother, more like a fellow-victim of the father's emotional abuse than a victim of the mother's sexual abuse. She forgives her mother, treating her as understandably suffering from unmet needs. Her anger is at her father and at men in general. She feels tremendously endangered by men in power and suffers from troubled dreams of victimization. She has a great deal of difficulty bearing her boss, who sounds to me somewhat, but not intensely, sadistic. Men, to her, are always ready to be gleefully dominating. Her empathy is more easily elicited by women, especially if they can at all be seen as victims of abuse by powerful men.

I frequently feel countertransference anger at the patient's mother when this part of her history is referenced. Would my patient be better off if she felt this anger at her mother, too? Does she need to feel it to heal the splitting, trust men more easily, and feel more "at one" with herself? More generally, how can I best help her mourn the loss of who she might have been if her mother had not sexually abused her?

While I have no clear plan, I do bring into the room a belief that I can help her bear her sadness best if our relationship renders her less alone with it and if we work on her guilty regret and shame. She has always felt implicated in the abuse, part of its cause, since she was finally able to get it to cease. Perhaps her greater anger at her mother will naturally result if she blames both herself and her father less. In any event, I believe she will benefit if she feels less loneliness because I am able to hear her suffering without turning away and without trying to eradicate it. If my actions, *most especially my treatment focus*, do not tell her I think it is a goal to get rid of the sadness, I believe she will be less alone with it. How I deal with her guilty regret, sadness, anger, and shame will communicate something about my own assumptions about healthy and appropriate emotionality. For example, the patient often takes the entire responsibility for my reactions to her. Transferentially, I think she is blaming herself for how her mother treated her, as if her failure to make her mother happier helped to cause the abuse. When I focus on my *own* contribution to my reactions to her, I am telling her, through my actions, that my assumptions differ from hers. At times I communicate this more explicitly, commenting on what I see as her pattern of taking all the blame with women, and none of it with men. But I believe that my explicit interpretation will have more power if what I implicitly express, through my focus, is consistent with it. In a paper on analytic integrity (2003) I described what I see as the analyst's potential for far greater impact when the content of his interpretations, his actions, and his focus all express consonant messages.

Several of the concepts discussed in Chapters 1 and 2 of this book guide my work with this patient. The idea that, for the most part, emotions serve as information, communication, and motivation, shapes my belief that we can learn from her sadness. It may evoke my empathy, and it may have other uses for her as time goes on. As is true for us all, her feelings operate as a system, so, for example, a decrease in the shame and loneliness accompanying her sadness will affect all her other emotions. If she becomes curious about why she has guilty regret for what her mother did to her, that curiosity will have an impact on the whole array of her other feelings.

Since I believe that the emotions of one person in an interaction affect the feelings of the other, I wonder how my countertransferential anger (at her sexually abusive mother) affects the patient. I know, for example, that rather than blaming, I feel curious about what enabled her to put a stop to the abuse when she was an adolescent. I assume that my curiosity has an impact on all my other emotions and it also affects the patient emotionally. On a conscious level, these assumptions do not tell me what to say or do in a session, but they are part of how I understand the work. I am sure that they affect my focus in conscious and unconscious ways. When I look back and wonder why I asked about one facet of the material I can often discern an assumption about emotionality guiding me, even when I am consciously thinking about something else. The basic assumption that emotions serve functions, as motivation and as communication to the self and others, often guides my focus. Because of this belief, I am looking for an emotion's interpersonal and intrapersonal function, and I am not conceiving of treatment as an effort to rid the patient of emotions, but, rather, as a process that works toward their integration.

This view of the emotions as having functions and the idea that emotions exist in a system, together with the concept of active empathy, gives me a way to think about my countertransferential anger toward the patient's mother. What feelings are missing in my response and why are they absent? Perhaps my anger, together with the absence of other feelings, functions as an expression of my regret for the patient's loss of an unharmed self. Active empathy would involve focusing on my own effort to emerge from this emotional state. I empathize not by feeling *her* emotions with her, but, rather, by feeling *my* feelings about her and grappling with them. Eventually, hopefully, I/we will be able to more clearly formulate my struggle and learn from it.

Regret for Acts of Omission in Treatment

In the late 1970s I vowed to myself to some day write up my confessions related to a few long-term analyses that essentially went nowhere. I knew back then that these analyses failed because of my own personal limitations, and how these qualities intersected with three male patients in particular. In this essay I will present one of these experiences in detail.

So began an unusually candid presentation by Irwin Hirsch (at the Clinical Services Meeting, September 20, 2005, W. A. White Institute, New York). Hirsch recounted his analytic work with B, a patient he had treated 25 years earlier. Briefly, the patient and analyst created a comfortable stasis, a kind of holding pattern that had benefits for each of them, but failed to take full advantage of treatment's potential for promoting change. B left analysis after 8 years, having gained in some areas but remaining limited in his interpersonal intimate life.

As I heard and later read this essay I thought about whether analysts regret their acts of omission any differently from their acts of commission. I believe analysts pay more public attention to our regrettable acts of commission, in which we do something irresponsible or inappropriate to our role. Here I would like to consider our regret for opportunities we missed, such as those discussed by Hirsch, and my own self questioning in the case of James that opened this chapter. In Hirsch's presentation the "road not taken" included a more direct confrontation with the mutually comfortable "deal" that allowed patient and analyst to "coast" (Hirsch, 2008) rather than truly engage each other:

> The two of us created equilibrium—I was well paid and adored, and he came at the times most convenient to me. He let me take respite from my demanding life and to sink into a self-absorption that was familiar to me. I never considered myself a particularly exploitative person, but I knew that I was engaging B at about 50% of my capacity. I rationalized that this was all he could integrate, but I knew otherwise—I was not pushing myself to be sufficiently present for him. (p. 8)

Later Hirsch summed up how two people can opt for convenience over challenge, "… our manifest tepid connection seemed just the right temperature for the two of us." Listening to Hirsch's self-reflections I felt moved by the struggle of an analyst with integrity. Such acts of omission seem so inevitable to me, and yet, for analysts, they can be so deeply regretted. There are always many roads not taken in analysis. Every moment of every session we focus selectively, choosing to respond to a part of the material, remaining silent, or even unaware of other aspects. Being human beings with human limitations, we lack the energy for some encounters, are too confused, or lack the courage for others. It can't be otherwise. And yet, the quality of human lives is at stake. If we feel we missed significant opportunities to nurture a richer life in someone we care about, regret seems to me inevitable.

But how we think about our regret matters, because it affects the emotions that will accompany regret. Do we approach it with shame about the inadequacies it reveals? Do we see our acts of omission as defining us? Do we feel that mourning and atonement are possible? What resources can modulate our regret, making it bearable enough to preserve its presence in our awareness as a useful reminder?

I would like to express how strongly I feel that we must temper our zeal for uncovering analytic sins with compassion for ourselves and our colleagues. While it is crucial that we face all the negative aspects of our impact, and all the ways we fail our patients, I think it is equally important that we use insight to promote our own health, as we (hopefully) do with our patients. Insight can be used destructively, demolishing self-esteem without extending help toward rebuilding it. We can, I believe, get lost in a frenzy of reproach or self-reproach. Like Savonarola setting fire to Renaissance masterpieces because they were not sufficiently "pious," we can get carried away with an intense need for purification. We live in self-righteous times, that, I believe, can make it especially easy to succumb to extremism. Even if the condemned is ourself, we owe him or her compassion.

I must stress that I do not mean these comments to be taken prescriptively. I am not suggesting that we can order ourselves to feel less shame with our regret, or more curiosity, or any other felicitous emotion. But I do believe our understanding increases when we pay attention to the intrapsychic and interpersonal impact of various combinations of emotions.

Regret Understood Interpersonally and Systemically

As outlined in Chapter 1, I feel strongly that the emotions that accompany a feeling can drastically alter its impact. Some combinations, I find, can be especially paralyzing for many of us. One such configuration is shame, or a sense of insufficiency/inadequacy, and regret, understood as sorrow and guilt about an outcome that could have been better. I believe that when we are ashamed as well as regretful the strength we need to face our regrets may be sapped. Instead of being able to "rise to the occasion" of courageous self-confrontation, we feel shame's need to hide ourselves. It is impossible to simultaneously satisfy the essential tasks set by shame and regret. *We may not be able to fully confront what we also deeply need to cover up.*

From this point of view, interpersonal/relational psychoanalysis has done our field a great favor. At least for many of us, I think it has changed the balance of the analyst's reactions to having intense countertransferential feelings. Shame about countertransference, the need to cover it up, and the sense of inadequacy for intense emotionality have been altered by placing a premium on the analyst's ability to disclose affect to colleagues and, at least at times, to the patient. Today, because I am less ashamed of having profound regrets about some of my work with patients, I am not as paralyzed by those regrets. I am sure this is partially a product of my greater experience in the field, but, I think theoretical shifts have also had an impact on me.

Returning to Hirsch's self-reflections, I ask what fosters his ability to publicly express his regrets about how his character issues limited his earlier treatment effectiveness. My belief is that one factor is an analytic climate that fosters unashamed disclosure of countertransference affect. Without shame about feeling and revealing regret we can, at least, more fully have our regrets. Hopefully, this allows us more opportunity for atonement, in Frankel's sense (as discussed above). That is, if we are less ashamed of our feelings about patients, whether they are regret, anger, enjoyment, anxiety, or other affects, we may be able to integrate them within ourselves, and in interpersonal dialogue. I return to Frankel's description of the Yom Kippur rite, which, for me, takes on new meaning in this context. Just as the spices of the *ketoret* are foul in isolation but not in combination, the analyst's emotions are thought of as more problematic when intrapersonally and interpersonally unintegrated. I now reflect on

Frankel's description of the Yom Kippur rite, thinking of my own regret about my patient who committed suicide:

> In order for us to come into our wholeness, all parts of the self must be held together as one. And when we join together as a collective, something greater constellates than the simple sum of individuals. Joined together, we atone for one another, for what one of us may lack another makes up for, and one person's weakness may evoke another's strength. In community, then, we find our wholeness and healing. (p. 162)

Thus, if I am not too ashamed about my guilty, regretful and other feelings about James's suicide I can, for example, integrate them with my love for teaching. I can find new uses for them in our analytic community, as well as in my personal development. Intrapersonally and interpersonally, my regret changes as it is transformed by its new uses. If my regret teaches me, and teaches others, I may find greater at-one-ment. A shorthand way of expressing this might be that love (of teaching) potentially transforms my regret, making it more bearable. But, on the other hand, too much shame could preclude my experiencing this intrapersonal and interpersonal healing. I believe that only by thinking about regret as part of a system of emotions, affected by the other feelings it joins, and affected by the interpersonal context, can we approach its complexity, and its potential transformation.

Shame and Regret in Supervision

Relatively little is written about any of the supervisor's emotional reactions in supervision. Whether we wish to call this supervisory countertransference, or a supervisor's transference to the supervisee, or use a different conceptual framework, there can be no doubt that supervisors have emotional reactions to supervisees and responses to the patients being presented. Of course, these responses reflect aspects of the supervisor's character style as well as reflecting on the supervisee and the treatment they are discussing.

I am sure I am not alone in feeling regret among my other emotional experiences as a supervisor. I can look back on work I have done and feel both sorrow and guilt about its limitations. While there are acts of commission for me to regret, I believe, at least for myself, that acts of omission have been more frequent in supervision.

Supervision can present even more temptations to "coast" than treatment does. I think it is all too easy to slide into shortchanging supervisees in one way or another. What may start out as a positive, collegueal atmosphere can easily become a subtle collusion to avoid anything potentially uncomfortable. This "slippery slope" is especially tempting for me when a supervisory hour comes in the middle of a long day of back-to-back sessions with patients. Seeing a supervisee in the waiting room, it is sometimes hard to stay as focused as I would with a demanding or worrisome and highly disturbed patient. There are so many convenient rationalizations available to the supervisor. Useful discussion of theory can slide into something like gossip about its originators. An hour that begins with genuinely helpful career advice can morph into an unfocused social chat.

What makes this regrettable is not so much the content, but the feeling (for both people) of getting through the hour and avoiding something more challenging. It is rather like the experience we have probably all had of escaping into the television or computer, wishing time away, rather than fully living it. Ultimately, it feels empty. We emerge as though from a time warp, perhaps a bit disoriented, certainly unfulfilled.

Many have explored the strains of an analytic life (English, 1976; Kepinski, 1981; Marmor, 1982; Buechler, 1992). Some blame the current managed-care culture and its consequences for the analyst. Others look within the process to understand why it can be so draining. In the past (Buechler, 2000), I have suggested that the unmourned losses of patients that accumulate over a career can be a factor. I also feel (Buechler, 1998) that there is a particular kind of loneliness we may suffer while doing this work. Although never alone in sessions, we may nevertheless be peculiarly lonely, though often (consciously) unaware of it. The strain of focusing intently, the bearing of feelings intuited, the paradoxes built into the role, vicarious traumatizations, and, I am sure, many other factors contribute to our depletion. Of course, that is only one side of the experience of being an analyst. There are also significant pleasures and fulfillments (Maroda, 2005) and potential stimulants of curiosity (Buechler, 2004).

Perhaps all of this can help us have compassion as well as ashamed regret for the supervisory hours we attempt to slide through. Seeing a supervisee can seem like just the thing to assuage the loneliness. Here is someone who may understand, who won't demand the impossible, who is "one of us." But giving less than 100 percent of my attention cheats a supervisee just as much as it would a patient. It *should* elicit my regret. But that regret should, I believe, point me toward atonement. Regret can be among our most potent teachers, focusing us on what can be lost when we merely glide, and what can be salvaged when we turn away from opportunities to coast and we face each other.

Regret For Acts of Commission in Treatment

A burgeoning literature identifies the analyst's overt actions that can be deemed "misdemeanors," or even analytic "crimes." These behaviors are carefully distinguished from the mutual enactments, by both patient and analyst, that are widely understood to be an unavoidable, and sometimes essential, aspect of the work. Most "crimes" violate a boundary intrinsic to the therapeutic endeavor, such as sleeping with patients or stealing from patients. "Misdemeanors," in contrast, are mainly secretive, temporary abandonments of our usual attentiveness, such as focusing on a personal list during a session. It could be asserted that when we steal time we are actually stealing, and, therefore, that there is a continuum between "crimes" and "misdemeanors," rather than a clear distinction.

I think when we distinguish analytic enactments, misdemeanors, and crimes we are often implicitly using several criteria for assessing the seriousness of the misbehavior:

1. Was it conscious and intentional on the part of the analyst?
2. Did the patient freely, willingly, knowingly participate?
3. Did the analyst attempt to bring the behavior into the dialogue, if at all possible, and use the experience to illuminate what was going on interpersonally?
4. Was it an act of "passion," where the analyst got caught up in an intense feeling?

Based on these, and perhaps other criteria, we assess the blameworthiness of the analyst's actions. Enactments may not be considered blameworthy at all (depending on one's theoretical orientation). The other categories differ only in the extent of opprobrium.

Of course, individual analysts are likely to feel guilty about these actions, since they clearly violate professional expectations. Guilt can be defined (Izard, 1977) as an emotional response to thoughts, feelings, or behavior that violates personally held standards. I think an important next step for those who consider the issue of analytic "crimes" would be distinguishing guilt about this conduct from regret and formulating some conceptions of feasible analytic atonements. The chance to atone allows regret one of its primary functions.

Regret, because it includes both sorrow and guilt, is a more complex set of feelings that focuses on what has been lost, as well as who is at fault. It seems to me, in a sense, to require a more profound understanding. Perhaps if we approach our own and our colleagues' "crimes" with heightened compassion, we can reach toward making our regrets do the work that sorrow and guilt can sometimes accomplish. Sorrow can bring human beings closer together in mutual appreciation of the human condition (Buechler, 2000, 2004). Guilt (and guilt anticipation) regulate and safeguard us as a society. How can we facilitate analysts' useful sadness and guilt when they have engaged in unacceptable practices? And how can we nurture the regretful analyst's capacity to atone? I suggest that we start with as nuanced an approach to ourselves as we have developed toward our patients. Each analytic "violation" is a particular individual action driven by an individual's emotional state. Understanding that state as fully as possible and exploring how the health of the analyst and the health of the treatment might be restored would have to be part of atonement. As was discussed in previous sections, atonement can be thought of as a movement toward integration of the "foul" in oneself, and integration of the "foul" individual into the group.

Regret That Teaches Us Transformation

> And suddenly it grew clear to him that what had been oppressing him and would not leave him was all dropping away at once from two sides, from ten sides, and from all sides. He was sorry for them, he must act so as not to hurt them; release them and free himself from these sufferings. "How good and simple!" he thought. "And the pain?" he asked himself. "What has become of it?" (Tolstoy, 1886, p. 279)

Love and concern transformed regret and pain as Ivan Ilych lay dying. Facing regret about his unlived life eventually helped him feel a love that could give his death its only possible acceptable meaning. He triumphs over death by transforming it from an unspeakable agony to a gift of life to those he could finally really care about:

"Where are you, pain?" He turned his attention to it. "Yes, here it is. Well, what of it? Let the pain be. And death … where is it?" He sought his former accustomed fear of death and did not find it. "Where is it? What death?" There was no fear because there was no death. In place of death there was light. (p. 279)

Regret was the vehicle that allowed Ilych the "light," or insight, that made this transformation possible. By facing the falseness permeating his life he could recognize how different and meaningful really loving is. He then understood that his death was not just a loss, but also, potentially, a way to free those he loved. Once his death became his most precious gift it no longer frightened him. Where there had been only pain and fear, there now was illumination. "In place of death there was light."

I think regret's most powerful role is as a teacher, a wise guide to what really counts. Perhaps we can take in its lessons only at certain times of life. Middle age seems to me to be a good season for regretting. The choices of the young often don't feel final. Coming upon aspects of life they have not known, the young may still be glad that there is so much uncharted territory. Unlived life can still speak to the young of promise, rather than defeat. Even loss is still, for the most part, temporary. But in middle age we begin to grow into our capacity for regret. Faster than seems possible, we close the gap between ourselves and the moment when even the opportunity to feel regret will be gone. Our unlived lives gather around us, a thickening throng that seems determined to remind us of every lost opportunity. Sometimes its lessons seem to come too late to be truly useful to us. But, perhaps, like Ivan Ilych we can still use regret to transform the seemingly meaningless. The pain is still there. But by illuminating what was and what was not truly significant, regret has enabled Ivan Ilych to transform the last moments of his life.

As clinicians, I believe we can often make a substantial difference in our patients' lives if we are willing to face our own regrets and theirs without expecting pain to be avoided, but hoping there will be ways to atone.

In his poem, "Something I've Not Done," W.S. Merwin (1973) caught the essence of many of my regrets.

Something I've not done
is following me
I haven't done it again and again
so it has many footsteps

like a drumstick that's grown old and never been used
In late afternoon I hear it come closer
at times it climbs out of a sea
onto my shoulders
and I shrug it off
losing one more chance
Every morning
it's drunk up part of my breath for the day
and knows which way
I'm going
and already it's not done there
But once more I say I'll lay hands on it
tomorrow
and add its footsteps to my heart
and its story to my regrets
and its silence to my compass.

Merwin seems to me to have an adversarial relationship with his regret. Which of them will get to suck in all the breath of life? Which will capture the other? In their closest encounter, Merwin fails to embrace his regret and instead tries to shrug it off, "losing one more chance." So the haunting goes on.

I, too, am haunted by something I've not done with my patient James, whose suicide I described in this chapter's first pages. As the hour with certain patients approaches I vow to myself that this time will be different. I will find the courage, the words, to name what I sense. But then, in the session, everything is enveloped in a gloomy fog and the words don't come. Even before the time is up failure is a foregone conclusion. As though intuiting where I wanted to go, blankness, my adversary, got there first. Worst of all, the memory of this hour will haunt the next. What if this patient is another James? What if finding just a few more words would have made a difference? What if I never get another chance?

5

Joy as a Universal Antidote

It seems to me that joy is well suited to playing a major role in promoting the emotional resiliency of the analyst and patient. Yet the psychoanalytic literature on joy in treatment is extremely sparse. I will speculate on the reasons for this and use my own clinical and some other professional experiences to suggest how joy can play a significant part in treatment's impact.

The Feel of Joy

Well before becoming a psychoanalyst I taught pre-kindergarten for non-English-speaking 3- and 4-year-olds. The first days were chaotic, with an unwieldy class size that the bureaucracy failed to notice. My sobbing class looked like a grief stricken UN in miniature. More than once I was tempted to join their despair.

In the midst of this melee was a tiny Chinese boy I will call Al, although his name was far more multisyllabic. Every morning Al was brought to class by his sister, a mid-teenager, and the only member of their family with a good grasp of English. Al would scurry to a seat near the door, perhaps so he could see his sister coming to pick him up at the end of class. He sat hunched, with his head touching the desk, crying silently most of the morning. The only giveaway was the trembling of his tiny bony shoulders.

My overwhelmed state can best be expressed by saying it took me a few days to register that Al was crying. Unlike most of the other children, he did not permit himself to emit a sound. The movement of those pitiful shoulders was the only observable sign of his sorrow.

When at last I noted Al's distress I caught his sister at the end of class and told her that Al was a bit young for this group, so he should not be forced to come to school yet. As you can see, I assumed that Al was being ordered to endure a trial-by-fire introduction to the American school system. Al's sister told me that Al begged to go to school each morning. He said he wanted to learn to be like the American children. Moved by this child's courage and determination I did everything I could think of to make him comfortable, but all my efforts seemed to fail. I tried including him in games, and not including him. I had no awareness of the use I would later make of these lessons about the gap between the effect I intended to have and my actual impact. Finally, I noticed that a Middle Eastern boy had the habit of leaving play materials near Al and then disappearing into his own activities. Al occasionally interrupted his distress to steal a peek at the toys. I decided to adopt the Middle Eastern boy's approach too, and it had better results than anything else.

Fast-forward to about 15 months later. It is the last day of the program for us, and as a farewell gift I allowed the group to choose our activities. To begin, they settled on a game of musical chairs. Most other days Al would have sat mute, curled over his desk until the game was over. But that day he got up to play with the others, perhaps moved by the notion of a last chance.

As the game proceeded I realized Al did not really understand its rules. When the music stopped, all the children except Al quickly found chairs, and Al was left standing, confused, sensing he had done something wrong. Then it happened. Every single child got up to give Al a seat.

A flood of joy rose in me then, and it rises in me still as I remember. Why? Is it because of Al's triumph over fear and shame? Here was a clearly terrified child alone in an alien language and culture, but determined to "make it." His hard-won victory was that, although he still did not know the rules of American games, his courage and determination had won the hearts of all of us. He had stuck it out, borne the waiting, the fear, the loneliness. He was "making it."

Or was my joy a response to the gentle grace of these children, caught, hopefully, before they were indoctrinated into hating each other for their differences? Their sweetness is certainly part of what moved me then and moves me still.

But perhaps my response was more self-involved. I was also "making it" through this extremely challenging experience. I, like Al, was overwhelmed and waiting for deliverance at the end of the day.

Regardless of its source I believe that what I felt and still feel about that moment is a joy akin to moments I have experienced in analysis, both as a patient and as an analyst. In this joy I feel the shoulders that shook stop shaking. I see the other children setting the game aside to give Al the second chance they would want in his place. The feeling wells up and takes over. It bolsters me, lends me a ballasting strength. I think it can have the capacity to tide me over rougher times, merely by existing as a memory, alongside them. It tells me, "This, too, is part of life. It happened, and can happen again."

While I know that what brings me joy is shaped by my personal history, I also believe that joy is a universal human experience and there are commonalities in how it feels to us all, and in its overall impact on intrapersonal and interpersonal functioning. What can we say about the nature of joy? What are some opportunities for joy in analysis, for patient and analyst?

Avoiding Joy

> It has been said there is not much *Freude* (German for joy) in Freud's psychoanalytic psychology. (R. Emde, 1992, p. 5)

At long last the positive emotions are enjoying much deserved attention. Until recently, psychologists and psychoanalysts were more preoccupied with anger, fear, anxiety, and depression than with joy and contentment. A leading emotion theorist (Ekman, 2003) frankly admits:

> We don't know much about most of the enjoyable emotions yet, for nearly all emotion research, including mine, has focused instead on the upsetting emotions. Attention has been focused on emotions when they cause problems to others and ourselves. As a result, we know more about mental disorder than about mental health. (p. 191)

After conducting a vast search for analytic studies of joy, Heisterkamp (2001) speculates that "Either analysts and patients in analyses and therapies have nothing to laugh about, or else their joyful moments have been deleted from published material" (p. 845). One would hope the second hypothesis is true. But why avoid focusing on joy?

Heisterkamp goes on to suggest that perhaps our psychoanalytic culture is at fault. At least for classical Freudians, expressing joy about a patient's progress might subject the analyst to censure for the failure to maintain adequate neutrality and abstinence. Worse, the analyst might be seen as indulging in a kind of acting out. In other words, we have been socialized to avoid mentioning our own joy with patients for fear of being shamed or made to feel guilty. But why would we be inhibited about focusing on the patient's joy?

No doubt personal reasons play a role in the absence of attention to joy in particular authors. But more general theoretical biases seem to be at play as well. It is interesting to note that Kohut is an exception to the trend toward avoiding the subject of joy. One reason may be that he is less preoccupied with a theory of instinctual pleasure. In classical drive theory an emphasis on increased or decreased quantities of libidinal pleasure may obscure the emotional experience of joy.

Thus, for many classical analysts, difficulties differentiating joy from other positive experiences have probably limited the study of joy. In contrast, Kohut (1977) emphasized that experiences of joy at his own progress are central to the child's development of a cohesive sense of self. It is also crucial, for Kohut, that we have the experience of being a "gleam in the mother's eye" (1971 p. 116). Being someone's pride and joy is so vital to our emotional growth, in Kohut's theory, that it is natural that he did choose to consider the subject of joy.

Joy's Place in the Spectrum of the Emotions

> Whenever we gain new land from the sea of unconsciousness, when we succeed in finding more satisfactory environments for the workings and longings of the id, joy emerges. (Heisterkamp, 2001. pp. 858–859)

What is unique about the role of joy in our emotional lives? To begin to answer this question we have to speculate about how our joy is affected by our other emotional experiences. This discussion is predicated on the assumptions about emotions outlined in the first chapter (for more extensive elaboration, see Izard 1971, 1972, 1977; Tomkins 1962, 1963). Briefly, it is assumed that a change in the intensity of any emotion has an impact on the intensity of all the others. For example, feeling great sadness or anger will color how sharply we know joy. In order to understand joy it will also be necessary to differentiate it from other pleasurable feelings. From a clinical perspective I think it is especially salient to appreciate how joy affects our anxiety, anger, sadness, and so on.

Joy, Excitement, and Pleasure

> While excitement is easy enough to induce in oneself (drugs, thrills, manic activity, violence, etc.), joy is much more difficult to counterfeit. The capacity for joy—whether in the context of a relationship, play, sexuality, art, or simply while living life—is an ability that is cultivated rather than something you can go out and get. I think that one could safely say that very few people who are able to really enjoy life ever come to therapy. If this observation is correct, then it has important implications for formulating the goals of the therapeutic process. (Jones, 1995, p. 97)

Freud's legacy includes our having to work to distinguish joy from other positive experiences. Freud interwove his understanding of positive feelings with his theories of infantile sexuality and the instinctual drives. This has contributed to our confusion.

Joseph Jones (1995) argues that it is clinically crucial to distinguish joy from excitement as well as from a more general notion of pleasure. Aside from Freud's influence, other factors make these distinctions difficult. Since both excitement and joy can accompany play, they tend to be poorly differentiated from each other. Yet the distinction seems clinically important.

Heisterkamp (2001) considers joy more encompassing than pleasure. Joy is about the total self, whereas pleasure may relate to only part of the self. This difference suggests that joy is not a sublimated form of pleasure, but a different and broader emotional experience. For example, while sensual pleasure may be intense, success can bring a total restructuring of who one feels oneself to be. In joy we feel a new and better alignment between ourselves and the rest of the world.

Thus, what I feel when I think of the children offering their chairs to Al is joy. Remembering that moment from so many years ago brings me a good feeling about life itself and my own relationship to life. Joy differs from pleasure and excitement in the time frame of the mark it leaves. Pleasure and excitement are wonderful moments now. But joy speaks to me of how deeply satisfying life can be now and in the future.

The Universal Antidote

Thus, because of what it can imply about life, I believe that joy is uniquely able to modify the impact of all the negative emotions. That is, feeling some joy is especially effective as a way to "inoculate" us against the negative impact of sadness, fear, anger, regret, anxiety, shame, and guilt. A bit of empirical evidence will set the stage for considering why I think the nature of joy as a human experience suits it to perform this role.

Fredrickson (2001, pp. 218–226) has developed what she calls a "broaden and build" theory of how positive emotions can balance the negative. Fredrickson has studied cardiovascular recovery from negative emotions, and concludes that "... positive emotions may help people place the events in their lives in broader context, lessening the resonance of any particular negative event" (p. 222). Part of how this works seems to be that the positive affect facilitates widening the array of thoughts and actions that come to mind, potentially increasing awareness of a variety of resources. Another way this can be stated is that positive emotions fuel resilience, or the ability to bounce back. Fredrickson suggests that more resilient individuals may be, wittingly or unwittingly, expert users of the power of a positive emotion to undo the effect of negative feelings.

Freud provided an example of the power of joy to counter negative feelings in his observation of his grandson's game of "disappearance and return" (discussed in Jones, 1995, p. 94). The child's joy at the "returns" seemed to help him bear the fear and anxiety of the separations. I believe we have many examples of joy vs. fear and anxiety in analytic sessions. A patient encounters something in himself he has always considered "not me" (Sullivan, 1953). Emotionally this can become an occasion for anxiety—the shock of encountering a stranger inside oneself. A woman who considers herself a frequent victim of sadistic men suddenly begins to see her own sadism. She responds defensively at first, feeling threatened. It is as though she were saying, "If I see my sadism, can I still be me? Will I see nothing else in myself? Will I lose me?"

But joy is also a potential outcome from the recognition of new aspects of the self. Heisterkamp puts it succinctly when (2001) he says that:

> Joy can be considered as a basic form of resonance. Psychodynamically, joy is complementary to the feeling of anxiety. Whereas anxiety reflects psychic distress in connection with problems of structuring, joy is the expression of successful (re)structuring. It is the feeling of self-discovery, of a new beginning, and of self-renewal. (p. 839)

A patient sees that she has a tendency to prefer being alone a good deal of the time. She remembers childhood hurt when her mother went into the bedroom to be by herself. She thinks of the famous phrase of the comic strip character Pogo, "We have met the enemy and he is us." She could get anxious about the realization she is similar to her mother in this significant way. Do others feel hurt by her, as she felt rejected and abandoned by her mother? She could feel anxious or depressed in response to this unwelcome piece of self-awareness. But a kind of joy is also possible as she makes new peace with her (long-dead) mother. It is as though her mother's "rejection" has lost some of its sting as it visits its new context inside the patient herself. And in being able to recognize this quality in herself she feels a kind of wholeness, or integrity. Perhaps she appreciates a bit of humor in finding that endlessly lamented mother hiding in plain sight inside her own psychic makeup.

There is something mellowing about these recognitions. It reminds me of a misty Turner landscape, where figure barely emerges from ground, all wistfully indistinct. The joy in seeing the "stranger" in oneself also seems to me akin to a certain type of ironic humor. Isn't it just like life to surprise me with a joke like this?

But, perhaps more importantly, as Mitchell (1993) suggests, we become stronger when we can encompass more selves within ourselves. The joy of successful restructuring must reflect knowledge that the broader definition of "me" means I won't have to waste as much energy defending against seeing myself fully.

To open to the joy of new selves contains a feeling of centeredness. It is as though I were expressing the self-confidence that I can afford to see this in myself. My love for myself is secure enough to encompass this new insight. This joy at more fully seeing myself can be greater than whatever feeling I may have about exactly what I am seeing. I have often felt that, especially with people who have been severely narcissistically injured, it is crucial to communicate that having the courage to look at oneself is admirable, regardless of what is seen.

So joy at having the strength to confront oneself, and the joy of expanding notions of oneself, can counter potential shame and anxiety. The joy of being able to look at oneself can balance the pain of what one sees. Put another way, these joys can be antidotes to the feeling of insufficiency. I think it is essential for each of us to believe, to some reasonable degree, that we have sufficient resources to meet our life as it unfolds. Without that conviction we are either terrified of life's uncertainties or mortified at our own limitations—or both. People who can recognize that they do not know what tomorrow will bring, but trust they will cope, have an essential form of security. So often, at least in my clinical experience, patients lacking this security devise costly ways of compensating. They limit their lives to the predictable, or, in the poet Rilke's (1934) imagery, live in only a corner of their potential "room." They make "choices" that are more compulsive than free, in that vital alternatives were not truly available. A woman who believed she could not accept a child who differed in temperament from herself "chose" not to have children. It is now (years later) painfully obvious to her that this was not a real choice in the usual sense of the word. She did not have enough faith that she could deal with child rearing as it unfolded, meeting whatever was difficult with sufficient resolve.

In addition to joy's role in balancing shame, anxiety, and sadness, I see many treatment outcomes as hinging on whether joy can adequately balance regret (for further discussion of regret, see Chapter 4). Piled-up regrets are, in my mind, one of the most significant challenges we face in our work (as well, of course, as in our own lives). The playwright Joe Penhall (2001) expressed it so engagingly that I would like to quote him at length. His play, *Blue/Orange*, is about a psychiatric patient (Christopher), his rather cautious psychiatrist (Bruce), and Bruce's slightly unhinged supervisor (Robert). Robert, who has climbed a portion of the psychiatric ladder of success, looks at his own past and future:

> Some days I get home from work, from a long night in the hospital, visiting, ward rounds, nothing untoward, nothing terrible, a few cross words with a colleague, some silly argument, I get home and I get in the door and I slump. All the life drains out of me. I think Why Am I Doing This? … Everybody Feels Like This. At some point. In their life. Everybody feels that they've … lost out. It's the Human Condition. The capacity to feel Disappointment. It's what distinguishes us from the animals. Our disappointment. Mm. It's true. The capacity to grieve for lost opportunity. For the lives we could have led. The men or women we may have become. It has us in an appalling stranglehold. And sometimes we say, Why Go On? And we want to end it all. The hell with it. Life's a sham. (p. 52–53)

I believe that regret is our greatest stumbling block more often than we realize. A middle-aged female patient, veteran of childhood abuse, has been through many years of treatment. She has created what could be a satisfying life for herself, with a meaningful career and marriage. Theoretically, she could be enjoying her life. But every potentially joyous occasion reminds her of her lost opportunities. The birthday party her friends throw her now reminds her that at 25 no one cared enough to remember her. Regret at wasted time wastes more and more time. What she can't have spoils what she (on paper) could. Loving moments with a friend's child bring pain about not having had enough support and self-confidence to choose to have a child of her own. Instead of being warmed by these moments she feels only sorrow, regret, and resentment.

As Penhall's character Robert so eloquently reminds us, disappointment when we assess our lives is part of the human condition. Yet some of us find a way to make peace with the portion we are getting. Why? Is this because some are able to mourn lost chances well enough to move on? Or is it, as many would claim, because some are genuinely more fortunate than others, and are getting a big enough portion to feel relatively blessed? These are questions of more than academic interest. According to the body of research amassed by Vaillant (2002) healthy aging depends partially on the ability to find "subjective life satisfaction." This is Vaillant's term for a dimension he equates with joy, or the "celebrant" sense about life. Referring to this quality, he advises the reader that it is an important component of adapting to life, and that "whenever I write pedantically of successful aging—think joy" (p. 15). Along with Jones (1995) I would say that, "At the core of their being, what humans long for is to enjoy life. In the long run, if joy is absent, it leaves people with a vague, undefined feeling that they are missing out on what life has to offer" (p. 92).

Love Anyway

Joy is, then, a paradoxical emotion. It is a feeling of appreciation for what can be in the midst of painful awareness of what can never be. It is a capacity to feel regret without drowning in it. We might reply to Penhall's character that, yes, disappointment is an inherent aspect of the human condition, but like any other form of love, a love of life itself requires us to "love despite" or "love anyway." That is, when we love a person, or family, or country, we are aware of flaws but still embrace. Similarly, to experience joy requires us to love life anyway. I think there is a kind of triumph in this. Joy says, in effect, "I see the reasons to feel regret, sorrow, shame, or rage, but I can still transcend them." This capacity to quicken despite life's pain is what makes joy a universal antidote.

What enables someone to love anyway? Why do some dwell in their bitterness over life's injustices, while others taste the bitterness and move on? I believe no single explanation answers this question. Some people seem to want to convict those who have wronged them more than they want to live their lives. I don't believe this is always because they have been more deeply wounded. The closest I can come to an answer is that willingness to forgive life comes most often from some kind of hope. However traumatized someone may have been, when they feel fulfillment is still possible they may be willing to move on. A patient, worn down by years of abuse, glimpsing a possibility for happiness, says about parents who tormented her, "I refuse to give them one more day." Thus, she declares herself unwilling to spend any more precious time and energy bemoaning what they did to her. Of course, this conscious resolve does not necessarily mean she is really ready to move on. But consciously she is willing to move on, which is, I would suggest, an important ingredient.

In short, I see willingness to love life anyway (the capacity for joy) as an antidote that can modify each of the negative emotions. To be able to find joy in the possible contextualizes anger, anxiety, sadness, loneliness, shame, guilt, and regret. It balances each in a slightly different sense. If anger is fundamentally a response to an obstacle, joy frames what cannot be overcome with what can. If anxiety and shame are ways of feeling insufficient, joy says sometimes I can be enough. If sadness spotlights loss, joy that exists alongside it makes figure and ground out of losses and gains.

Analytic Joys

I think it is possible to see joy as pivotal in the experience of being an analyst or patient in treatment (in addition to its being a key component of overall emotional health). In fact, it seems to me that the analytic situation is especially rich in opportunities for joy. On the other hand, without significant moments of joy analytic inquiry seems likely to be limited in its impact.

This viewpoint is based on a series of assumptions:

1. As I have suggested, joy is uniquely suited to balancing negative emotional experience and making it more tolerable. Joy potentially counters the loss in sadness, the powerlessness in anxiety, the stymied frustration in anger, the isolation in loneliness, the pain and hopeless longing in regret, and the sense of failure in shame and guilt.
2. Since analysis dares to investigate who we are, it challenges comfortable assumptions about ourselves. This can create opportunities for anxiety, but also for joy.
3. The process of analysis facilitates awareness of what we have in common as human beings, as well as what makes us each uniquely ourselves. In different senses these two aspects of analysis may occasion joy (for both participants).
4. Analysis can provide chances to nurture, experience, and witness leaps forward, self-transcendence, immersion in a creative process, exhilarating movement, miraculous second chances, healing understanding, profound acceptance, self-discovery, and generativity. Each of these can be associated with joy. I briefly illustrate them in the remainder of this chapter.

"… Clearing the Sill of the World"

We watch a child we love take her first faltering steps and we beam all over. Just like other people, analysts and patients celebrate the thrill of a triumph over obstacles. I suggest that this thrill can be considered one of joy's many forms, and I believe it can punctuate the analytic experience for each of the participants. Analysis provides so many chances to see some challenges being met while others are avoided, perhaps awaiting future growth. The analyst listens to the patient digging for a truth about him or herself, perhaps painfully gaining ground. Similarly, the patient may hear the analyst's struggle toward greater authenticity. No matter what results from the moment, the effort itself can be an occasion for a kind of joy.

This joy is certainly not confined to the analytic relationship. As a college student I volunteered to read to the blind. Fortune connected me with a man I will call John, a prizefighter who had recently lost his vision in a terrible accident. During our first meeting in his home, I suffered uncertainty about what to do for him as he groped around, trying to learn how many steps to take to get to the bathroom, etc. He suggested we have a cup of coffee. All too eagerly I got up to make it, relieved at having a clear activity. He became extremely angry with me, exclaiming this was his home, he invited me to have coffee, and he would be damned if he would let me make it. I sat down, taken aback, trying to integrate another lesson on the difference between intention and effect. Of course I meant well, but if I wanted to help John I would do better if I sat and ignored his fumbling with the cups and stilled my impulse to take over.

Joy frequently accompanied my experience with John. He was a young man who had never had much interest in academic subjects, preferring to express poetry with his physical grace and strength. Now life was asking him to radically change, to focus inward, to develop himself in unprecedented ways.

The moment that stands out for me was the time, years later, that we began teaching a night course in mythology together. Before John perfected his knowledge of Braille I had to read for us both, and we decided to begin with some fighting heroes John and I could both relate to. I remember the swell of feeling I had as John introduced himself to the class. I could not have understood then how this experience was preparing me for my own career. I thought I was helping John and, as a bonus, learning something about Greek mythology. Actually, I now believe, I was learning something about the joy I craved then and still need today.

I believe this craving expresses a great deal about my personal history, but it is also not unique to me. Why does the crowd roar when the come-from-behind horse Seabiscuit crosses the finish line? Why do we cheer pluck, the refusal to give in to daunting obstacles, the determination of a child like Al, (the Chinese boy whose story began this chapter) the extraordinary tenacity of the participants in the Special Olympics?

Transcendent Joy

Not surprisingly, for me it is a poet who expresses this joy most movingly. I will call this feeling "transcendent joy," in an attempt to describe the thrill it brings. The poet, Richard Wilbur, writes about a time when he listened at the door of his daughter's room, hoping to hear the clack of her typewriter announce she had been able to triumph over a block in her writing. I think the poem superbly illustrates several components that are often present in transcendent joy: (1) a seemingly overwhelming obstacle to something that matters; (2) a sense that whatever is being attempted has symbolic, as well as concrete meanings; (3) a feeling of being able to identify with that goal, or the person pursuing it; and (4) an unexpected, or unlikely triumph over the obstacles.

In Wilbur's poem "The Writer," as he listens at his daughter's door he remembers:

> ... the dazed starling
> Which was trapped in that very room, two years ago;
> How we stole in, lifted a sash
> And retreated, not to affright it;
> And how for a helpless hour, through
>   the crack of the door,
> We watched the sleek, wild, dark
> And iridescent creature
> Batter against the brilliance, drop like a glove
> To the hard floor, or the desk-top
> And wait then, humped and bloody,
> For the wits to try it again; and how our spirits
> Rose when, suddenly sure,
> It lifted off from a chair back,
> Beating a smooth course for the right window
> And clearing the sill of the world
> It is always a matter, my darling,
> Of life or death, as I had forgotten. I wish
> What I wished you before, but harder. (p. 23)

The starling's takeoff, the daughter's access to words, the prize-fighter's successful self-transformation, and Al's overcoming of difference and isolation have something in common. I believe they all represent meaningful human triumphs. At first the obstacles appear daunting, but perseverance wins the day.

Such stories are hardly unknown to us, either as patients or analysts. For example, Balint (1968) tells a vignette about a young woman who came to analysis to work on her inability to achieve professionally or enter a romantic relationship. After 2 years of painstaking exploration:

> ... she was given the interpretation that apparently the most important thing for her was to keep her head safely up, with both feet firmly planted on the ground. In response, she mentioned that ever since her earliest childhood she could never do a somersault; although at various periods she tried desperately to do one. I then said: 'What about it now?'—whereupon she got up from the couch and, to her great amazement, did a perfect somersault without any difficulty. (pp. 128–129)

Discussing this case Hesterkamp (2001) remarks, "... the tremendous joy that a scene like this awakens in patient and analyst alike contains the powerful efficacy of immediate and mutual resonance" (p. 852).

When people cheer the liftoff of a space capsule what are they celebrating? The triumph over gravity (as in grave sorrow, or death's grave, or the weighty, serious, or dangerous? Or, perhaps, as in "engraved," that is, forever stamped)? Just as in philosophy transcendental knowledge rises above human experience, and in religion Jesus transcends death by rising above the earth, concrete upward movement can represent a symbolic triumph over something daunting. It is no accident that Wordsworth begins his poem, "My heart leaps up when I behold/A rainbow in the sky ..."

The feeling accompanying this breakaway from "gravity" can be joy, whether it is experienced by a patient, a father, an analyst, or a devout worshipper at the feet of his risen lord.

An interesting comment on the joy of breaking away from confinement is provided by Altrock (in Heisterkamp, 2001, pp. 852–654). He tells of a time in his training analysis when he felt a tremendous need to get up from the couch. Unable to stop himself, but fearful and ashamed, he jumped up. Daring to look at his analyst's face, which was beaming, he felt tremendous joy, although afterward he wished that the two of them had discussed what happened so its meaning could have been better understood, and it could have felt more like a release and less like a blunder on both their parts.

Transcending Self

Perhaps not unrelated is the joy of reaching beyond oneself to connect with essential humanity. Some believe this impulse is at the heart of joy:

... when we feel part of a greater whole, we experience a sense of joy and well-being.... The Hebrew word for one-ness—*echad*—comes from the same root as the word for joy—*chedva*. We experience joy when we feel a sense of oneness and connectedness. This is the central aim of all Jewish spiritual healing—to restore a sense of unity, joy, and connectedness in a world in which brokenness seems inevitable. (Frankel, 2003, p. 22)

Thus, one time-honored understanding of joy is that it is a profound feeling of being part of life itself. Emotion theorists have favored this interpretation. Izard (1977), for example, says that joy is "often accompanied by a sense of harmony and unity with the object of joy and, to some extent, with the world. Some people have reported that in ecstatic joy they tend to lose individual identity, as in the case of some mystical experiences associated with meditation" (p. 27).

A similar sensibility is the association of joy with the feeling of being part of Nature. Bernard Berenson put it eloquently, "... I climbed up a tree stump and felt suddenly immersed in Itness. I did not call it by that name. I had no need for words. It and I were one" (quoted in Jones, 1995, p. 88).

For that glorious instant there was no boundary between inner and outer reality, and no need to tell them apart. As we would expect, romantic poets trumpet this understanding of joy. In his poem "Intimations of Immortality from Recollections of Early Childhood," Wordsworth represents them when he bids us to remember "truths that wake, to perish never; which neither listlessness, nor mad endeavor, nor man, nor boy, nor all that is at enmity with joy, Can utterly abolish or destroy!" (pp. 153–154). Remembering that we are part of the vast tapestry of Nature can bring deep joy.

Psychoanalysts have been more ambivalent about shedding boundaries. An exchange of letters between Freud and Romain Rolland is telling. Rolland (quoted in Jones, 1995, pp. 88–89) said he thought an "oceanic feeling" was the source of religious experience. Freud replied that he could not find this feeling in himself and could not convince himself of its validity. Jones sees Freud's attitude as dismissive and his tone as indicating that such experiences were regressive aberrations. Jones suggests:

This tendency to subtly pathologize ecstatic states has left theorists with a very real ignorance of the full range of joyful experience. This lack, in turn, has been a major handicap in developing a comprehensive theory of affects. These ecstatic states are not regressive but are the experience of intense joyfulness. Perhaps because of our ambivalence about the subject, the psychoanalytic literature contains remarkably few studies devoted to the emergence of the capacity for joyfulness. (p. 89)

An interesting exception is Marion Milner's (1956) case study subtitled "The Yell of Joy." In it she calls the absence of boundaries "cosmic bliss," and associates it with a shout at the moment of orgasm.

I suggest that several aspects of this vision of joyousness can trouble psychoanalysts:

1. The idea of an absence of a boundary between inner and outer reality is associated with psychotic pathology.
2. The passivity and receptivity of this union with nature may be threatening to some.
3. This view does not accord human beings a special status over other forms of life.
4. To some, joyous bliss may sound like a form of submission (Ghent, 1990) as opposed to dominance (of nature).
5. It may raise the specter of being lost forever, like an Odysseus remaining with the temptress Circe instead of stoically sailing away.

I think Jones is right that a tendency to pathologize this form of joy has contributed to joy's relative absence from the psychoanalytic literature. Nevertheless, clinically, I believe, we have probably all had experiences of joyous union. Jungians, whose training may help them be less intimidated by these feelings, differentiate states of union from states of fusion. Fusion can be confusing and threatening (Schwart-Salant, 1989, pp. 36–47). Calling moments of genuine union the "conjunctio" Schwartz-Salant credits them with a great deal of treatment's potential for healing.

To me this seems similar, in spirit, to Schachtel's (1959) understanding of "real," as opposed to "magical" joy. For Schachtel, real joy is "a feeling of being related to all things living." It is a continuous turning toward the world, the "felt experience of the ongoing acts of relatedness" (pp. 42–43).

As analysts, we are uniquely situated to realize that nothing human is alien to us and joy can accompany each stretch and every recognition that this, too, is potentially me. Differences of gender, age, cultural background drop away. I hear a woman's struggle to take adequate care of herself as she also attempts to give care to her pitifully dependent, grievously ill mother. I wonder what it feels like to have a mother who is a lost child, who can't remember her daughter's name. I have never been that daughter, but I delve into being her now. It is not a difficult entry. How sad it is to love someone who is gone, but still physically present. This live corpse of a mother can't be buried and mourned, will not be still, pipes up in irritation. She is a child without any future, permanently perplexed. All she knows is that she is at some disadvantage compared with everyone else and she wants to lodge a complaint.

I do, too. Is this how a perfectly decent life has to end? As T.S. Eliot says, not with a bang, but with a whimper? Isn't the physical pain, fear, and loss enough? Why add indignity?

Seemingly hardly a setting for joy, and yet it is also there for me, partly because I am adding to my understanding of our fragility. With this heartache I know a little more of life.

But, at least for me, it is not just added experience that evokes joy in this situation. It is also the freedom to lose track of who I (generally) am, and what part of my experience is coming from inside. Winnicott (1971) characterized this as the freedom we can have in transitional space, where there is no need to know what is coming from inside vs. what is external. It is true that when I look at a self-portrait by Rembrandt I can easily get lost in a twilight, in some part his brush strokes, in some part my reverie. No one is likely to demand that I sever one from the other.

Although I am aware there are dangers implicit in what I am saying, the truth is that I don't wait to go to a museum to have that kind of moment. For me, patients very often become transitional objects, and the analytic hour is a transitional space. This is a tremendous source of joy, although it brings in its wake a heavy responsibility. I relish momentarily relinquishing the work of differentiating where an experience is coming from. But I also know this is a fleeting joy, and I always have to be ready to take up that work again.

I see the joy of losing track of oneself as a democratic joy, equally available to analyst and patient. Patients are, in my experience, just as likely to be afraid of this confusion as analysts seem to be. The relative absence of orienting stimuli on the couch can sometimes facilitate losing track. Sometimes it also exacerbates fears of being influenced, invaded, taken over by the analyst. Temptations so often form the fabric of our fears. Patients, like their analysts, can be all too aware that as human beings we must limit ourselves to brief vacations from the work of differentiating I from Thou.

Finding Myself

> Joy, then, is what we experience in the process of growing nearer to the
> goal of becoming ourselves (Fromm, 1976, p. 106).

It may seem paradoxical, but I believe sharpened self definition is
as frequent a source of analytic joy as is losing track of oneself. Like
the joy of losing oneself, this joy is also equally available to analyst
and patient. All of us define ourselves, at least in part, by contrasting
with someone else. I can think of no interaction better suited to this
task than psychoanalysis. Whether verbalized or not, a patient and
analyst are constantly comparing notes on their reactions, assumptions, and ways of processing life. One of our opportunities to learn
who we are comes about when we can see someone else take a very
different message from an interchange. In this sense self-definition is
inherently an interpersonal process.

Erich Fromm consistently cheered us on to differentiate ourselves
from others. He championed full self-awareness, the courage to
embrace and not escape our freedom. I think there is a potential joy
in self-recognition. Like children in front of mirrors we see a characteristic tilt of the head and smile, just as we would register the familiarity of anyone else we knew and loved.

Fromm (1947, p. 192) defined joy as an achievement that requires
productive effort. His is an active, purposeful joy, a kind of reward for
healthy living. Striving toward full self-actualization brings Fromm's
joy along with it. Conversely the failure to individuate incurs potential
depression, in Fromm's view. It is as though the self, unrecognized,
can wait only so long for rescue before it withers from neglect.

Self-awareness as a source of joy has a long history. As an example,
we might turn to the writings of the Stoic philosopher Seneca, who
understood joy to be "born inside" (quoted in Nussbaum, 1994, p.
401). Seneca goes on to suggest that the soul of "solid" joy is brisk and
confident. He advises us to "Look to the true good and take joy only
in that which comes from what is your own. What do I mean by 'from
what is your own'? I mean you yourself and your own best part."

As analysts we have all gone through what I think of as a second
adolescent self-defining process—the development of an individu-
ated analytic voice. In a paper on joining the psychoanalytic culture
(1988), written shortly after my own graduation from analytic training, I described what I see as some of the vicissitudes of developing a

distinct analytic voice. Like any other separation–individuation process, it has its inherent possibilities for raising anxiety levels. But it also has great potential for evoking joy, if our analytic "parents" and we, ourselves, can celebrate our differences.

A female patient tells me about a professional meeting she attended, and I hear nothing about her own contribution to the discussion. I begin thinking out loud about what might have kept her quiet. I am assuming something inhibited her. She points this out, asking why she could not have merely preferred to be quiet.

This moment is significant to me because it opens up the possibility for us both to verbalize assumptions we might not ordinarily examine. It is not, I feel, a matter of whose assumptions are better, but rather how her assumptions are characteristic of her and mine speak of who I am. There is something fulfilling, intensely satisfying about this kind of exchange. In an atmosphere that is affectionate, sometimes humorous, occasionally wistful, we are saying to each other, "So you think that way about it. I don't. I think this way." It can be wistful because it points to roads not taken, but it is affectionate and humorous because we are dear to each other. We are, in effect, saying, "Isn't it just like you, to think that way." Like an oft-repeated family story, it carries the intimacy of being fully known and accepted.

The God in the Details

Many curses and blessings between people who know each other well begin with "You always" or "You never ..." Those of us who have done couples counseling can attest to the angry assault this phrase can presage. Yet what do we mean, in a positive sense, when we say someone is familiar? When someone dies, don't we miss exactly the characteristic little idiosyncrasies we might earlier have caricatured, chided, or even resented?

I think psychoanalysis provides a unique opportunity for the exploration of seemingly unimportant details. Even though they might appear much less significant than the assumptions referred to above, they sometimes acquire more meaning when they are explored in treatment. A patient tends to end sentences with a slight question mark. To me, her tone suggests that she is asking for permission to think as she does. The little question mark is of no real importance in itself. But it can be used as a window into something potentially significant.

The joy we can feel when such a detail is explored has, I think, something in common with a kind of humor, or irony. We are amazed that we reveal ourselves in such minuscule behaviors. We may also feel gratified someone is paying such close attention to us. We feel "found," without, perhaps, even having known we were "lost." There can be a childish delight, a feeling of having been "caught" (which, of course, is only pleasurable when we wanted to be caught in the first place).

When I think of patients I miss, it is often tiny details I remember first. A nod of the head, a way of putting a briefcase down, a frequently used phrase or word, all evoke vivid recollection. Like the madeleine that is so evocative in the writings of Marcel Proust, the tiniest details are often the surest triggers of the texture of a life. It can be a source of joy to know, and be known, by these manifestly insignificant, yet enormously important details.

Other Analytic Joys

It is a joy to be involved in an analysis because of the inherently challenging nature of the process. In the beginning of a treatment two people are strangers to each other. A conversation begins. As I see the work, part of the process is the development of a common language. As is true in any intimate relationship, analyst and patient forge a shared understanding about what "we" mean when we say X. That shared language is created in the service of improving the patient's life, in some sense.

Many types of creativity are required of both participants. To name a few, both must find words for inner experiences, prioritize some thoughts over others, and bear simultaneously feeling alone enough to be adequately centered and connected enough to relate to the other. Eventually, at least in how I see the work, both must become participant observers, interacting with each other while also observing that interaction.

For some, the strange, limited, and limitless analytic relationship is a new kind of inter-relatedness. How many times in our lives do we get to live in a new way with someone? How many new types of relationships do we ever encounter? How many times do we get to see the world, and life itself, through someone else's eyes?

As I have expressed elsewhere (Buechler, 2004) psychoanalysis is an interchange about curiosity, hope, kindness, courage, the sense of purpose, balanced emotionality, the bearing of loss, and integrity. It engages us in the fundamental questions about how we live our lives. The choices we each make in a session reflect who we are as people. Our souls express themselves in what we privilege every moment of each hour.

The challenge inherent in the treatment exchange can be a source of joy. The opportunity for unlimited expression of curiosity is also, I believe, at the core of its joyful potential. When we are "on," when we feel the process is going well, we may have the feeling of exhilaration that comes with any difficult fast movement. Especially when it seems to take off, to have a life of its own, it is like riding a wave.

Like an athlete, we can have the sensation of finding a groove. I imagine the feeling is similar to that of the tennis pro hitting the center of the ball. It feels solid. Baseball players talk of the ball "connecting." I think joy in treatment is sometimes a similar experience. When we are "connecting" there is a particular texture in the back and forth. The words feel right and the rhythm feels natural. As the ballplayer becomes one with the bat, as the violinist becomes one with the instrument, we seamlessly lock together in words and silences. We are at one with ourselves, and, in some particularly joyous moments, with the patient as well. We are not "gravely" tied down (to a theory, an urgent goal, or anything else predetermined). We dance lightly, gracefully free.

I am sure that this very personal vocabulary expresses much about who I am as an analyst and person. I cannot know how much it reflects only my own particular needs. I wonder how much the texture of my joy differs from yours. Can we ever really know? How might knowing this be useful to us as clinicians and as human beings?

It is astonishing to me that Al, the little Chinese boy I mentioned at the outset, is a grown man now. In my memory he is still 4, and his shoulders still hunch, tiny and painfully fragile, over a wooden school desk. It is both sad and a joy to wonder what became of him. It is painful because I will never really know, so the story will always remain incomplete for me. Although I was totally unaware of this at the time, this experience was a harbinger of what it would be like for me to be a clinician. Almost every patient I have ever worked with leaves this permanent question mark behind.

But it is also joyful because I believe I helped him some. However unquantifiable and unknowable it is, I feel I had some good impact on his life. He was not my patient but this feeling is familiar to me as an analyst. A long parade of faces makes me grateful I chose this field.

Perhaps it is easier for me to isolate joy about Al because he was not my patient. As suggested earlier in this chapter, as analysts we are socialized to remain silent about joy with our patients. With Al things were simpler for me at the time, and in retrospect. But some of the inner experience of joy does not differ. My heart leaps as I think of myself helping him transcend obstacles and as I remember connecting to him across our barriers of culture, age, gender. I hope that, to some degree, Al had a second chance to find his way in this strange, alien place, where the music suddenly stops and the children all mysteriously know when to sit down. I would like to think that the miraculous moment, when all the other children stood to protect Al, lives on in minds other than my own. I want to hope that, somewhere in the world, a few middle-aged people have had a harder time hating another person for their differences, because they, too, keenly felt Al's confusion when the music stopped. I hope they took away into their lives that Al's terrified yearning to belong was not male, or Chinese, or 4 years old, but was simply human.

As is true for me as an analyst, sometimes joy seems to be about transcending myself and about participating in a leap forward over initially seemingly overwhelming obstacles. But analysis encompasses many joys. Treatment also provides opportunities to ride its wave, feeling the exhilarating power of the process. In treatment both people can lose track of who they are, and of time and place. They can also increasingly discover who they are, partly through discovering who they are not. In a process I think of as inverted mourning they can encounter the minute details that give substance to identity. That is, in mourning we gradually let go of someone by remembering, for moments, how she took off her hat, and then, later, how she carved the turkey (Freud, 1917). The opposite occurs in psychoanalysis, where we build up a sense of the other through accumulating such details. The other comes alive in our minds, borne of moments of knowing and being known. This is, at least for me, an important source of joy.

As can be true in treatment, my experience of Al allows me to fantasize that I have made a difference in how another's life is lived. I have promoted health in someone, perhaps enhancing his capacity for joy. All of the pleasure of generativity is contained in these fantasies. By touching Al I invested, just a bit, in another life, and in life itself. The dividend is joy.

In Balance

I have called joy a "universal antidote" because I believe it can help balance all the negative emotions. In connecting outside myself I am less lonely. In soaring over an obstacle or helping another soar I am less entrenched in anger. In riding the wave of the process I know exhilarating movement is possible, so depressing limitations are less encompassing. In constructing a new inner object relationship I am less saddened by other losses I may be mourning. In participating in the affirmation of life my guilt and my regrets lighten. In losing track of myself I let go of the anxiety of constriction. In finding myself I feel stronger, clearer, and more whole. I shed some shame and sorrow and invest more fully in life.

Facilitating Joy

In a witty essay on forms of supervision Levenson (1991, pp. 115–116) illustrates algorithms by describing the belief, popular in the Middle Ages, that to avoid ague you had to close the windows at night, among other safeguards. While they did not know about the anopheles mosquito, they developed a stepwise procedure that worked. They thought it worked because night air spread evil humors. Despite the inaccuracy of their explanatory theory, the process was effective.

Analogously I believe that the clinical stance advocated by Greenberg (1991) works, but my explanation of its impact differs from his. Greenberg advocates that the analyst should maintain a position equidistant between being the old transference object and a new relational experience: "The neutral analyst occupies a position that maintains an optimal tension between the patient's tendency to see him as a dangerous object and the capacity to experience him as a safe one." (p. 217)

In other words, if we are too much a "new" and therefore safe, object, we will not sufficiently evoke the transference. But if we are too much the "old," dangerous object the patient will feel too threatened to take the risks successful treatment requires. This explanation of why the analyst's equidistant stance works privileges the issue of safety. I believe it is very valuable and true but it emphasizes the avoidance of anxiety as the core of human motivation (as, of course, did Sullivan, 1953). It highlights our need to avoid negative experience, rather than the motivating power of joy and other positive affects.

For example, with a woman whose mother was depressed, if I am sufficiently similar to the mother to resonantly engage the patient, yet significantly different in my capacity for repair, I think joy can play a vital role in the curative potential of the treatment. I matter enough partly because of my similarity to her mother, a beloved person from her past. Only if the analyst can matter will the treatment attain vitality. Otherwise it easily becomes an arid intellectual exercise.

But, of course, the experience the patient has with me will not help her if it simply repeats the pain of the past. Expecting her impenetrable, unrelentingly depressed mother, the patient needs to find someone else. One day, this patient came into her session in an agitated state, fiercely denouncing her husband. He is hopelessly insensitive, emotionally absent. Once again he didn't hear her, despite her effort to express her needs clearly. She seems to be telling me all effort is useless. Anything I say falls short, because it has a glimmer of hope in it, which proves the limitedness of my comprehension of what she is up against, in her husband (and mother). Saying anything at all is too hopeful, since it implies that words could make a difference.

In the complicated way clinical material unfolds, the patient is her impossible mother and expects to find this unbearable mother in me. I am struck by the myriad ways I could disappoint her. I could talk, not talk; hope, not hope; try, not try. I open up a discussion of which might be the best way to fail. If I keep "pitching" I will seem impervious, above her pain. But if I give up she will have deadened and lost me. I tell her I have decided to take a chance on the first approach. I know it will be better for me, and I hope it will also be better for her.

In retrospect I believe that I have been enough like her mother to involve us with each other, but enough different, in my ongoing emotional availability, my capacity to observe as well as participate, and my palpable adequacy at taking care of myself. Because I am enough like her mother, my differences matter. The differences do, in a sense, make me "safe." But they do more than that. It is not just the absence of the negative but the presence of positive, hopeful emotional experience that has the potential to effect change in this clinical situation. I am not just safe. I manifest the possibility that the future can be different from the past. The patient has a chance to feel the joy that she can become more than she has been. Transcendent joy is a kind of affirmation of life's possibilities. Albert Camus once said that in the midst of winter he found, in himself, an irrepressible Spring. That Spring is more than just the absence of something negative. It is the presence of the healing power of joy.

6

Grief

I don't miss Iris. Perhaps because I don't "remember" her. Not in the ways that I remember things and people in the past, who are truly gone. No wonder she did not want a memorial service. She knew I would not need to remember her in that way. I sleep quietly now, with Iris quiet beside me. I drop off in the daytime, too, and wake up feeling calm and cheerful, as if Iris were there. But one morning recently I caught the tail of my vest on our Windsor chair and spilled my mug of tea. I wanted to tell Iris about it, but when I got upstairs I found that she was not there and I couldn't tell her. (Bayley, 1999a, p. 43)

In the 1950s John Bayley, a struggling young English literature scholar, had the cheek to court the brilliant philosopher Iris Murdoch. There followed the kinds of adventures such extraordinary intellects are made for—journeys where the destination is awe in each other's presence. Theirs was a tight community of minds, though not without its sensual and sexual components.

But for Iris in the 1990s the gentle encroachment of aging gave way to the more rapid course of Alzheimer's disease. The once dazzling imagination became the mind of a stubbornly recalcitrant toddler, insistent on bursting out of a moving vehicle or refusing to eat her breakfast. The loss of the familiar Iris in the presence of this bizarre version was almost more than John could bear. And yet, with stunning loyalty, he cared for her at home for nearly 3 agonizing years. With patience, tolerance, and a saving sense of humor John corralled his infantile wife, pressing spoonfuls of cereal into the mouth of the woman he loved.

Iris died (at last?) in 1999. John writes that, "When she died, I closed her eyes and then opened them, as if we could still play together. She had looked and not seen us for days, but now she seemed to see me" (p. 43).

Is this the moving expression of a genius at describing grief, or is it the raving of a man who cannot face the reality of his enormous loss? Is it "normal" to need to go into her room to recognize that his dead wife is no longer available for a conversation? When must we bow to the boundary between life and death, real and imaginary, wish and fulfillment, self and other? Does unimaginable loss confer any special dispensations, permitting us to defer full recognition of reality and still remain within the fold? Or must we label Joan Didion "mad," when, after the death of her husband, she compares the feelings she expected with her real experience (2005):

> We might expect if the death is sudden to feel shock. We do not expect this shock to be obliterative, dislocating to both body and mind. We might expect that we will be prostrate, inconsolable, crazy with loss. We do not expect to be literally crazy, cool customers who believe that their husband is about to return and need his shoes. (p. 188)

Are these people exaggerating, taking advantage of literary license? Or, are they describing rare intensities of grief, qualitatively different from grief at the loss of less notable relatives? Or were both John Bayley and Joan Didion literally driven mad by their profound losses?

We need not ascend literary heights to find examples of grief's effects. It is frequently the foreground, most of the time part of the background of most treatment sessions. As clinicians we are sometimes called upon to judge someone's grief as within or outside "normal" limits. Just how do we make that frequently consequential assessment? Where do we get our own notions of "normal" grieving?

I think that most often we silently render a judgment about whether someone's grief is being lived normally without speaking of it to the patient and, most of the time, without ever consciously fully formulating our own thoughts about it. The patient tells his or her life story, which includes grief. What we focus on as problematic, as worthy of therapeutic attention, results from our (often unformulated) judgment of the normality or pathology of his or her grief's expression. This subtle interpersonal interplay can make a significant difference in the patient's subsequent treatment and, more generally, life experience. I believe that once we meet patients we participate in their ongoing process of self-judgment about the quality of their coping. Our focus is our most frequent expression of what we really think. That is, what we ask about, ignore, comment on, privilege, tells patients what we feel is worth examining therapeutically. This is bound to affect how patients present themselves to us and, cumulatively, how they think of themselves. But much of the time we don't consciously formulate the basis on which we evaluate whether people's way of bearing their losses is psychologically problematic. Elsewhere (1999), I have suggested that we prefer to see ourselves as neutrally following the patients' self-assessments. But we participate in these assessments more than we care to acknowledge. In sessions, as elsewhere, the patients' expression of grief is shaped by interpersonal factors. In addition, it is also affected by the state of the rest of their own emotional systems. That is, since grief is a part of a system of emotions (see Chapter 1) we can't really say anything about others' grief without also considering their loneliness, anxiety, and what they are ashamed of. But, then, how does this interpersonal and emotion systemic vision of grief affect our assessment of the boundaries of what is "normal"?

A female patient I treated who was extraordinarily close to her mother describes herself as not yet mourning her death. The patient is in her 40s, and her mother suffered a painful, lingering death a decade ago. Can grief's *absence* be considered evidence of pathology? How much grief would she have to express to fall within "normal" limits? To what extent is grief's absence or presence in the eye (and the imagination) of the beholder? When she tells me of her loneliness in her marriage and I hear echoes of her loss of her mother what does this mean? Is it evidence that she is really grieving, so her feelings are normal? What if I hadn't seen grief in the background of her marital dissatisfaction? Perhaps along with Winnicott's belief (??) that there is no such thing as the baby we must accept that there is no such thing as the mourner. We shape the mourner we see; her grief and its normal and pathological boundaries. Recognition of this may help us use our clinical experience and psychoanalytic literature in the service of finding ways to treat grief that more fully respect its interpersonal and emotionally complex nature.

Peter Shabad (2001) has contributed extensive clinical examples and thoughtful discussions of the grieving process. But, even when a clinician makes a concerted effort to recognize the subjectivity of our notions of normal mourning, it is extremely difficult to shed idealization of a kind of freedom, or letting go of the lost object. For example, in describing the difference between grief and mourning he says:

> Whereas grief is an emotion of overwhelming sadness, mourning can be viewed as a process of internal transformation by which the old is relinquished and the new is engaged with an open heart. ... Survivors of loss and disillusionment do not really turn away from their most cherished desires, they merely divert them inward. In the deepest reserves of their heart, the bereaved rebel secretly against the facts of loss that have been shoved down their throat, and hold on to what they supposedly had given up. In such circumstances some survivors do not accept that the loved one is lost permanently; they may say that they have worked through the loss, but somewhere inside they may save a place for the loved one's eventual return. (pp. 299–300)

In many extremely sensitive passages Shabad asks what facilitates the process of letting go that he sees as normal mourning (p. 303). He describes the mourner's willing relinquishment of the object as an act of generosity or trust that the environment cares enough to hold his experiences if he cedes them. Shabad sees the task in mourning as a paradoxical process of accepting our unrealistic desires, but giving up irrational demands for their fulfillment. Our wishes can, then, lead an interior life. "The generosity of mourning the loss of a loved one—relinquishing a demand that the dead person be present in the flesh—depends on these internalizations of the imaginary" (p. 311).

To me it seems as though Shabad's vision of healthy mourning is that we make a kind of bargain. We accept the absence of the person we loved if we can hold on to his or her ghost. There is, for me, a religious or spiritual quality to this vision. Something that still lives compensates us for that which ceases to exist. It sounds consoling, but what would John Bayley and Joan Didion say to that bargain? If Didion were willing to settle for her husband's spiritual presence would she still be expecting him to need his shoes?

What seems hardest to accept is that, in mourning, we yearn for the body of the beloved as much as for the soul. We may even miss the physical presence most of all. When, for example, a parent loses a child what would we say is a normal response? Does a notion of "getting past" the loss make any sense? What would it mean? Don't memories of precious moments when the child was still alive play over and over with all their physicality? Don't we long for the person's smell, skin, or laugh?

My understanding of Interpersonal theory helps me conceptualize why representations and identifications cannot compensate for the loss of the actual physical other. As I elaborate below, I believe that one of the hallmarks of interpersonal thinking is its capacity to do justice to the enormity of loss's impact on ongoing relational life and the sense of self. For example, in the moving play "Rabbit Hole," a young boy has died in a tragic accident. That his parents have an internal representation of him does not do much to comfort them. They are distraught. They keep his toys, his clothes, his picture. They long for 1 more day of hearing the sound of his voice. They want their living, breathing son back so they can be his mother and father again and anticipate a future of helping him grow up. Shabad's bargain, that we can willingly relinquish the object, seems unrealistic in this context. Nothing would entice these parents to give up their "irrational demands" to have their son back. There is no interior life that is meaningful enough for their wishes. They want real interaction with their son today and they want to be surprised and delighted by him tomorrow. An internalized object doesn't learn football and fall in love and can't give his parents the joy of *evolving* in their parental role.

In my opinion, conceptions of mourning that suggest we can willingly relinquish the flesh-and-blood person so as to hold on to an internalized object representation or identification do not do full justice to real life experience. They exaggerate the power of the cognitive idea of a person to replace the palpable person. In our deepest attachments we love more than just the idea of someone. We love their bodies. We relish their ability to surprise us. Internalized objects don't have a living being's capacity to surprise. An object representation can't change on its own and it cannot elicit changes in us. It can't amuse and delight us with its unexpected developmental twists and turns. I imagine Joan Didion keeps her husband's shoes because she loves his feet, not an internalized representation of them. When we need to be held we yearn for a *body* to cradle us, not an idea.

But however I may see most analytic descriptions of grieving as falling short of the reality of the process, our failings pale before those of the popular press. Consider this description of the benefits of treatment for elderly patients in despair, "Another kind of therapy helps people understand, express, and resolve longstanding feelings of grief over losing a husband or loved one" (*New York Times*, Tuesday, March 21, 2006, p. F8). I discuss this quote more fully below, but here I note that it sounds wonderfully neat, to "understand, express, and resolve" longstanding grief. To me it seems like an amazingly naïve faith in cognitive insight. It is as though if we name pain well we eradicate it. Pain's power is entirely a product of its ability to hide. Once we bring it into the light of day pain, like some kind of vampire, vanishes. Grief simply can't survive daylight. Sometimes I think of the current popularity of cognitive behavioral treatments as a retreat to Freud's youthful, naïvely optimistic belief in the power of verbalized insight. Just by uttering the demon's name we defeat it. Put the proper labels on our agonies and we "understand, express, and resolve" them. Perhaps we all succumb, at times, to the fantasy that relief can be that simple and accessible. But it is not a harmless fantasy. It leaves Joan Didion shocked and perplexed by what her loss is really like. Fortunately, she believes her experience, and not "expert" opinions. In one of the most poignant passages in the book, Didion relates her attempt, researcher that she is, to study psychiatric explanations of the grieving process. One that particularly missed the mark, leaving her feeling outrageously misunderstood, describes the treatment process in which, "Using our understanding of the psychodynamics involved in the patient's need to keep the lost one alive, we can then explain and interpret the relationship that had existed between the patient and the one who died" (quoted in Didion, p. 56). Reading the next paragraph I imagine Didion's eyes flashing as she asks:

> But from where exactly did Dr. Volkan and his team in Charlottesville derive their unique understanding of "the psychodynamics involved in the patient's need to keep the lost one alive," their special ability to "explain and interpret the relationship that had existed between the patient and the one who died"? Were you watching *Tenko* with me and "the lost one" in Brentwood Park, did you go to dinner with us at Morton's? Were you with me and "the one who died" at Punchbowl in Honolulu four months before it happened? Did you gather up plumeria blossoms with us and drop them on the graves of the unknown dead from Pearl Harbor? (p. 56)

In other words, Dr. Volkan, how dare you smugly, condescendingly, approach my grief as though you understand what I lost better than I do. Didion does not see the shortcoming as only Dr. Volkan's, but, rather, views our society as wanting to hide from the real pain of loss by "diagnosing" more conspicuous sufferers from loss as pathological. She agrees with the English social anthropologist Geoffrey Gorer (1965) who saw a trend in England and the United States toward treating mourning as morbid self-indulgence, partially by giving approval to the bereaved who hide their grief well. Describing her own upbringing, Didion remembered that, "When someone dies, I was taught growing up in California, you bake a ham. You drop it by the house. You go to the funeral. If the family is Catholic you also go to the rosary but you do not wail or keen or in any other way demand the attention of the family" (p. 61).

By prescribing limits to normal grieving, or by ascribing to beliefs that once the loss is understood properly it will be muted, we pretend its pain can be brought under control. While this may work in theory, I suggest it can do harm in practice. The strongest patients may, like Didion, become outraged and feel we are patronizing and insensitive. They may dismiss us, and move on. But the less firmly centered may blame themselves, rather than us, for their failure to benefit from our ministrations. We may then compound their losses, adding the shame of being stigmatized to the inevitable pain of grief. If they accept that they have failed to "get over" their loss in a timely fashion, and that this failure to "move on" is a form of pathology, the bereaved may suffer a loss of a sense of their own normality, along with their loss of a loved one.

Pathologizing the grief that inevitably punctuates life is consonant with the subtly negating attitude toward all emotionality that I think is still prevalent in the wider culture, and in the culture of the mental health professions. We adopt what I like to call "pus" theories, that if we get an emotion "out" it "heals." We strive to "express" our anger, fear, rage, guilt, or shame, hoping to mute its intensity. We fail to recognize the Faustian bargain we are striking. By pathologizing and trying to eradicate aspects of the human condition we barter away some of our passion and the potential meaning our life can have. Ironically, given that emotions are the most powerful modulators of other feelings, we may unintentionally blunt our capacity to recover. For example, a woman who recently lost her husband, believing she is supposed to "move on" as quickly as possible, takes medications because she finds she can't do it on her own. This deadens all her feelings, including the loneliness that might have driven her toward making new connections. Wanting to decrease one emotion, we may use approaches that truncate all of them. We may cut ourselves off from our most powerful tools for regulating affect, including those that can eventually help us bear sorrow. By choosing to be numb we alienate ourselves from each other and from our own most vivid life experience. Like people killing time, in killing off our grief we kill ourselves.

Specifically in relation to grief, we hope to "let it out," and "get past it." But I believe that an expanding array of clinicians realize the potentially detrimental effects of this approach. In the 1970s Henry Krystal (1975) developed treatment techniques to help drug addicts feel more able to fully live their painful feelings, and, therefore, rely less frequently on drugs to cope with them. Seeing the human condition as inevitably burdened with sorrow, Hoffman (1998) has focused our attention on our mortality rather than away from it. Gaines (1997) saw the process of mourning as including preservation of the inner tie to the object, not just navigating the pain as quickly as possible. Picking up on these thoughts Frommer (2005) and, to some degree, Glennon (2005) wrote of the therapeutic value of a view of health as a full embrace of the pain of the human condition.

But it is hard to shed the legacy of an analytic tradition that privileges insight as an instrument for gaining cognitive control over emotionality. It is equally difficult to distance from a wider culture that prizes mastery, and a medical or scientific culture that values quick and measurable cures. These values find their clearest expression, I would suggest, in the psychological treatment of responses to loss. Here, more than anywhere else, our tendency to want to tame pain takes hold. We are tempted toward pain relief as clinicians most of all because we, ourselves, long for it as human beings. No less than others, we would like to believe that human suffering is like a substance that can be isolated from life itself, confined in time and space, categorized, and, eventually, cured. We look for ways to feel less, as though an emotion can be turned down like a thermostat. Like the paranoid patient who believes that when his enemy is vanquished all will be right with the world, we act as though life will be peachy once we "get through" sorrow to a magical state that is purified of the pain of being human.

Winding Sheets

In his nuanced, evocative reading of Seamus Heaney's "Clearances," Ogden (2001) explores the "coexisting forms of love that together shape an experience of grief" (p. 293). In Heaney's poem I find a bereaved son remembering the mother with whom he had folded newly laundered sheets. Because this sonnet was written in the year of the poet's mother's death, in my mind the sheets become a shroud.

The poem and Ogden's discussion suggest to me that the death of someone loved leaves a silence whose texture depends on the feel of their silences in the past. I have found this way of thinking clinically useful. Death's new, infinite texture is of familiar fabric. Heaney's mourning is formed from the homely cloth of ripped-out flour sacks.

> So we'd stretch and fold and end up hand to hand
> For a split second as if nothing had happened
> Beforehand, day by day, just touch and go,
> Coming close again by holding back
> In moves where I was X and she was O
> Inscribed in sheets she'd sown from ripped-
>   out flour sacks. (2001, p. 304)

I see a shy son leaning toward his occupied mother until the tiny aftershock of their touch frightens him just enough to scurry away. Perhaps the space between them was always defined by these skittish skirmishes, so when she died the silence around her still felt temporary. Any moment she would pull her end of the winding sheet toward him again. Her death could be an ongoing surprise for Heaney since he is so accustomed to losing, but then always regaining her. Why isn't she still acting "as if nothing had happened"?

"Coming close again by holding back" strikes me as love made silent by a determination not to disturb. Countless experiences come to my mind, with patients and others, most especially adolescents. Those years have so often evoked careful love from me. I do not want to frighten off the man/woman/child whose right to separate selfhood can still so easily feel threatened.

But when death grants a liberal guarantee of infinite, unlimited separate space, when the danger of her intruding passion is forever past, how do we mourn a woman who understood tick-tack-toe so well? How do we remember a mother subtle enough to play her "O" against our "X" without ever needing to name the game? Given the analytic idealization of naming games (see previous section) and a similar bias in our wider culture, as analysts we may not be well suited for this task. Drunk on our (relatively) newly granted permission to name our every countertransference passion we may have forgotten how to come close by holding back. Yet the act of love that is a necessary part of Heaney's mourning, and that might enable us to participate in it with him, would require our capacity for just such a feather-light "touch and go." But our cultural and professional heritage gears us toward what I see as a naïve one-sided view that naming always relieves, and in order to "get over" loss we must explain and eventually contain and control it. As an example, we can cite Freud's (1914) distinction between the normal process of mourning and pathological melancholia: "… in normal mourning time is needed for the command of reality-testing to be carried out in detail, and that when this work has been accomplished the ego will have succeeded in freeing its libido from the lost object" (p. 252).

Mourning is rarely seen as an ongoing loving experience. Along with Didion, who eloquently protested against her grief being pigeon holed, I suggest that mourning does not generally submit to Freud's definition. The bereaved may, at times, counterfeit acquiescence. Just about everyone would like to be taken as normal. My experience is that most people tend to stop telling me they still talk to their dead partners years after the funeral. Once in a while they permit themselves to let me know they are still advising them on certain matters, such as financial investments. Some may consider themselves as having permission to continue listening to their spouses in their areas of special expertise. I have also found that older patients, those, say, over 70, seem to regard themselves as free to reference the dead more easily than their younger counterparts. It is as though closeness to death gives them the right to start up an ongoing conversation with loved ones who have already died. Or, perhaps, they are less worried about my evaluation of their state of psychological health. In any case, it is always possible that my experience is idiosyncratic, and my patients are simply responding to my own attitudes about normal grieving. I can't know to what degree this is true, by definition. But by writing about the subject of normal mourning, I hope to contribute to an ongoing conversation in which analysts can examine our own attitudes, and consider their impact on the treatments we participate in.

I think of a woman, now in her 80s, whom I have treated for more than 20 years. In that time period she has lost both of her parents and her husband, in addition to many close friends and relatives. Physical ailments constrict her life in various ways. Sessions can easily become catalogues of her losses. Sometimes I feel she is trying to prove to me that life is too cruel to be worth living. When I bring to the session a reluctance to accept this conclusion tension can permeate our interchange. It seems to me to be impossible to remain analytically neutral in what I choose to focus on in the session. I could focus on the anger I hear in her complaint, the unrelenting progression of her illnesses, her terror, her loneliness, what they evoke in me, and so on. Freud's (1912) "evenly hovering attention" seems very far off to me. Whatever I let myself linger over, whatever I fail to notice, whatever I respond to and remember next session reflects how I understand being a human being and bearing the losses inherent in the human condition.

For example, when my elderly patient tells me that she spent Sunday talking to her (dead) husband about their children, what do I feel? What does my feeling encourage, permit, and preclude for her? My patient and I continuously co-create the limits of normal grief. Sometimes we imply that it includes passionate regret for what was never said when there was still time. In those moments I may have the strength to bear being near unfathomable pain. I don't always have it. Sometimes I am capable of playing Heaney's silent tick-tack-toe, the love that *chooses* not to speak its name. I can listen to my patient, almost touch her, move away without naming anything. To me, this is mourning alongside her. Internally my own mourning may differ qualitatively from hers in many ways. But if, that day, I can mourn without any end in sight, I can ease us into doing it side by side. I have this kind of psychic availability sometimes, but not always. Like many creative processes, I cannot order it around, but just appreciate it and hope it returns soon.

Treating Grief

In a trenchant series of papers and replies (*Psychoanalytic Dialogues* 15.4, 2005) several analysts expressed what treating grief means to them. From my perspective, the discussion crystallized some of the central issues we face when we attempt this work:

1. If we accept Gaines' (1997) proposal, that Freud's emphasis on decathecting the lost object is too narrow a view of grieving, what must be added to his formulation?
2. Given the perspective that the self is shaped by interpersonal interchange, what aspect of self do we lose when a significant person dies? For example, let's say my friend deeply appreciated my sense of humor. When he dies I still retain my memory of this, but I lose the chance for new experiences of it. What part of my *self* have I

lost? If I feel that his pleasure brought alive something in me, does some part of me inevitably die along with him?

3. In what senses can we maintain a tie internally, and in what senses is this impossible?

4. Is healthy emotional life generally enhanced by the presence of a focus on our mortality? Put another way, is denial sometimes an adaptive approach to bearing the human condition?

5. What can be the health-promoting benefits of experiences of grief?

6. What are the most common emotional components of grief? Should we, along with Freud, privilege "ambivalence" as the most frequent complication of normal grieving? What other emotions are particularly likely to make its pain unbearable?

7. What are the limits, or boundaries, of normal grieving? If the bereaved refuse to acknowledge the death, behaving as though the dead were still alive, is this by definition pathological? Does grieving grant us special privileges in our relationship to reality?

8. What is the specific contribution the analyst can make to a patient's experience of grieving? In what way does our professional training prepare us for this task? Is there some way our training could better equip us?

To this formidable list I add some personal views. In the rest of this chapter I spell out how I see loss as an ever-present, ongoing human experience, concretized and made manifest by a death. Briefly, for now, I suggest that the frame of analytic treatment is especially suited to engage us in a dialogue about the limits inherent in being human. While the full spectrum of our grief goes unformulated most of the time, treatment during moments of acute loss provides a chance to bring it into focus. Our training as analysts can prepare us to witness grief and to bring to the fore its separate emotional strands. Grieving does inevitably change the aspect of "self" that was cocreated with the person who died. But change is not necessarily depletion. Physical absence of the "other" often brings certain aspects of the "self" into sharper focus. Grief as an ongoing human process is highlighted by the frame of the treatment. The frame can serve to remind us of all that has been incomplete, truncated, and tragically curtailed in our interpersonal lives. Grieving is interpersonal and recursive in its essence. Just as Freud suggested that the *finding* of the object is always a re-finding, so the *losing* of the object also inevitably recapitulates other losses. It reconnects us with our personal collection of sorrows. The friend who dies reawakens all that has ever been taken.

Loss also shifts the ever changing balance of emotions in each of us. For example, with the sharp pain of sadness in the foreground, minor irritations may fade to insignificance. They pale in the presence of a powerful reminder of what most matters.

Freud's (1917) most influential conception of normal grieving was predicated on his drive theory. From this vantage point, the mourner would have to decathect the lost object in order to invest in new relationships. If there is a fixed quantity of libidinal cathexis old attachments must make way for the new. However, Sussillo (2005) points out that this does not fully represent all of Freud's thinking on the matter. His understanding of the mourning process evolved over his lifetime, moving closer to our more current conception of the complexity of normal grieving. I would suggest that an attraction to the idea of "letting go" of lost objects has complex roots. Human beings have found many ways to support the notion of mourning as relinquishing attachment. Note, for example, the statement from the popular press that I quoted earlier (*New York Times*, March 21, 2006, page F8) that what helps elderly people who have lost life partners is to "understand, express, and resolve longstanding feelings of grief over losing a husband or loved one." I would argue that using the word "resolve" is yet another attempt to imply that we can overcome the pain of loss, and put it behind us. We sometimes use words to paper over reality in our effort to believe we can achieve mastery over grief and be finished with it.

Some (Gaines, 1997; Frommer, 2005) have argued that this outcome would not be desirable even if it were possible. Continuity of the relationship with someone significant who has died is a necessary aspect of full human relatedness. Working with patients who sustained the loss of a parent during their adolescence, Sussillo (2005) argues that, optimally, the relationship with the dead parent continuously evolves as the patient's age-appropriate needs change. Frommer suggests that confronting the inherently unending nature of the mourning process can enhance our appreciation of the human condition and help us bear an awareness of our own mortality. In a particularly moving passage Frommer's patient asks him if he was "over his grief yet" about recently losing his mother. Frommer replied that "my grief was still present, but that it was changing and was different from the way it had felt immediately after my mother died." Directly addressing the question of whether grief ever ends Frommer said:

> I told him I was sure that, in one way or another, I'd be grieving for her for the rest of my life, but that grieving for her did not mean I could never feel happiness again. I told him that my mother's death had affected me deeply; it made me more aware of my own mortality and fueled my desire to live the rest of my life as fully as I could. (pp. 492–493)

As has already been suggested, a profoundly complex question is the issue of what we really lose when someone we love dies. First, just what do we lose of the aspect of ourselves that was an interpersonal product of the relationship with the deceased? Also, to what extent can we really preserve the essence of the lost object, either through an internalized object relationship with them, or through an identification with them, as Freud (1917) and others suggest? I think it can be tempting to create a sanitized version of mourning that tames its agonies and fails to do justice to our need for palpable, living, embodied, unpredictable others, and not just notions of others. As I have already suggested, I believe that a true grasp of our interpersonal natures forces us to conclude that the loss of actual, specific, intimately known others is irreplaceable. We need to feel their breath, to hold their hand, to watch them laugh, to experience them in the living moment, through every sense, and not just in memory. This need is given poignant voice by survivors like Didion and Bayley who will settle for nothing less than the continuing presence of their beloved. Anything else denies the importance of the body, of surprise, of the unpredictable moment. No matter how mature and well developed our inner life, there is no object relational substitute for an alive partner when you want to go dancing.

These issues are extremely controversial in that they bring into focus our understanding of the nature of the self. I would suggest that it is here, more than on any other issue, that the analyst's fundamental theoretical orientation determines his or her outlook. To what extent do we each believe that the self is primarily a product of *ongoing, real* interpersonal interchanges with living others?

From my own understanding of human grief I would suggest that it is extremely important to differentiate the sorrow that is an inherent aspect of the human condition from pathological states. For example, a woman consulted with me, stating that she was "depressed" because she found out she could never bear a child. While it is, of course, possible that she was suffering from a depressive disorder, I would not assume that this must be so. It is common, in our culture, to use the words "sadness" and "depression" interchangeably. After considerable discussion I came to see this patient as extremely sad about what, for her, was a significant loss, but not clinically depressed. Developing this distinction together proved valuable to us both.

I see significant losses as affecting the whole balance of a person's emotions. This affords clinicians a wider range in their focus as they listen to patients. If we don't privilege sadness, but remain open to hearing about, for example, the patients' loneliness, we may find that addressing that feeling first might have greater impact. Patients and analysts frequently get stuck trying to soften a sadness that is simply a human response to loss. Sometimes a focus *away* from that sadness is more effective. Believing that the emotions exist in balance, with every emotion affecting the intensity of all the others, means to me that I can have an impact on patients' sadness by facilitating their curiosity or becoming a presence that modulates their loneliness.

I see loss as an ongoing aspect of human experience, not a discrete event. It is a part of every hour of every day, including every treatment session. Some moments are not formulated as losses until much later in the work. Concrete losses crystallize the ongoing experience of loss and bring it from background to foreground. In every session, for example, I fail to understand some of what patients are trying to communicate, and, therefore, I confront them with the inherent loneliness of being human beings. They feel the loss of the hope they may have had that I would "get" their experience. Then, if a more concrete loss occurs, it is likely to evoke the pain of all their accumulated losses. For example, if I tell them I will be away for a week, they may seem to "overreact" to this temporary loss, but I believe that reaction is really a product of the many types of loss we are living out at that time.

Treatment affords a unique opportunity for dealing with loss. For me, this is an aspect of the significance of the treatment frame. It crystallizes the omnipresent limitations of human relatedness. This is part of the reason that the frame so often elicits strong reactions. An interesting example of this occurred in Sussillo's (2005) paper on working with people who had lost a parent during adolescence. Sussillo describes her treatment of Judy, a 24-year-old socially withdrawn patient whose mother's death from recurrent cancer occurred when the girl was 16; her father succumbed to a longstanding heart disease when she was 17. As this depressed woman poignantly explained, "I feel all alone in the world; I am no one's daughter anymore; I don't know who I belong to" (pp. 514–515).

Sussillo describes a complicated enactment that developed in the treatment. For some time Judy had been chronically late to sessions, sometimes failing to appear or call. Then, one day, Sussillo confused the appointment, believing it to be on another day, and was not in her office when the patient arrived for her session. How are we to understand the meaning of this mistake? In an evocative discussion of the case Cole (2005, pp. 539–549) highlights how the frame became the locus of an enactment of the patient's need to resist the new attachment to the analyst and hold on to her old attachments. Cole asks whether this actual interaction around the frame was the only way Sussillo could come to understand the pull of the patient's old object world. As analysts do we have to actually live something out with the patient in order to understand it? Must we violate the format of the frame in order to grasp what it symbolically stands for in this particular treatment? Cole implies that the relational analyst privileges the need for an *actual enactment*, while more traditional analysts would not. Responding to this issue, Sussillo replied to Cole (2005) that "… there was an unconscious communication in my forgetting of the session; however, in my view, it's not essentially about the frame." She goes on to argue that the frame was not "the heart of the matter," but, rather, the enactment was about "unbearable affects of loss (and the sense of intersubjective vulnerability) and the need to regulate them …." (p. 563).

I think that, as analysts, we are so used to the frame, and, perhaps, so dependent on it, that we dare not fully comprehend its tragic dimension. Sussillo seems to me to differentiate the frame from the "heart of the matter," while I would see them as one and the same in many senses. Sometimes the patient's heart (and sometimes the analyst's) can be broken by the frame. The frame guarantees that we will not always be available when we are most needed. It can bring home to each participant how frequently, in any relationship, the presence of the other is ill timed from the point of view of the self. Sometimes, as the analyst, I feel the hour ending way too fast. I want more time, and have to experience, yet again, the same regret we feel when someone dies before we have had the chance to express something vital. Of course, the ending of a session is usually not as fraught with meaning as this implies. In an ordinary day, hour follows hour with no hearts actually broken. Through the frame we enact the limitations of all human connection in a muted form. But once in a while it is a very real reminder of the ache of endless love and need, and how that ache begs for more than it can have. The frame is both symbol and symbolized. It *represents* the limitations of human connection, but is also an *actual* limit. It is a lived experience, a real example, of how badly timed human connection often is from one's own point of view. But it also symbolically represents how this can occur in every relationship, and not just in treatment. No one most needs someone else every Tuesday, Thursday, and Friday at 4 o'clock. For everyone there will be an occasional Wednesday full of yearning, and there will be a Thursday when it would feel wonderful to be left alone.

But in any relationship nothing violates the "frame," the expectation of contact, as much as the permanent absence of one of the participants. When someone we love dies, "Wednesday" stretches into eternity. For us, as analysts, every hour of every day has the potential to become an endless Wednesday. We can see this reflected in how badly clinicians sometimes suffer when patients abruptly terminate treatment. In effect, the patient is saying, "You may not have realized it, but you already had your last chance to engage me. Now, and for the rest of time, you can live with wondering why I left, and what could have happened between us if we had continued our work."

Ordinary and Extraordinary Grief

I suggest that grief about the limitations of human connectedness is embedded in the fabric of life and inherent in every session of every treatment. Therefore, every session presents an opportunity to work on this issue. We "work on" it in many ways. We live out these limitations with our patients. We talk about them when we discuss the frame. Termination epitomizes the point at which "we" no longer exist together physically.

Thus, looking back at the questions I posed in a previous section (see "Treating Grief") we might ask how different orientations about grief would influence analytic technique. For example, if I believe that decathecting lost objects is desirable, how do I live out the termination phase of treatment? If I think that human ties require the actual living presence of the object in order to be fully realized and cannot be fully maintained internally, how does this affect my handling of the frame? Would I deal with my own vacations differently? If I think human beings are "healthier" the more we address our mortality how would I handle the patient's lateness?

If I personally believe denial is sometimes an adaptive approach to bearing the human condition, how would that affect what I focus on in a session? If I think we lose an aspect of "self" when someone dies, how would that impact the way I schedule appointments?

Along with William Blake, then, we can see the world in a grain of sand, and a treatment hour as a microcosm of the human encounter with limitation. With some patients, for example, I find myself more inclined to mention, toward the end of a session, that our time is almost up. Why? I think, sometimes, I am obliquely referencing how abrupt endings can be, how suddenly they can intrude, how unprepared for our last moments we can feel. Perhaps I am asking if there is a way to ease into the silence of separation. Can we ready each other for loss if we prepare? Can, perhaps, my very *wanting* to soften loss actually modulate the loneliness of it?

When the content of the session is actually about a significant loss the "ordinary" losses of everyday analytic life take on added significance. Thus, for example, in Sussillo's treatment of Judy, the patient who lost both parents during her adolescence, it seems to me inevitable that the frame would become an important focus. The ordinary rhythms of connection and disconnection take on extraordinary meanings in this context.

Of course, I am not suggesting that we deliberately manipulate the frame so as to bring up significant human issues. Rather, I feel we should recognize the frame's many layers of meaning. It is my own belief that how we bear the pain of the frame makes a profound difference. It is a pain that must be endured but that should not feel sadistically or arbitrarily visited on either participant. In how we live the frame we can indicate that the sadness, yearning, and regret that are inevitable in all human contact can be somewhat modulated by love, kindness, and mutual recognition. I would not suggest that we try to eradicate the pain of disconnection, since that would block the use of the treatment relationship as a microcosm for the rest of life. But, perhaps even more importantly, I do think that by visibly, palpably trying hard to reschedule missed appointments I am saying I am not deliberately imposing my absence as an expression of my power to do so, or as an arbitrary punishment. I think that the goodwill inherent in my stance may, to some extent, clarify the pain of (once again) recognizing how seldom the other is "there" at just the right time. Notice I did not say my goodwill eliminates the pain (which would be unrealistic, and would rely exclusively on new experience as the agent of change) but that it *clarifies* the pain. Pain can then be experienced as inherent in human relationships (rather than artificially imposed by a set of arbitrary analytic rules). By palpably giving all I can within the confines of my role, I am saying to the patient, "This is how life is. It can't be helped. Inevitably, sometimes, we leave each other hungry." I understand that many analysts would object to my approach. Some would feel I am heading off the patient's sorrow and anger and precluding important transference experiences. For some, my approach raises the specter of the "corrective emotional experience." They might suggest that I am trying to fashion a kindly interchange that will teach the patient a healthier way to bear absences. These objections all have merit. But, ultimately, I believe that it is even more important for patients to realize that some of the pain they feel is inherent in life, and not deliberately, wantonly inflicted. It seems to me to be ironic that I see my actions (giving all I can within the necessary limits of the frame) as making possible the kind of undistorted experience that neutrality and abstinence aim for. How can patients come to understand loss in its purest form if we don't take care to separate it from imposed, unnecessary, arbitrary loss?

I believe that the lessons about human connection and vulnerability that we take from the experience of losing someone can radically change over time. A female patient's mother died during a protracted emotional struggle between them over whose view of their past relationship would prevail. At the time, her mother's death provided the woman some relief as well as grief. But now, years later, she has so many more things to say to her. Given how much she would cherish the chance to say them, her mother's continued absence is very poorly "timed," from the patient's perspective. In a sense, her loss is much greater now than it was when the death occurred so many years ago.

Loss as a Continuous Experience

To sum up, I think of loss as an ongoing aspect of treatment (as well as the rest of life). For example, a moment that clarifies my mis-attunement highlights the limitations of (our) connection, for both me and the patient. Rather than a dramatic event, loss is most often a strand woven into all human experience. But a particular major concrete loss brings this part of life into focus. We are unusually aware of loss at a funeral. We come face to face with it. But the feelings we have are engendered by the whole flow of loss in our lives. Losing a hope, an idealization, a belief, a possibility, augments other losses. To me, loss is like a great river fed by countless tributaries.

Another way to say this is that when we confront concrete losses we are reminded of our ongoing losses. In Donnel Stern's sense (1998), loss becomes a formulated experience. A death reminds us that life's every spark is temporary, but so does the ending of the session, or the onset of cold weather in early winter. No wonder art has so frequently envisioned a relationship between winter and death, as have mythology and so many other cultural expressions. Summer is always being lost, even at its height. So is life itself, including everything we cherish. Loss is always near at hand, but that is especially clear and highlighted at certain intense moments.

From this perspective, it is meaningless to think of loss as "resolved." We don't "get over" a loss, any more than we can "get over" being ourselves. Losses become integral parts of who we are as human beings and what living means to us. Every loss brings this aspect of life to the foreground of our experience, and modifies our ongoing knowledge of what losing is like. Another way to put this is that, like the experience of September 11, 2001, any significant loss changes how we view the world, human life, and ourselves. Losses we bear now will contribute to our response to the losses we face tomorrow.

Revisiting the passages written by John Bayley and Joan Didion that began this chapter, I would suggest that their sense of their loved ones' being present for them, in physical, and not just spiritual or psychological senses, is not about denial, the absence of reality testing, or any form of pathology. Rather, it is an effort toward balancing the knowledge of loss with a deliberately conjured experience of the presence of the person they loved. Iris Murdoch is still present, in many senses, for John Bayley. He knows what she would laugh about and how she smelled. When he wants to tell Iris about catching the tail of his vest on the Windsor chair he is compensating himself for the ways Iris is absent, with the ways she can still be present. Just as those who are blind may have a heightened experience of another sense, Bayley is augmenting the Iris-sensations that he can still have, in order to bear the Iris-sensations he can no longer have. Bayley is not accepting the "deal" Shabad (2001) and others posit—that we can bear physical loss because we still have an inner object relationship with the departed. Bayley has an internalized object relationship with Iris, of course, but he wants more than that. He wants to see her eyes still loving him. I would call this wisdom, and not any kind of pathology.

Returning to some of the issues raised by Ogden, Gaines, Shabad, Frommer, Sussillo, Cole, and others, I would suggest that when someone dies we change. It is oversimplifying merely to say we lose parts of ourselves, since we may find ways to balance lost sensations with those that are even *more* available now. For example my patient whose mother died years ago during a stormy passage in their relationship can better experience aspects of her mother now than she could while that difficult old woman was still alive. My patient changes as she weighs what she has lost against what she has found. She may, then, relate to life a bit differently. She hasn't exactly "lost" who she was with her mother, but she has changed as a result of her experience of trying (and partially failing) to recreate her mother. Similarly, in Heaney's poem about his dead mother ("Clearances," discussed above) Heaney reframes their old dance of "touch and go." Whereas before his mother's death their game may have signified her unavailability, now that she is dead it may take on other meanings. From the vantage point of her current vast absence, "touch and go" may now represent his mother's delicate understanding of the limitations of their contact. Her feather-light touch may now seem to Heaney to be a way she taught him her rhythm of holding back and coming close. Heaney can use this recreated mother to help him bear what he can no longer have. He has not wholly lost the "self" he was with her, but that self has changed its meaning, as she has changed, for him. Previously her "touch and go" may have signaled the limited availability of an everlastingly occupied parent. After all, Ogden (2001) tells us Heaney was the oldest of nine children. Now their "dance" also could be understood as an expression of her quintessential form of loving, her way of "coming close again by holding back." This reinvented mother still can change Heaney. He *has* lost the self springing from ongoing, potentially surprising interchange with his teasingly alive but exhausted mother. But against this loss is the "gain" of the self he can be with his freshly constituted, maturely understood, internalized "mother." This "mother" inside his mind does not have the power of embodied otherness, that surprising magic we discover as infants, in a dance with a (hopefully) responsive face.

The imagined mother may give some comfort but she is no substitute for the real thing. Heaney has lost the tingle of the self he was when his mother was alive and ultimately unpredictable. It is true that he has also "gained" a more fully considered mother and self. In short, Heaney's self-in-relation-to-mother is altered—added to, as well as diminished.

If Only

My own clinical and nonclinical experiences tell me that the emotion that most frequently complicates loss is regret and not, as Freud (1914) posited, ambivalence. I am not suggesting that ambivalence doesn't play an important part in many grief reactions. Of course, it does. But even in these emotional states, I would say that regret may be a significant aspect.

Since regret is the subject of another chapter (4), here I briefly describe the role regret can play in grief. A woman now in her 80s looks back on her long marriage to a man who has recently succumbed to chronic heart problems. She and I know how hard she worked to keep him alive and well as long as possible. Yet she is constantly subjecting herself to cross-examination. The list of her possible "crimes" is always the same. Maybe, toward the end of her husband's life, she didn't try hard enough to get him the best care. Maybe she didn't say the right goodbye. Maybe she didn't communicate how deeply she loved him. Maybe she wasn't nice enough to him while he was still alive. Maybe she didn't appreciate how unusually good he was.

What accounts for the tenacity of her energetic self-criticism? I have no doubt that ambivalence plays a key role. Given how recently her husband died, I am cautious about pointing out her relief, and how much of a burden his last years were for her. While these feelings are extremely important, I feel wary about bringing them to the fore just yet. Is this my clinically apt sensitivity to her talent for self-flagellation or a countertransference I should challenge internally? Or both?

The patient's ambivalence toward her husband is, of course, highly significant. But I think what makes this nearly unbearable for her is vast regret. I believe, she (correctly) intuits that the regret will always be with her although other feelings may fade. Over time her guilt will soften. She may forgive life more for what it took from her and be less angry. The vague cloud of irritated depression may lift somewhat. But I don't believe her regret will end. How do any of us bear that we didn't fully live the time that was precious? That we let chances for joy pass by? That we looked the other way?

It is hard to face the limitations in our capacity to love. Surely sorrow plays some part in our emotional reply to this recognition. Anger or ambivalence is usually implicated in the cause of these limitations. But I think it is regret that most often brings the pain to its height. For example, while there are many ways to understand why Oedipus blinds himself, I think the role of regret has not been sufficiently recognized. Often, like Oedipus, we would wish to understand the meaning of each crossroad before we choose our path. If only we could see ahead in time to avert unbearable sorrow. Loss complicated by regret stars in so many tragedies, on and off the theater's stage. Ultimately, I believe, the greatest pain in loss very often stems from our regret that we didn't divine more, love more fully, stretch our selves and live a wider, emotionally richer life while we still had the chance.

A question I frequently raise in treatment hours is, "What do you think will be your deepest regret about how you are living now?" I know how little impact merely asking this question has, and yet I still ask it. Of course *when* I ask it is a product of who I am, what I regret, what, to me, is a "wider, richer life." Once again, I bump into my own inevitable subjectivity. But I feel that asking this question can, sometimes, shift us into searching for what is still possible in situations where much is outside our control. A patient rails at her husband, bemoaning his inadequacies as a father. I ask her what she thinks she will regret most when she remembers these years. Perhaps nothing much happens when I ask the question this time. But maybe, at least, I have interrupted a well rehearsed diatribe and something new has had a chance to occur. Later on we may be able to revisit the sequence and better understand the diatribe itself.

We all know (at least in theory) that loss is part of life's deal and that it hurts. The question that comes up for me is how can we live with it? Not how can we accept it, or adapt, but live? Once again, my own answer brings the balance of emotions into play. I believe that John Bayley knows that he gave Iris Murdoch as good a death as he could. I imagine that knowing this somewhat delimits his guilt and regret. I would differentiate guilt and regret here by saying that I think guilt refers to standards we feel we have violated, while regret, in this context, is for opportunity lost. While Bayley could well have personal, conscious, and unconscious issues that exacerbate his guilt and regret, I think it likely he also knows how hard he did try. Securely knowing this might enhance Bayley's ability to continue to turn toward Iris so she can keep him company. If we live as hard as we can, if we embrace all the loss, the love, the hope, do we bear the pain of life any better?

Ultimately it is my heart and not my mind that tells me my answer. Theory only confirms it for me after I have already arrived at it, but it isn't what convinces me. Participating in the lives of others and my own life has acquainted me with some of the shades of bearable and unbearable pain. I have come to believe that regret often colors the darker shades.

The Analyst's Grief

> I have some concern that emotionally focusing on one's mortality can cross over from empowering existential anxiety to pathological preoccupation and paralysis. (Glennon, 2005, p. 534)

> Living the terror and despair that come from really looking at what we know to be true about our existence, like living through losses of all kinds, requires a sustained relational engagement if we are to be able to mentalize our experience and construct the psychic space necessary to continue to create or restore meaning for our lives. (Frommer, 2005, p. 555)

Are human beings "healthier" if we are always keeping one eye on the clock? Should consciousness raising about mortality be part of the job description of the psychoanalyst? Are analysts particularly well suited to this task? How would we integrate this work with the rest of our analytic functioning?

It seems to me that analysts are uniquely qualified to comment on the broader issue of bearing loss. The analyst is, in a sense, a specialist in this area. Elsewhere (Buechler, 2000, 2004) I have catalogued the extraordinary variety of losses analysts regularly face. I would top the list with the fact that throughout our careers we lose touch with most of the patients we treat. I believe I am not alone in maintaining that once patients terminate treatment under usual circumstances I should not make any contact with them, so as to avoid pressuring them in any way. My goal is to preserve the possibility of resumption of the analysis, should the patient feel the need arise. Consequently, I can conjure up, in my mind's eye, a long parade of former patients. I would love to know what happened to them, out of natural curiosity in all cases, as well as genuine concern in a few. I still feel very much as I did in 2000:

> ... for those of us who feel post-treatment contact should be very limited there is a unique kind of loss at the termination of an analytic treatment. Never to hear what became of someone you have known so intimately is an incredible loss. Yet it is a regular occurrence in our professional lives. Loss comes with the territory. (p. 85)

But our analytic experience includes many other regularly occurring losses. Aside from planned terminations, there are the abrupt disappearances. Patients who simply never return for their next appointment or terminate the work with a mysterious phone message can cause us severe pain and doubt. For us, the story always remains unsettlingly unfinished. We wonder if we could have done something differently to make it possible for the treatment to go further. We feel responsible for any "mistakes" we might have made, and can regret that we may never have a chance to repair the damage.

Those of us who work with children may suffer the pain of having the child's parents withdraw the youngster from treatment often, from our viewpoint, just when the therapeutic relationship seems to be developing. In addition, there are less well defined losses, such as burnout or the loss of faith in the profession. Our professional culture and the wider social climate provide us with demoralizing encounters as we deal with managed care in an era that values pharmaceutical solutions to life's problems, the bottom line more than the quality of a life, one-dimensional, simplistic, one-size-fits all treatments, and so on.

In learning to bear these repeated experiences, do we gain any wisdom that we can use in approaching the losses at the heart of this chapter? Do we learn something of value to ourselves that can also be helpful to our patients?

I can say that I have learned to gather resilience from frequently losing myself in sessions. That is, without consciously engineering it, I often lose track of time, among other things. I am not as rooted as usual. I could be anywhere, anyone, any age. As I would in the theater, I let go of the boundary between here and there, reality and fiction, me and not me, possible and impossible. Temporarily, I am free of the usual constraints. I don't have to keep track of what is reasonable, likely, preferable. I have no history and no future. As I have written elsewhere (2002) there is joy in this unmoored state, at least for me. I feel liberated, as though I am able to dance lightly, quickly, gracefully.

These moments of escape strengthen me as I bear losses I am experiencing now, as well as those I anticipate. Another way to say this is that living in transitional space fortifies me, enabling me to feel better equipped when I return to the harsher realm of reality.

Visits to timelessness are what enable me to bear glimpses of mortality. These vacations are more than just rejuvenating. They frame life differently. They transform the constraints of time, place, and person into temporary conditions. Thus, sessions where I lose awareness of time and of myself as a separate entity change the meaning of moments when I face the constraints of my life. They balance the constriction of mortality with the joy of participating in the limitless.

Just as getting lost in a symphony, a painting, or a book refreshes me, some sessions provide a chance to get outside my self. Sometimes I feel I am "in" someone else, for a moment, or just not "in" my self. Sometimes I am alternating, in a personal version of Sullivan's (1954) participant observation. I momentarily let go of my self, only to return to it and think about what just happened.

These forays into otherness somewhat modify the experience of mortality. The more they happen, the more they make mortality the exception rather than the rule. The joy of generativity is, in part, the pleasure of escape. I become part of life and not, merely, my time-limited self.

While I don't believe that constantly concentrating on mortality is desirable in treatment (or elsewhere) I do think the play of its shadow is an important part of life. Unconsciously, without any premeditation, analysts model the alternation between losing ourselves and refinding ourselves. In other words, while this usually remains unformulated, I believe we can sometimes demonstrate how being a participant in timeless life makes being time-bound bearable.

Loss takes three fundamental shapes in this chapter. While on the surface they seem quite different, I believe they merge in our experience of life. Losses of beloved others, lost hopes for attunement in others, and our own mortality all bring sorrow. The loss of a loved one, the losses attendant on a treatment's frame, and the ultimate loss of our own lives seem to have little else in common. But I see them each as similarly coloring life's fabric and as contributing to the pain of the other two. If we can face the unavoidability of all three, if we can look them square in the eye, if we can find enough joy in other aspects of our lives, perhaps we can balance the equation. We will, however, never succeed if we deny the depth of our losses. For each, there is no comforting easy compensation. Internalizations and identifications offer some solace but they do not make it all fine. Nothing can substitute for the electric charge that comes from a profoundly attuned, alive, embodied, sensate, unpredictable other. No memory, no idea is as elastic. None vibrantly promises future. We know this, and cannot be fooled into accepting substitutes for what we crave. When the truly cherished dies we conjure because it is the best we can do.

When I look at someone I know I have touched who will live after me, my own mortality doesn't mean quite as much as it otherwise would, because it stands side by side with ongoing life. I can then peek at mortality more often. I am well aware that this is a very personal statement and I am not suggesting that it applies to others. But I think it would be worthwhile for us, as analysts, to think about how our work (among other things) gives meaning to our lives, sustains us, and fortifies us to face losses, including, eventually, our loss of life itself.

A female patient and I have worked together for many years. In my mind's eye I have watched her four children grow from infancy to the brink of adolescence. She casually mentions how words of mine helped her deal with a minor incident. Along with narcissistic gratification I can also find joy in the idea that something from me now lives in these children. This ripple effect extends my reach. I have participated in something that cannot be located in time and space. This will frame and modulate the next time I experience how I am also locked into time and space.

Being analysts gives us a fine vantage point for experiencing both time and timelessness. Our daily schedule demonstrates an essential absurdity that is inherent in the rest of our lives as well. From 3 o'clock to 3:45 a patient and I exist together. No matter what is happening we must stop at 3:45. Like Cinderella dashing away from the prince at midnight, we must obey the clock and not our hearts. However wonderful (or terrible) the ball might be, when the clock strikes 12 it is over. Sometimes hours, like some lives, end just when they are really getting going.

Treatment lives within a time slot. But sometimes magic happens. At the very same time as we are obeying limits we also overcome them. Like Heaney and his mother, we come close by holding back. Staying within our time and role constraints we also break through them. The hour takes off, the process carries us, and we are free of any awareness of limitation. We know the joy of floating outside time and self. We help generate growth that renews itself and takes us into the future.

Each session is an opportunity to make a difference to each other. In a circumscribed period of time we have a chance to have an experience that feels limitless, and will endlessly reverberate in our memories.

Sometimes, at the end of a session with the patient who is a mother of four, I regret how we used our time. I look back, wishing I had kept better hold of my own sense of purpose with her. I am sad this chance is gone, but also relieved that the session is over. I think she has similar feelings about parenting. She wishes it would never end, and will miss her children painfully as they scatter into their adulthoods. At the same time, she longs for her work to be done. She knows she has profoundly affected their lives, yet wishes she could have had more impact. She is more aware of her own aging process when she is around their budding youth. But, near them, she sometimes feels an expansive, wordless joy at participating in their lives. I feel all of these things, at various moments, with her. I am sad and relieved to see her go. When my work is done with her I am sure I will regret its limitations and be glad for every moment we got lost enough in each other to fully meet. Those are the moments when my self awareness falls so completely away that the end of the hour is a jolting surprise. The aliveness of those moments will outlast our work together.

When she leaves, whatever grief I feel will not result solely from the loss of her presence. Rather, it will be an accumulation of feeling made palpable to me by the event of termination. That is, knowing I may never see her again will bring my feelings about losing her to an intensity level that is high enough for me to recognize. Partially, I believe, I will be responding to all my lost chances for the "now moments" (Stern, 1998) that might have made a difference to us both. I will regret all the times I took it easy, stayed locked inside myself, and counted out the seconds until she left. All those hollow moments will gather together at the "termination" and add to its hurt, because then my chance to make them up will be officially over. On the other hand, to the extent that we really knew each other, at least this one form of regret will not complicate my loss. Like John Bayley with his Iris, I will know that conjuring her will not come at the expense of my peace of mind if I feel that I have used the opportunity of knowing her as fully as I could. This might somewhat leaven my sadness. The fullness of our contact has provided me with sensations, words, and memories. While not all I might yearn for, this is something. Our effect on each other was sharpest in its immediacy, but it may yet develop new meanings for each of us over time.

7

Empowering and Disorienting Anger

People tend to feel guilt in this man's presence. We know we should be more tolerant, less impatient. As I listen to a painstaking account of his day's work, replete with implied criticisms of his arch rival's behavior at a meeting, I grow sleepy. I try to focus on what he is saying. After all, it is his time, his session. He is being appropriate (why am I thinking of the most overused word in the therapeutic lexicon?)

I feel as though he has taken his role as a patient to some kind of mad extreme. "Mad," I reflect, in several senses. Yes, he is supposed to tell me what is on his mind. And I am supposed to be willing and able to hear him. I wonder how much he means to drive me to distraction (literally). I begin to pun, the word "distraction" having given me something to play with. But why am I engaging in word play at this patient's expense? Maybe I need to take some time off.

I think about Joyce Slochower's (2003) concept of analytic misdemeanors, those moments we steal from patients by letting our attention wander. She describes our furtive glances at shopping lists, magazines, photographs, and so on, all while we are supposed to be paying attention to a patient. Even though there is no magazine in front of me I feel as if I am stealing time. Am I a thief?

But then my inner defense lawyer takes the floor. No, this is an enactment, not a misdemeanor, since the patient is playing a significant role. I find myself parsing. Enactment or misdemeanor, our fault, his fault, my fault? Countertransference that can be useful to this treatment, or (mostly) a personal warning to alter my schedule?

I am ready to tell him what just happened and see where it takes us. Perhaps I am a bit too smug about my honesty as I describe my difficulty in paying attention to what he is saying. What was he feeling as he spoke?

What follows can be likened to a tug of war. He tells me he would be happy to repeat everything he has said so far so I would not miss any of the details. I wince, momentarily distracted again, inwardly musing that this would be cruel and unusual punishment. I say that I am bringing it up because I think it could be meaningful for us to consider what just happened between us. As though I hadn't spoken, he starts to replay the team meeting, with special emphasis on the behavior of his arch rival. I feel he is testing whether I pick up on the outrageous, unwarranted, insensitive behavior of the rival. He doesn't ask me what I think, but spreads the situation in front of me and waits to see how I react.

Now I *am* furious, but not entirely sure why. I am, however, aware that what has changed for me is that now I don't like either of us. While I understand why I am angry (or at least some of the reasons) I am not sure why I am *this* angry. Is it because I feel he is trying to control me? Is it because he is succeeding (although neither of us is getting what we want)?

I am next more fully aware that my humor has been at his expense all along. I was ready to become angry at him even before the session began. Why? Is there some way I can make use of this situation for us both?

In retrospect, I think my anger and my humor were ways to assert separateness. I was, in effect, saying he could not control me, force me to look where he wants me to look, think what he wants me to think, and say what he wants to hear me say. I was insisting that I am not a marionette. But why did my assertion of separateness take this form?

In addition to considering my countertransference as a form of anger, I could think about it as my obsessive response to his obsessive indirectness. One of the fascinating aspects of obsessive behavior is its exquisitely contagious quality. A supervisee describes the bind in dealing with a patient who is insisting on controlling the scheduling of sessions. The supervisee feels caught up in the very struggles that need to be illuminated. To accede to the patient's demands feels like collusion, but to refuse feels punitive and an enactment. The issue of conforming versus rebelling that plays such a major role in obsessive dynamics is increasingly central to this treatment exchange. The supervisee feels this is engaging in the power struggle, and not just analyzing it. Sullivan's (1956) analogy of obsessive dynamics' being like sticky flypaper comes to mind. It is impossible not to get stuck in it. I think some of the stickiness results from our effort to be "above" needing to have our own way. Trying too hard to avoid being engaged in a tug of war guarantees our involvement in it. We then become angry because we feel forced into being "bad," out of control, and childishly retributive.

Anger seems to me to be an emotion that very often operates in disguise. Just as steam is water, although it does not look like water, my sleepiness was anger. Bonime (1976) once insisted that a patient's yawn was anger. Similarly, I think my sleepiness and jokiness with my patient didn't merely indicate anger. It *was* anger. I am not content with demonstrating that he cannot control me. I am punishing him for trying. I am also fighting fire with fire, so to speak. I return his anger with mine, his efforts at controlling the session with my own, and his linguistic preoccupation with my own wordplay. Two are engaging in the tug-of-war.

While I could say that I had a therapeutic intention to help the patient see himself more clearly, my emotional state does not fit that description. I did not merely want him to see something. I wanted to *make* him see, just as he wanted to order me to see that his professional rival was being outrageous.

It is interesting to me that someone overhearing us might not catch our fierceness. Although we were both enraged, it was a quiet rage on both sides. It specialized in its ability to be overlooked or mistaken for something else.

I think of another patient, a woman who is driven wild by her husband's ability to get away with his covert controlling behavior. Everyone thinks he is a saint. Only she knows the truth about him. And she can't stand that. He is getting away with (soul) murder. Is my need to punish my patient similar to her desire to expose her husband? Is the intensity of my feeling born from a similar insistence?

I think I am so angry because of the power the male patient has or, more accurately, the power he and I give him. My effort to point out how he is trying to force me into a corner *forces me into a corner.* If I try to escape his control I am still reacting to his agenda. The intensity of my feeling stems, I believe, from a sense that I have lost my self. In Sullivan's (1953) language, I have lost the "good-me."

From my point of view I have lost something even more precious than a good opinion of myself. I have lost time. Trying not to steal from my patient is a full-time job. I can do little else when I am preoccupied with conforming or rebelling. I am off balance and unable to focus. I am reminded of a female therapist who consulted me in the midst of a terrible battle with a long-time female patient. An ugly and potentially endless legal battle was brewing. The patient wanted to continue a treatment that, for her therapist, had become torture. The therapist found herself dreading their accusation-filled sessions. Her preoccupation with this patient was causing her sleepless nights and anxious days. The patient was clearly using legalistic language to formulate a case of "abandonment." After more than a decade of treatment the patient had been complaining of little progress, but when the therapist suggested they might terminate, the patient became enraged. The therapist quite reasonably offered to arrange a consultation or a transfer to another clinician. This further inflamed the patient, who insisted on her right to decide when their work was done. Increasingly, the therapist felt stripped of everything she liked about herself. She felt ungenerous, untherapeutic, unable to think. The potential for years of defending herself in court was constantly on her mind. Every word out of her mouth became either an admission or a self-defense.

Along with Epstein (1979) we could imagine that if she had more anger-inclusive criteria for being a "good therapist" she would not lose so much of her self-esteem just because she is having a conflict with her patient. Consequently, her anger might not escalate to such a degree. I think this is true, but I also believe that avoiding the anger is not the goal. What I would like to consider is, could she remain connected to this patient and still fully use her anger's empowering potential? Also, does she have to bring her anger out into the open to effectively point out the patient's indirectness? Is that contrast, or some other sort of contrast essential to this work? More generally, can we be strengthened by the assertive force of anger without being disabled by its destructive power?

I would suggest that the ability to express anger is treasured in some analytic circles much more than others. Informally, members of the interpersonal schools often find fault with noninterpersonalists because they are seen as deficient in that capacity. Less experienced colleagues are also often subject to this criticism. Like other stances, this can be taken too far in a macho version of let's see whose anger capacity is biggest. On training committees, the candidate's capacity for expressing anger can become, I would say, an over-valued fetish rather than merely a therapeutic option.

Elsewhere (1997), however, I have also described treatments I see as stalled because the analyst cannot reach into his anger and use it to motor the work. This previous paper described a treatment deadlock in which a therapist was unable to connect to her anger at a patient's stubborn withdrawal from her. A kind of stalemate was the unhappy result. The therapist's usual curiosity was completely absent, to a degree that was stunning for me as her supervisor. The patient, a 35-year-old depressed man, had a successful career and no personal life. His awkward stony silences were punctuated by animated descriptions of his work. His therapist found herself enacting a painful parody of neutrality, asking stale clichéd questions, parroting what the patient had already said, or ambiguously wondering how the treatment was making him feel. Listening, I was reminded of the fog Sullivan described as engulfing some treatments (1956). Finally I suggested that the therapist was avoiding her anger at the patient's unwillingness to talk about anything besides work. In trying so hard not to be angry, the therapist was left with nothing to say. I knew that this therapist was usually an intensely curious person, an avid, lifelong learner. In this treatment, however, anger was an elephant in the room, taking up all its space, sucking out all its air.

More generally, I would suggest that the capacity to experience anger and use it to be a separate, effective analyst (and person) depends on its cost. If anger costs one all sense of being oneself the cost is too high. In treatment I am interested in understanding how each participant can bring the cost down to a reasonable price. In other words, how can we still be ourselves, in our own eyes, while enraged with each other? How can we still feel connected, even though anger has a tendency to distance people? I think one of the most important ways we can make a difference in patients' lives is by helping them access their anger as an empowering resource.

Anger has been thought of as promoting a sense of separate self-hood (Bonime, 1976). Infancy research (Izard, 1977) regards anger as an early response to obstacles. From early in life, we tend to swat at whatever (or whoever) is in our way. The 4-month-old swipes at the blanket that stands in his way, and the adult unleashes rage at someone psychologically barring his path. Sullivan (1956) suggested that, early on, we notice that states of anger do not usually include the experience of intense anxiety, so we learn to rely on anger to help us feel cohesive, centered, empowered. As opposed to anxiety, which often destabilizes us, anger can help us coalesce if we can become adept at recognizing it in ourselves before it escalates too much to harness its power. For example, some people who are angry at what is being done to our environment use their passion to motivate them to fight for its preservation. I think anger can also play a role in more personal battles, like the fierce determination to survive a life-threatening illness.

Whether some are born more aggressive is an issue with a long complicated history in analytic theory (for a succinct summary see Mitchell, 1993). Regardless of one's position on this question, human beings clearly have an innate potential for anger and its related emotions such as rage and hatred (see Fromm, 1964, 1973, for one point of view). In any case, analysts have taken from Winnicott (1949) and others the notion that the patient must be able to experience our negative reactions in order to trust the validity of our positive responses. So one use of anger is, clearly, as a contrast. This reframing of the analyst's anger can grant us a kind of permission to feel and express it. This can operate to mean that our anger at patients will cost us less of our sense of therapeutic viability.

I suggest that if an ability to express anger at patients is considered a developmental milestone for analysts in training, this has a profound, long-range impact. It lowers the cost of anger at patients. We can be angry and still retain our therapeutic reputation with ourselves. This cost-trimming probably frees us from a nonconstructive, intense, snowballing emotional state. Perhaps we can then feel anger at a patient without its escalating into entrenched hatred. In my mind the distinction between anger and hatred is that, while anger is a feeling of opposition, hatred includes an intense desire to obliterate. Nazi propaganda did not spread mere dislike of Jews. It fostered a desire to rid the world of the Jewish "plague." It was a matter of extermination, not just opposition. If what we feel toward a patient doesn't cost us our sense of self, perhaps we can oppose without needing to destroy.

But this leaves me uneasy. In ennobling the analyst's capacity for angry countertransference have we declawed anger itself? Has it gone from an unmentionable secret to a privileged state of grace? I believe our field has a culture as replete with a set of values, leaders, outlaws, and etiquette as any other culture. Anger at patients used to mean the analyst needed more personal treatment. Now, squeamishness about anger at patients is more likely to be noticed as such an indicator.

From my point of view, a problem with each of these positions is that it creates an emotional hierarchy. One emotional state is considered superior to another. We are prescribing a profile of the emotionally healthy analyst. This is problematic to me because it presupposes knowledge I don't think we have (see below for a fuller discussion of conceptions of "normal" anger). Is it more or less effective for the analyst to be intensely emotional? Are certain countertransferential emotions more helpful than others? When, and with which patients? If we can't answer these questions (and I would suggest that we can't) how do we know what attitudes about countertransferential emotionality to promulgate in training?

For many years I have thought about Winnicott's (1949) statement that sometimes we have to put our feelings toward patients in storage until the patient is deemed ready to hear them. But, he continues, the treatment is not complete until that milestone is passed. Year after year candidates ask me how these decisions are made. To store or not to store becomes the question. Lately storage has gone out of fashion. Perhaps this is because it seems so unequal for one person to decide when another is ready to hear something. In any case, I think the questions are valid and important. If I decide to store my anger at the obsessive patient I described in this chapter's first pages, but I don't store other emotional responses, who am I protecting? Doesn't this have most to do with what is in vogue in my analytic culture and what is personally comfortable for me? It is often a bit too easy to subtly blame the patient, considering him too "fragile" to confront yet. In effect, we hand the patient the storage bill. His fragility is held responsible for our need to store anger. We promise ourselves we will take back responsibility for what we do with our anger at some future nebulous time when the patient will be better able to absorb it.

But, is it always self-serving to store our anger at patients? Storing anger can be seen as privileging tact over truth. It says timing matters. There is a long analytic tradition of believing this. Have we completely lost this belief along with so many other forms of certainty?

I suggest that sometimes when we decide to store we are unwittingly substituting the expression of our own pride for the expression of our own anger. However subtly, to indicate that I know someone is not yet ready to hear what I feel reflects my belief that I sit perched above him. So, when I decide to store anger at a patient, I could be modulating my anger with my pride (not necessarily on a conscious basis). Also, I have a secret that, among other things, is itself an assertion of separateness. I am expressing the feeling that I am entitled to a privileged position, above the treatment interchange. I am a separate, protective presence. I know best, even when my own emotional self interest is involved.

While it is easy to see what is flawed in this assertion, I think it equally important to see its possible functions. However misplaced its faith, it does suggest a way to modulate one emotion with another. I am moving from a state of anger toward my patient, in which I might barely recognize either of us, to a state of protectiveness. I can value the patient and our work together. Perhaps I am also making a kind of reparation. I could be seen as recovering my capacity for empathy. After feeling unhorsed by a power struggle with my patient I am now feeling restored. Aside from the value of my personal equanimity, what seems to me important is the decrease in the cost, to me, of working with this patient. I have found a way to economize, so I will probably be able to afford the work. That is, having decided to put my anger at the patient in storage I am now able to work again because I have become recognizable to myself. But is the price of this too high? Is it deceitful and therefore wrong on principle? Is it based on an assumption of a kind of omniscience we just cannot really have? Is the analyst's storage of personal anger ever, on balance, wise?

Rules of Engagement

The word "engagement" can refer to involvement, but it can also mean "to enter or bring into conflict with, as in "we have engaged the enemy" (*American Heritage Dictionary*, p. 433). In this section I explore some of the ways analytic involvement can subtly express the analyst's or the patient's anger. I suggest that anger is often an unacknowledged subtext in case reports in our conferences and published literature.

Christopher Bollas (1999, pp. 106–127) describes his treatment of Antonio, an engineer who often seemed to be playing out a private set of rules of engagement (in the sense of involvement and in the sense of conflict). With employers and with his analyst, each relationship seemed highly promising in the beginning until Antonio started to withdraw. In Bollas' words, "Within a few weeks of beginning analysis Antonio, who initially seemed talkative, composed, and alert, was transformed into an often mute, distraught, and lifeless looking self." Among other interpretations, Bollas told Antonio "… it felt like he was leading me up a very meaningful path saturated with feelings, but that he stopped his narrative at crucial moments to gain my increased interest in order to thwart it" (p. 107).

Some time after this exchange Bollas reports a session in which Antonio echoed his analyst's every word:

> ... he sat down very calmly and looked at me unblinking. I waited for five minutes or so and then said "Well ...?" and he responded, "Well ...?" Thinking I had been misheard, I replied "What occurs to you?" and he said "What occurs to you." It was a flat empty echo. (p. 108)

Unsurprisingly, Bollas was confused by Antonio's behavior. This had never happened before, and Bollas confesses he was unsure how to proceed. He remained silent for most of the hour, only occasionally commenting on Antonio's behavior. Toward the end of the session Bollas suggested that Antonio was "trying to dislodge me from my analytic position, to mock it and myself, and that something cynical and disturbing about himself seemed to be occurring." Bollas goes on to understand Antonio's behavior as a kind of mimicry, meant to show Bollas "someone else, a hated person who was meant to be shoved aside" (p. 109).

In the next months Antonio became overtly paranoid, believing people on buses were talking about him. There followed a period of violent fantasies, in which Antonio thought of punching people on the bus, or knifing people on the Underground, or blowing up buildings. Bollas understood these fantasies as peculiar thoughts that overcame him "like visitations of the bizarre, sweeping over him, and carrying him off from himself, just as they swept through the occasional fellow traveler, who would see a man shifted by passing thoughts into an uncomfortable frame of mind." Antonio then described occasions when he would be talking to a passenger on the bus, until he had "a bad idea pass through his head, which would then end his social engagement, rendering him a kind of headstone for the departed" (p. 111).

Bollas eventually understood these sequences as a form of memory: "His remembering took the form of mutating himself in the presence of the other, transforming what appeared to be an ordinary amiable relation into a bizarre eruption that drove the other into a corner" (p. 114). Bollas felt he helped Antonio by occupying a position "outside the scene, outside the transference, outside the analysis and it was from there that I could speak to him ..." and "by speaking from the outside, I gradually put Antonio back into life itself, a necessity forced upon me from communiqués transmitted from the strange country we call transference and countertransference" (p. 126).

I have the fantasy that thinking in terms of bizarre eruptions and communiqués transmitted from strange countries may fit Bollas' British culture more easily than it does my own. When I listen to this case report I think of ghosts bedeviling, possessing, and inhabiting a helpless host. Suddenly Antonio is no longer himself, but has been mutated by the ungrateful dead. By taking a position outside the interchange, Bollas has been able to understand this otherworldly transformation, capture all its bizarre details, and heal his patient by describing them to him. For me, this conjures up witch trials.

Is it my American pragmatism or a less culture-driven and more personal need that renders me more comfortable describing Antonio as a very angry man who discovered an effective way to disturb his analyst? I see Bollas as engaging in an angry tug of war with Antonio. While he theoretically justifies why he has to speak to Antonio from "the outside," I hear them both as withdrawing from each other. Mimicry went both ways, as each pantomimes the other's withdrawal. If a patient were to echo my every word I imagine myself quickly becoming enraged, feeling mocked, and asking what kind of game this was and why he was playing it. I also imagine asking myself what I might have done to provoke him, rather than what kind of ghost was inhabiting him. My taking up a post outside the interchange would not surprise me, as an expression of my own anger (at least partially). I would see the therapeutic challenge as finding a way to use the anger in the service of our work. Other emotions would have to come to my aid, such as positive feelings for Antonio, curiosity about what was going on, emotionally meaningful identifications with my own analytic forebears, and a determined attitude about the effort to promote aliveness in myself and others.

This perspective meaningfully differs from Bollas' in several ways:

1. I understand taking a position outside the transference–countertransference as impossible. I am reminded of Stephen Mitchell, who often emphasized his belief that we cannot interpret outside the transference–countertransference, because we are inevitably affected by it.
2. The *idea* of going "outside" strikes me as an angry withdrawal on the analyst's part that is parallel to the patient's withdrawal, and may be a form of retribution.

3. I do not think of patients, or of myself, as inhabited. Of course we are affected by our past experiences and people we have known. But it is rare for these figures or events to be "swallowed" or regurgitated whole. We are influenced by them but they are always incorporated into an already somewhat formulated self. That is, whatever happened to Antonio was affected *by* him, as well as affecting him, as it occurred. Antonio was never a blank slate or a piece of clay to be molded. He was always a particular person who had an impact on others and on situations he was in. He can't be merely a carrier of past events or people who impinged on him.

4. Antonio's echoing, withdrawal, and impenetrability to Bollas' influence are anger. They don't merely indicate anger's presence. They are, themselves, forms of anger. As such, they operate like any other expression of an emotion. They are interpersonally formulated and affected by any other feeling that is also present.

5. Bollas' silence the rest of the hour that Antonio echoed him was as much a form of anger as was Antonio's mocking echo. They were both angry. Antonio was probably angry that Bollas had interpreted him as gaining Bollas' interest "in order to thwart it" (see above). For Antonio, I imagine, that may have felt like being accused of something. It may also have felt intrusive. How did Bollas know this was Antonio's motive? To me it certainly seems understandable that what followed was a period of paranoia "in" Antonio. Each of them, I suggest, was focused on negative motives in the other.

6. Like all forms of emotion, the anger Antonio and Bollas felt was shaped, partially, by the other feelings it joined (see Chapter 1). In this instance I would guess that both Bollas and Antonio had anger profoundly shaped by hurt pride. I imagine that, at first, Bollas anticipated feeling special to this unusually promising patient. Others had failed the patient and were failed by him, but this would be different. But it wasn't. What feelings did that evoke in them both? Disappointment, along with hurt pride? Similarly, I would bet that Antonio's pride was hurt by some of Bollas' interpretations, and his withdrawal as well, perhaps, as the analytic frame itself—at least as Bollas lived it with him.

Intense anger and wounded pride can be a particularly lethal combination. Impulsive, destructive, and self-destructive behavior often results. For example, a woman is so hurt and enraged by men who don't want a relationship with her that she "has" to confront them, forcing them to explain why they have withdrawn. Now defensive, every date may wound her further, perhaps feeling outraged that an explanation is demanded of him for not desiring further contact. In treatment I feel (ironically) that the best response I can give is to appeal to her self-interest. I believe that narcissistically vulnerable people very often don't understand how they put their own sense of self-worth at risk. Appealing to their self-interest seems to me to be a way we can interrupt the self-hurtful cycle. So I am, in effect, trying to help a narcissistic patient be *more* attentive to preventing wounds to her self-esteem. My understanding of this is that I am focusing on the balance of emotions "in" each of us. I am hoping that if I help her feel enhanced pride in her increasing capacity to handle the situation well, that self-esteem boost will change the balance of emotions she experiences. I am also counting on my own curiosity ("what do you think would happen if you …?") to stimulate hers. In a sense, I am betting that pride in coping well with what life brings can heal hurt about what life brings. As Victor Frankl (1985) so movingly portrayed, the freedom to assign personal meanings to our experiences is inherent in being human. If the date's withdrawal becomes a challenge to my patient's capacity to cope, rather than a humiliating sign of her worthlessness, she may actually feel different about it and not merely behave differently. The balance of her emotions has shifted. My feelings about her have probably changed as well. My curiosity and genuine admiration of her are likely to have heightened.

Returning to Bollas' work with his patient Antonio, I would suggest that anger was coconstructed by analyst and patient, at least in part. It was not a visitation of Antonio's possessive ghosts. Neither Antonio nor Bollas is merely a host, like a previously healthy being inhabited by microbes. Each brought a history of experiences with other people to their interchanges. For each of them, that history is interpersonal. Nothing human occurs in a vacuum. Even the newborn infant is increasingly seen as far from being a blank slate and as having a significant impact on his human surroundings.

Conceptions of Normal Anger

Elsewhere (2004, Chapter 6), I have suggested that all of us bring our own theories of healthy and abnormal emotionality to our work as clinicians. I believe that we are often unaware of its sources in our life experience, in the values of those who have influenced us professionally and personally, and in our clinical work with patients. This partially unformulated theory guides our clinical focus in a session. How depressed can someone be and still be regarded as normal? How much anxiety qualifies as pathology? Under what circumstances does the intensity of grief over a loss, fear about a medical condition, jealousy with a lover, or rage at injustice trigger our judgment that the emotion is not a normal response? When is the absence of emotionality pathological? We all have our own guidelines for these judgment calls.

Some clinicians see the intensity level of an emotion as key to differentiating normal from abnormal feelings. Thus, if the *intensity* of rage, for example, is high enough, these clinicians would consider the rage abnormal under most circumstances. Other clinicians rely more on a judgment of the appropriateness of the emotional response in a given context. For these clinicians, their judgment of the rage as normal or pathological would depend on whether the situation seemed to warrant rage. I suggest that without having thought much about how we arrive at judgments of appropriateness, we tend to use our own emotional responses as a kind of template of normal human reactions. Probably all of us consider our own responses to the situation the patient presents as a kind of average normal response. I think we then construct a rough, partially conscious bell curve in our minds. If the patient's response falls within a few standard deviations of our own imagined response to the patient's situation, we consider the emotion normal. But if it differs significantly from our own, we begin to look for pathology (in the *patient*).

Another standard I believe we use to judge the normalcy of an emotional response is the interaction between the emotion and the patient's cognitive functioning (see, for example, Barnett, 1980). Do the patient's emotions tumble out too quickly to be modulated by cognition? Or, does the person express thoughts in a flat, totally unemotional monotone? For some of us, the effect of the patient's emotionality on the clinician can be a factor. For example, Epstein (1979) has written of how we assess borderline rage on the basis of our countertransference.

What I would like to emphasize is how extensively our unformulated theories about healthy and abnormal emotionality affect our clinical work. One extremely important issue is how this loosely constructed theory affects our focus in sessions. What we even notice depends on our own conceptions of normal emotionality. For example, a woman tells me about her weekend, including many angry interchanges with her very young children. What is my own standard for the limits of acceptable punishments for children? What do I consider abusive? Where do I, personally, draw this line? This will deeply affect what I notice about her story, what details I retain in my memory, what I pick up on, what I dwell on, what I question, and so on. But do I ask myself where I got my standards? Have I formulated a belief system about normal anger feelings and normal anger expression in parenting? Have I thought through where these beliefs come from in my experience as a child, parent, psychologist, reader, citizen, member of a socioeconomic class, consumer of art, film, and other products of the culture?

Our notion of treatment's goals is also, I suggest, profoundly affected by our beliefs about normal emotionality in general and normal anger expression in particular. I think we would probably all have a similar view of some acts of outright violence. But what about angry words from husband to wife? What about the tone of a critique of a piece of writing? What about the limits of acceptable censure of students in a class? What about the behavior of the police and other officials? How much anger is appropriate for an irate driver? Is it ever normal to throw the plate of artichokes at the waiter (as the painter, Caravaggio, is said to have done)? After the fifth time the insurance company insults our intelligence (from our point of view) what are the limits of a normal response? I suggest that it is impossible to be entirely neutral about these issues, and that they profoundly affect our notions of the goals of treatment as well as impacting on our judgment of how well the work is going. If I, personally, feel it is never appropriate to throw artichokes at a waiter and my patient makes a habit of it, I am likely to see her as having an ongoing problem with her out-of-control rage. I think I would tend to consider the treatment unfinished. I would oppose her wish to terminate treatment if she expressed it. I might cite the artichoke throwing as an example of her unresolved problem. If she argued that she never throws artichokes unprovoked our theories of normal emotional expression might openly collide. I might, then, articulate a belief that it is never an appropriate action, regardless of the provocation. She could question me. How do I know this? Hypothetically, I might consider why I take this stand. Not unlike Fonagy's (2001) conception of mentalization, my self reflection might result in an examination of some of the sources of my personal theory of healthy and pathological forms of anger, rage, hatred, hostility, aggression, frustration, annoyance, irritation, and fury.

I believe that a similar process goes on in relation to normal sadness, guilt, shame, joy, loneliness, surprise, curiosity, envy, fear, anxiety, jealousy, and other emotional experiences. For each, the clinician has a set of (mainly unformulated) standards about normal experience and expression. Frequently, clinicians have never examined the sources of these standards and how they affect their behavior in a session. For example, do I believe that human beings are inherently curious, so if my patient is not showing any curiosity I then assume something must be interfering? Do I believe it is normal to feel sad forever about certain losses? Do I, personally, value forgiving and forgetting? Do I see health as requiring an absence of intense loneliness, anxiety, envy, and so on? Do I assume that comfort with surprise is an aspect of emotional health? How much grieving for a dead parent falls within the limits of my personal conception of normal sorrow?

While clinicians often hope we can be neutral in helping patients actualize their own values about healthy emotionality, I suggest this is impossible in practice. Of course, we want to help people find their own ways to live fulfilled lives, and we don't want to impose our personal values. But, I would argue, many of the tasks of a clinician do not permit us constant awareness of how our beliefs about healthy and pathological emotional experience and expression are affecting our work and, most especially, our focus. Consequently, I believe it is part of our task to reflect on these beliefs and frequently examine their origins to the extent that they can become conscious.

The Angry Analyst

What determines how hard I try to reschedule a missed appointment? I suggest that the state of my countertransferential anger often plays a key role. Anger can take so many forms in treatment that it is frequently extremely difficult to recognize. I believe that this is further complicated by the analyst's anger really being a cocreation of both participants. It is very difficult to articulate this point, since language tends to refer to the anger as belonging to one participant. Thus, we speak (and write) of the analyst's anger, the patient's anger, and so on, as if the anger resided in one person. If we believe in the inherently interpersonal nature of all emotionality this is inaccurate, but we express ourselves this way for the sake of clarity. To further complicate the picture, anger is part of an array of emotions modulated by the levels of all the others. To refer to anger without mentioning strong accompanying shame, for example, may not capture the reality fully. Ashamed anger can be a very different experience from anger unaccompanied by notable shame. But, for clarity's sake, we discuss emotions as though they existed in isolation, just as we refer to individuals with feelings, without examining their interpersonal aspects. Let's say I feel goaded into anger by what I see as a patient's passive–aggressive withholding. My behavior expresses this anger, which evokes more passive aggression on her part. Given her history, I think about what we may be enacting. Some might see one of us as expressing the anger for both. Can we say that the anger I feel is wholly "mine"? In what sense is it mine, in that it originates "in" me, and is typical "of" me and in what sense is it a cocreation?

A partial list of how we act out anger analytically would have to include these subtle, and not so subtle forms:

1. A patient completely "forgot" a session (perhaps an expression of "her" anger). I call her on the telephone to find out if she is coming. She says she is sorry, that since she was concentrated on other things the session time slipped her mind. She then grows silent. I feel she is waiting for me to say it is fine. I say nothing, momentarily blank. I feel a flash of anger. I won't say it is fine. But then I feel childish, and wonder why I am so angry (not, why I am angry at all, but why it has this flashpoint intensity). This leads me to reflect on my relationship with this person and my own background. But, whatever the outcome of these reflections, I believe that saying nothing at that moment was partially an expression of "my" anger. It probably is not only anger, of course. Was her "forgetting" narcissistically wounding to my pride? Did that increase my anger's intensity?

2. A patient won't leave the session on time. She slowly gathers her things, putting on each glove with (infuriating) care. I think, "Why can't she do this in the waiting room?" She makes small talk about the ghastly weather. I consider whether she is deliberately stalling to get me angry, or to hold on to me. Then I ask myself if her motive would make a difference to me. In any case, she is making it difficult for me to end the session. I reflect on the infancy research, on anger as a response to obstacles. Then I start to wonder if I am obsessively avoiding my anger by escaping into theory.

I next remember Winnicott's (1949) belief that the analyst expresses hate by closing the door at the end of the session. Why am I so anxious to get this patient to leave? What was going on between us before the session ended? Aside from the complexity of the interpersonal nature of "our" anger, I would suggest that "my" anger is probably heightened by my uncertainty about what to do. If I confront her I am prolonging the session. If I don't confront her, I am, in a way, colluding. I don't like this choice, so I am angry at the patient who "put" me there, not reflecting, for the moment, on how we both participated in putting me there.

I believe that "my" anger is expressed in the pattern of my thoughts at each point in this interchange. For example, seeing her as unwilling to leave rather than unable, may be an expression of my anger. In how I construe her actions I am justifying my anger. It is impossible to keep tabs on every aspect of this interchange. While it is a small moment in time, it illustrates how each participant is constantly affected by emotions that are intricately interwoven with the feelings of the other person and with other emotions occurring at the same time.

3. A patient seems to me to endlessly embroil me in triangles. Describing a discussion with her husband, she illustrates his empathic qualities. He is in her professional field, and so he gave her great advice about what to do in an altercation with her employer. She does not (overtly) make the comparison between her husband's advice-giving and mine. I make it. Then I wonder where my perception of the triangle came from. Am I creating a competition with her husband, wanting to be the better advisor?

In this situation I think one form my anger takes is impatience. I want the story over with. I feel I know its ending from its beginning. I am angry I have to listen to it in painstaking detail. But would I be so impatient if I didn't sense that I am losing a competition? How is my anger shaped by my envy and other emotions I am feeling? I believe that my impatience is a product of the overall balance of my emotions.

Furthermore, impatience is certainly not a new experience for me. Its history in *my* life affects how I experience it with this patient. The patient is not simply projecting a feeling into me. My feeling is partially shaped by my own lifelong relationship to impatience. Sorting out what is creating my impatience might take more time than I can give it, since I am also trying to attend to the rest of the session. But as always, at least in theory, the anger is an interpersonal event, and shaped in part by other emotions it joins.

4. I think that probably the most frequent expression of anger on the analyst's part as well as the patient's, is the failure to respond to what the other expresses. By its very nature this is hard to formulate. It strikes me as having amoeba-like simplicity. I make an interpretation to a patient that, in retrospect, wounds her pride (perhaps an expression of my own anger at how difficult our work is for me. I am saying, in effect, I will not let such considerations slow us down any more. I will ride roughshod on her pride if I have to in order to make "progress"). The patient changes the topic. This is, in a sense, a neat expression of anger. She simply wipes me out.

But I can see, in retrospect, times *I* have refused admittance to some aspect of *her* self-expression. For example, when she mentioned still missing her (long-dead) father I used to muse to myself that she still could not recognize her profound ambivalence toward him. Now, I believe I was refusing to hear her simple, genuine yearning for him. I can imagine several reasons for my refusal, including my envy of her strong attachment to this hurtful father. I can see that in the past I did not *want* to hear that she still felt so attached. I think I was angry, as though her ongoing attachment to her sometimes abusive, sometimes loving father was responsible for our slow progress. While this may (at least partially) be true, my anger about it is my (not necessarily inevitable) reaction. It was easy to pathologize her attachment. I heard it as a symptom and refused to take it in in any other way. Not hearing aspects of what the patient says, or over-pathologizing it, can be subtle expressions of countertransferential anger.

5. By now it must be clear that I am more interested in the expressions of anger that might easily go unnoted, since I believe that these are harder for analysts and their patients to recognize and fruitfully engage. Most analysts would probably think of anger as a possible explanation when they grow unaccountably groggy with one particular patient. A supervisee tells me she got so sleepy she almost drifted off, yet she was perfectly awake with the patients before and after the hour we are discussing. Is this about her anger at the patient, or at me, or both? Or could it express some other feeling, such as anxiety?

In any case, when we grow unusually tired we generally ask ourselves why. But do we self-reflect when we forget something the patient has already told us? Do we consider countertransferential anger as a possible explanation? Simply forgetting can be an extremely suave way of refusing to let something or someone in. When patients forget a session we are likely to think of anger as a possible explanation. But what about when we forget the existence of their sister or their father's occupation? I am not suggesting that anger is always involved. No emotion is always involved in any type of behavior. But it *can* be involved.

6. Another way I think I express countertransferential anger is by attending more carefully to frame and boundary issues than I otherwise might. I think when I am less angry I have a more comfortably casual stance. If either of us strays from a strict observance of the frame it can be explored for its meaning, but I am confident we will return to observance of the usual parameters. But if I am angry I may, in a sense, hide behind the frame. I end the session precisely on time, as though I need to be careful about how much of myself I give away. Hoarding minutes, I hold myself apart. When I am not angry, I think I am more likely to lose track of time, floating in the process, creatively engaged. The absence of this state in me, like the absence of compassion, memory, and curiosity, can be a subtle form of anger.

7. Angry rhythms can be discernible from angry content. I think an angry rhythm is often staccato. I can listen to the "music" of a session without consciously focusing on the words, and register the degree of anger in each participant.

8. Anger in the analyst can be extremely constructive, at times. For example, after a long and (from my point of view) very productive period of treatment, a patient began contemptuously criticizing me, and, basically, trashing our work. After listening to this for a while, I got angry enough to say something. In retrospect, I think what I needed was enough anger to propel me to stand up for the treatment as well as for myself. There followed a fruitful discussion of why the patient needed to create distance between us by dismissing the value of our work.

9. Sometimes I think anger in analysts allows us to express a separate point of view that can be interesting and useful. An unforgettable experience for me was a moment when I returned to work after a week's serious illness. On the morning of my second day back while I was still quite weak, a patient I had treated for some time entered the office complaining about how long I had been out. Absences due to illness are extremely rare for me, and I believe that any patient of mine would conclude that when they happen they must have been warranted. Perhaps because I was making considerable effort to come back to work quickly, I took offense at this patient's complaint that I had stayed out too long. My anger was strong enough to cause me to say something without much thought. The patient quickly recognized my feelings, which I acknowledged.

This incident proved helpful in many ways. We were able to use it to explore why we each reacted as we did, and also how different vantage points can profoundly affect perceptions.

10. Quick flashes of anger in me sometimes can play a constructive role in the work. With one woman, I never felt like I understood why friends so frequently mysteriously disappeared until one day I got angry at (what I felt to be) her over-entitlement. What had happened was that, on the day before a scheduled session the patient called with what seemed to me a valid reason for needing to try to reschedule. But before I could get back to her she called again, mentioning that I must not have gotten her first call. While listening to the message I recognized my own flash of anger. Indirectly, but clearly, I felt accused, tried, and found guilty of neglect. My anger at what I experienced as the injustice of this focused me on our interchange, which eventually helped us explore important material.

11. And finally, one last example of how anger can be productive: a woman confined to a wheelchair most of her life became extremely angry that I was not in a similar situation. In her rage she fastened on the fact that even in order to angrily "walk out" of a session she would have to enlist my assistance with her chair. In response to this humiliation she decided there was one rebellious thing she didn't need my help to do. She took my tissue box and, quite methodically, shredded every single tissue all over my office floor. For some moments we stared at each other in silent rage. My own anger enabled me to understand an aspect of my countertransference to her. As I thought about my experience of the session I realized that this was not the first time in my own life that I felt blamed for my good fortune. For the patient, her action provided a visible expression of her lifelong rage at the inequity of her position in life, not just in a wheelchair, but in many other senses.

Anger at the Patient vs. Anger on the Patient's Behalf

When we write about the analyst's anger, we usually mean the analyst's anger at the patient. But I would suggest that an equally frequent occurrence is our feeling anger on the patient's behalf. Examples include very strong feelings of anger, or even hatred, toward those who have sexually abused our patients. In addition, I believe that those who treat children quite often feel intense anger at their parents, whether they have been abusive or not. This very common countertransference can be difficult to bear. My experience is that it is often strongest in the therapist's earlier years in practice. Perhaps this is partially because the clinician may not (yet) have faced the daunting task of being a parent. Life experience is a factor we don't take into account enough, in my opinion, in our discussions of our differences in technique. But my own clinical experience of treating children when I was in my early adulthood and many experiences of supervising child treatment suggest how common it is to feel intense anger on behalf of children who suffer at the hands of their parents.

In treating adults we can have similar countertransference feelings, perhaps especially if we work with sexually abused or battered patients. But anger on behalf of a patient can also occur in less obviously abusive situations.

Anger on behalf of a patient has something in common with anger at a patient, regardless of its personal and interpersonal sources. It provides the analyst with an opportunity to experience the anger within a balance of other emotions. I believe this to have great therapeutic potential, as I will illustrate shortly. In other words, if I feel anger on behalf of my patient I have a chance to do something with that anger. Whatever I do with it will, I believe, be experienced by my patient. If my personal struggle with this anger includes an eventually successful modulation of the anger by other emotions, this experience will tell me something that might be valuable for both me and my patient.

Before I turn to some examples, I would like to consider some of the problems with my approach and some of the more common ways it can be misused or misunderstood.

1. I am not prescribing corrective emotional experiences for the analyst. I do not believe analysts can aim to feel anger on behalf of the patient any more than they can aim to feel shame or any other emotion. While this sounds obvious, I believe it is not always understood. I think some analysts do expect themselves to feel compassion, or curiosity, or hope for every patient who walks into their offices. I don't think it is possible for us to deliver a preordained emotional response of any kind, even if it would be helpful to the treatment.

2. I do not mean to imply that we know the right way to live life, for ourselves or for other people. My technical suggestions can sound like a version of logical positivism. I believe it is very dangerous for us to think we know the healthy way to live, and that it is our job

to spread the word. Since patients often, in my experience, come to treatment hoping for such a blueprint, it is especially important for us to be clear that we don't have it.

3. The emotional modulation that works for one person may not be effective for another. All we can (sometimes) provide is a way of modulating anger, not *the* way.

4. As already mentioned, I differ with the theory of projective identification as it is commonly described. I do not think it likely that patients can "put" their anger into us, as though we were neutral containers waiting to be filled by the patients' experience. All analysts are human beings with life experiences, values, emotional patterns, and theories that we bring to work every day, and that affect all our responses to patients. We bring a lifetime of experience of our own way of being angry, as well as our "reputation" (with ourselves and others) for being quick tempered, afraid to express anger, holding grudges, or some other tendencies. Our feelings with a particular patient may reinforce or challenge our beliefs about our patterns. But we have anger-related tendencies that predate our professional lives, and have a significant effect on what can and can't easily be "projected" into us.

Early in my work with a female patient she described her childhood as the older of two siblings born to an obviously severely disturbed couple. Her father had all the characteristics of a classically paranoid character, while her mother was extremely depressed, barely able to get up in the morning. With evident pride, the patient described her ability to care for herself and her sister, fixing breakfast from a very early age. She lauded her "independence" as having given her an exceptionally good start in life. Many of her earliest memories left me shocked, saddened, and angry for the child who had become so precociously adult. But I felt she probably couldn't afford to have feelings similar to mine. Her positive framing of her early experience had helped her make peace with the only life available to her at the time. For a long time I was alone with my anger for this patient. In fact, any evidence of it disturbed her. She wanted me to share her admiration for the plucky, sturdy survivor she had learned to be. I could genuinely feel admiration, but not without anger that no one in her extended family, school, or neighborhood noticed the undernourished, inappropriately attired child with the spotty attendance record who rarely did her homework and only sporadically received medical care of any kind.

My anger, of course, had many personal sources, which I thought about a great deal. At first, it seemed anything but helpful to the patient. As a result I found myself focusing on other feelings I also had, such as curiosity about how she learned her coping skills. This helped me join in some of her feelings about what she had gained from her early responsibilities that stood her in good stead later in life. I continued to feel angry and sad as I watched, in my mind's eye, the child she had been cope with challenges way beyond her comprehension. But gradually I also felt more joy at her triumphs, and better understood her pride in her ability to shoulder enough to make her sister's life easier than her own.

Over time my anger faded. It never disappeared, but seemed to become less relevant to my understanding and treatment of the patient. I believe she was able to identify with it when it took a more muted form. She came to feel angry at her upbringing, what it had failed to provide for her, and how these gaps had affected her adult life. But for her, as for me by then, anger was not intense, but shaded by sadness and modulated by more positive feelings. Whether this gentler form of anger was mutative can certainly be questioned and, even if it was, we may speculate that she could have come to it in other ways. I accept these formulations, but believe it is also possible that I helped her by finding within me emotional resources that allowed me to modulate my anger on her behalf. It means a great deal to me to emphasize that I believe my anger was not her experience projected into me, but rather an emotional experience of my own, reflecting, at least in part, the human being that I am. I felt it as *I* have come to feel such things. It was largely shaped by how I have come to experience anger, as a particular human being, with a particular history of life experience and, most especially, anger experience. I modulated the anger to help myself cope, not to provide an object lesson in anger management for the patient. I did not set out to model something "corrective." I wanted to remain able to learn what it was like to be this patient. But as I dealt with the anger more successfully, I think its decreased toxicity helped enable the patient to identify with it, own it, and feel it for herself. My struggle for emotional balance played a vital role in hers.

Anger in Supervision

I think of anger in supervision as playing a role similar to its functions in treatment. As an example, I will describe a pattern that is
very familiar to me. Frequently, in my role as a supervisor, I hear
about the treatment of a patient by an analyst in training and I
become enraged with the patient's entitlement. I suggest a more confronting stance. The analyst may follow my advice and have a very
hard time with the patient. Sometimes the analyst balks. We discuss
our differences and deal with them in one way or another. I get past
my anger, and become more sympathetic toward the patient. Time
passes. Seemingly suddenly, the analyst becomes totally enraged with
the patient, practically throwing her out of the treatment. I counsel
considering the patient's point of view and, once again, we examine
our differences.

What happened and why does this recur? Of course, it could be
understood as simply an aspect of my particular character and style.
To some extent, that must be true. But I also think something else
is going on. Initially the male analyst is responding to the female
patient as a whole person, and I am (at first) responding to the *issue*
of narcissistic entitlement. Later, having extended himself (perhaps
beyond endurance) the analyst is fed up. He has bent over backward
for too long. He feels guilt because he knows he has participated in
allowing the patient to mistreat him. He also may feel shame that he
has inadequately handled the treatment frame. But mainly he is outraged at the patient's lack of empathy and her feelings of entitlement
and grandiosity.

I think part of why this recurs is that the treatment usually starts
before the supervision, and the analyst has already intuited that, to
keep this patient in treatment, he has to accommodate some. Before
I came along he found ways to make it feel acceptable to bend over
backward or he found ways to selectively inattend to how much he is
accommodating. I do not feel the same degree of pressure, guilt, or
shame, so the balance of my feelings can tip toward rage.

Another possibility is that the analyst takes my advice and is more
confrontational and the patient terminates. The analyst may overtly
or covertly blame me. I become the fly in the ointment, a familiar
role for supervisors. Yet this is hardly a good outcome, for the treatment or for the training. Can it be avoided?

It might be easy to say I should simply curb my enthusiasm (for confronting narcissism). Or, we might recommend that I recognize the beginning phase of this pattern faster, telling myself to think more carefully about my supervisory influence. Another alternative might be that I increase my respect for the analyst's style, hesitating to suggest any changes until I know the case better. All of these seem perfectly reasonable until I am actually in the supervisory situation.

Supervisory countertransference receives less attention than countertransference in treatment, but I doubt it is less powerful or important. In fact, I would argue that it may be more powerful, since the supervisor is responding to a characterization that may resemble caricature, while the analyst is encountering a real patient. Descriptions of "cases" might lend themselves to stereotyping more easily than live people do. An actual human being will elicit an array of feelings in me, but a case report may evoke an oversimplifying, one-dimensional response. This may be part of the reason case conferences elicit so much splitting in the audience. Discussions frequently follow a predictable pattern, with some suggesting that the analyst confront more, while others recommend a softer, gentler approach. As Levenson (1984) has remarked, supervision accrues its clarity from its higher level of abstraction than treatment. It is easier to see the whole landscape from above it. Similarly, it is easier to have "super" vision when not eye level with an actual patient. This confers both advantages and disadvantages. We think we know the score when we are responding to a *category*, rather than an actual human being.

I think this makes it more likely, at least initially, for the supervisor to feel unmodulated anger at a "type" of behavior. Meanwhile, the candidate has already modulated his anger with other emotions, perhaps including anxiety about facing the consequences if he loses a training case. But the candidate may have also developed positive feelings in response to the patient. Just as a parent may well have enough love to bear the outrageous behavior of her teenager, partially because she still remembers him as an adorable 5-year-old, so can the analyst savor endearing moments shared with the patient. Many analysts in training have sounded as though they would like to tell me that they know patients are being outrageous, but they are not *just* outrageous; they are also suffering, or struggling with themselves. They are reclaimable in some sense.

We eventually change places, I think, because the candidate directly experiences the patient's entitlement and, eventually, can't tolerate it. Meanwhile, as the supervisor, I have heard more about the patient, who has become more of a complex human being to me, and not just an example of narcissism. My feelings are now more balanced and less intense, like colors muted by combining them.

Of course there are other possibilities, but I believe this pattern is not uncommon. While all three people have responsibility for themselves, I believe it is mainly the supervisor's job to make every effort to become aware of supervisory countertransference and attend to its impact.

Anger in Balance

> Hatred is a passion requiring one hundred times the energy of love. Keep it for a cause, not an individual. Keep it for intolerance, injustice, stupidity. For hatred is the strength of the sensitive. Its power and its greatness depend on the selflessness of its use. (Moore, 1992, p. 83)

Believing that all the emotions can sometimes serve positive functions, and that the meaning and experience of an emotion depends on the other feelings it joins, directs me to think about the possible functions of hatred, anger, rage, and related experiences. How does each affect the balance of emotions "in" and between the participants in an analytic process?

Much can be said about the differences among these feelings. Rage is considered by some to be the simplest of the three, since it pushes the individual toward immediate discharge of the impulse (Arieti, 1967, 1972). For Kernberg (1990) the most extreme forms of hatred dominate and destroy the object relationship. Sullivan (1956) understood anger as:

> ... one of the ways of handling anxiety that we learn early, at the time of the empathic linkage with significant adults before there are any particular analytic thought processes.... In this way the child learns the given pattern of being angry, the social expressions of anger, in the mild degree that parents show it toward people in late infancy. Thus anger takes on the beginnings of social conditioning. At the same time it takes on a very important justification of existence in that it spares one anxiety. (pp. 95–96)

Thus, for Sullivan, anger may sometimes be the lesser of two evils. We feel more coherent in anger than we do in anxiety, and may be able to function more smoothly.

This explains one way we can understand the functional aspect of anger and anger-related emotions. In a moving passage of *King Lear* Shakespeare eloquently conveyed how towering rage can save us from dissolving in tears. The old king knows that sorrow could unhinge his reason and dissipate all resolve. He is determined to use anger to fight against emasculating sadness:

> ... touch me with noble anger,
> And let not women's weapons, water drops,
> Stain my man's cheeks! No, you unnatural hags,
> I will have such revenges on you both
> That all the world shall—I will do such things,
> What they are, yet I know not, but they shall be
> The terrors of the earth. You think I'll weep;
> No, I'll not weep:
> I have full cause of weeping
> but this heart
> Shall break into a hundred thousand flaws
> Or ere I'll weep. O Fool! I shall go mad.
>   (Act II, scene iv, pp. 274–284)

A similar viewpoint was held by Bonime (1976), who saw anger as a possible basis for a sense of self. I would say that the impact of anger depends on the other emotions that accompany it. For some, anger tends to disrupt functioning more than it empowers and coalesces. Perhaps these people respond to being angry by feeling guilty or ashamed of "losing control." Or they may immediately become anxious about potential reprisals. Anger can solidify and empower or disorient, depending on our history of anger experience and the other feelings it recruits.

In a previous contribution (1995) I suggested that hatred is most likely to focus and strengthen the individual's resources in situations that threaten profound grief. We hate the destruction of our environment, envisioning and, to an extent, already feeling the loss. We hate bigotry because it destroys the humanity of its perpetrator and victim. We hate the Nazi scourge because of our sorrow at the devastation it caused. We hate in order to hold together in extreme pain. In the context of supreme sadness, hatred can provide strength to the sensitive.

In more ordinary moments, anger can firm resolve. A woman, reflecting on how much her parents' physical and psychological abuse have cost her, became determined not to spend the rest of her life in sorrow about her losses. In a furious tone she announced she would not give them any more of her time. This declaration might not be entirely actionable, but it did signal her resolve not to waste more of her life on regretting the past.

Similarly, I believe that anger sometimes helps us manage impulsive responses (damn it, I won't let this get the better of me). At other moments it may delimit inhibitions that stem from shame sensitivity. For example, a 40-something single woman, desperate to be involved in a relationship, overcomes her reluctance to go to singles events because she refuses to give in to her discomfort at them. Or, a man in his 50s refuses to resume smoking because he would be damned if he would let that habit control him.

We could say that anger, and related emotions, supply the force to fight for what we need and believe in. Anger can be a hidden ingredient in any determined effort, including the will to fight an illness or any other obstacle to life. Of course, anger and related emotions can also disorient us and they have tremendous destructive potential. It is no accident that our language speaks of fits of bad temper, paroxysms of anger, boiling over, flying off the handle, blowing one's top, convulsing with rage, being mad, and falling into a rage. These phrases emphasize our native belief that anger can possess us and make us feel out of control. On the other hand, we also use phrases that emphasize how anger makes us powerful: towering rage, breathing fire, fierce rage, showing one's teeth, and stamping the foot. Language signals the contradictory possibilities in the intrapersonal and interpersonal impact of anger and the other anger-related emotions.

Like most human emotions, anger can serve many functions. More than most others, it can empower or unhinge, create or destroy. The Greeks expressed anger's power to quell fear, I believe, in the story of the god Prometheus, who stole fire to give it to humankind (Slochower, 1970, p. 77). Like anger, Prometheus' gift of fire can wreak terrible destruction, but it is also the basis of civilization and, ultimately, human freedom. Strikingly, Prometheus emphasizes his freedom from fear of retribution for his crime. Just as Lear called upon rage to steel him against weakening, Prometheus, threatened that his body would be encased in rock and Zeus' eagle would feast on his liver, stubbornly declared, "There is no fear in me." Using words not unlike Lear's, Prometheus emphasizes that he "will not grow woman-hearted.... It is not my nature." In Aeschylus' version, Prometheus is "punished not merely because he gave fire to man. What Prometheus bequeathed is the fire of revolt, the spirit of defiance, that is, man's freedom from fear" (Slochower, 1970, pp. 78–79).

Freedom from overwhelming fear can be anger's gift. With fierce determination we may be able to face what otherwise might engulf us. Whether as supervisors, patients, analysts, or in any other role in life, sometimes anger is what enables us to find the strength to persevere.

Why is anger constructive and empowering at some times, and at others destructive and disorienting? I wish I had a more comprehensive answer, but I can contribute some thoughts.

As every analyst knows, anger that is obsessively defended against can inhibit or otherwise disable people. Usually the anger shows despite the defenses, but in a strangulated, muted form. For example, a man who is angry at his wife asks her a seemingly innocent question:

Husband: How was your day, dear? (spoken in a sharp, accusing tone)
Wife: (confused by the disparity between his words and tone) What do you mean?
Husband: (exasperated) God, can't I say anything to you? I just asked how your day was ...
Wife: (crying, but also getting pretty angry) What do you want me to say? Just *tell* me, for God's sake!

Although this is not verbatim, it would probably sound familiar to any clinician who has treated couples. The obsessive person is trying to communicate and obfuscate at the same time, and ends up being very unclear, but vaguely discomfiting to himself and others. As would probably be true for both my fictional husband and wife, the anger never dissipates because no one understands it enough to do something constructive in response to it. The obsessive patient himself does not get communication's usual benefits, including better self-understanding and better attunement from others. In addition, his anger is too diffuse and vague to empower his own actions. Worst of all, the anger pervades his mood, making it less likely that other, more positive interchanges will serve to modulate it. A vague pervasive cloud hangs over everything, stalling action, blunting every enthusiasm, choking curiosity, muting joy. Others may instinctively steer clear of him or, depending on their own characters, get locked into obsessive battles for control.

Thus, the anger does not have its potential bracing, strengthening, coalescing effect. Other emotions, such as joy, curiosity, love, and pride (in taking a position, or in taking courageous, inspired, purposeful action) don't have a chance to provide balance.

Obsessive anger between two people tends to escalate into full fledged but inconclusive warfare. Often, when I have treated couples, I have seen my role as helping them fight *better*, rather than helping them fight less often.

Perhaps most dreary is obsessive anger's tendency to hang around, spoiling the rest of life. Nothing has a sharp tang. It is not uncommon for depression to be the ultimate outcome.

What I am suggesting is that, at least some of the time, the problem is not *that* we are angry, but, rather, *how* we are angry. How we use our anger, our rage, our hatred, determines whether it serves as the "strength of the sensitive" or our undoing.

Special Section

Training
Nurturing the Capacity to Make a Difference

Have you ever wondered how admission committees decide which applicants to accept for analytic training? What are the criteria? Perhaps more importantly, what should they be?

I believe that psychoanalytic practice, like any other profession, includes skills that can be nurtured, if not taught. But unlike some fields, ours rarely spells out what these skills are, how analytic aptitude can be assessed, or how it can be developed. Medical training is often criticized for its failure to instill some of the qualities that being an effective doctor requires. Studies persuasively argue that prescribing medications is useless if the doctor has not adequately explained their benefits to the patient or has not made it clear how the drug should be administered. But although there is a long history of research on the ingredients of psychologically effective treatment, the application of this body of work to our training selection process remains vague and unexplored. In medicine there is, at least, an effort to isolate what makes an effective doctor and how medical training can nurture these skills and interpersonal qualities. Why isn't a similar effort being made in our own field, where, it can be argued, interpersonal skills are even more essential to good practice?

Perhaps part of the answer to this question is that psychoanalysts have traditionally resisted clarifying the skills our profession requires, as though demystification would damage our field. Like the wizard of Oz, we don't want people to look behind our curtain. They might discover that the wizard is not a wizard at all. In other words, our own insecurities have hampered our quest for clarity. Thus, while Levenson (1991) (among others) has highlighted the role of demystification in treatment, I think we have not paid adequate attention to demystifying the analytic process for candidates in analytic training.

With this goal in mind, in these chapters I describe some patterns of thinking, feeling, and relating that recur in my own work. I am well aware of many objections this might reasonably elicit from the reader. First, the patterns I discuss may sound non-analytic or even anti-analytic to some. But like the proverbial blind men in their description of the elephant, I can only describe analysis as I experience it. Hopefully, if enough of us reveal our analytic process to each other we will emerge with at the least a better understanding of our differences.

Another danger I court in these chapters is the possibility that what I am describing will be misunderstood as a kind of "cookbook" of psychoanalytic method. I would suggest that the fear of being seen as providing an oversimplifying, watered down, superficial version of psychoanalytic praxis has probably discouraged many of us from writing about the process at all. I think that is a costly mistake. Candidates may graduate with a sense that they still have no idea what they are doing but it would be imprudent to mention this to anyone, since that would reveal how little they learned in their training. Depending partly on their own characters, defensive patterns, and life experiences, some may register this as a product of personal inadequacy, while others may feel cheated and outraged at their institute. In any case, I would rather give candidates a template of what is in my mind as I work and initiate a process of exploring its strengths and weaknesses as a model. Like any other identity formation, the process of analytic training requires someone to be willing to provide a clear enough demonstration of *a* way (not *the* way) to function, so that the learner can formulate a personal style that is similar in some ways and differs in others.

What does it mean to think analytically? How does that differ from any other thought process? Of course, dividing the analytic thought process from other aspects of the work is potentially misleading and, at times, arbitrary. Analytic thought, empathic immersion, and interpersonal relating are inseparable. I discuss them separately only for the sake of clarity.

How can we nurture the capacity for analytic thinking, feeling, and responding in the course of training? Should aspects of analytic process be separated and "taught" to candidates? Should we teach candidates how to "think analytically," if that phrase has any meaning? In a subsequent chapter I discuss the more emotion-driven aspects of the analytic task. If a capacity to promote emotional growth is a significant aspect of treatment, how do we select and nurture clinicians to be able to engage in it? Given the concept that each emotion is a specific self state with a unique history for each of us, how do we develop the candidates' own capacity to be curious and to elicit their patients' curiosity? How do we develop the candidates' capacity to feel and elicit joy? How do we help them become comfortable with surprises about themselves and elicit that comfort in their patients?

Similar questions can be asked about the emotions that are usually labeled negative, but also have functions in human experience. For example, how do we nurture the clinicians' capacity to bear the sadness and loss that will be a frequent aspect of their experience with their patients? Can we help develop candidates' resources for strengthening their patients' capacity to live with sadness and loss? How can training facilitate working with both participants' anger, fear, shame, guilt, jealousy, and other "negative" feelings, each of which has a place in the human repertoire?

If we believe these emotions are important aspects of conducting treatment, I think we should focus on them in training more than we do. As a start, we should discuss whether it is possible to choose candidates based, in part, on their potential to deal with each of these emotions. While coping with emotionality is probably a major focus in much analytic supervision, the content of supervision varies greatly, so that some emotions may not come up, especially if they create discomfort in the candidate or the supervisor. Bringing them up in theoretical as well as supervisory contexts might encourage their exploration in the candidates' personal analysis.

My effort here will be to name some of the skills and talents I see as crucial to analytic practice. I hope others will voice agreements and disagreements with my list, and the reasons for their positions. From my point of view this, in itself, would be valuable, if only because it could clarify these criteria for prospective applicants. The vague question, "Do I have the right stuff to become an analyst"? might morph into "Can I develop the capacity to create analytic analogies from disparate information"? or "Can I remain curious and self-exploratory when a patient is not at all (overtly) interested"? To my way of thinking, while we might argue about the best list, it would be edifying to have that argument.

In the next three chapters I outline some of the cognitive, emotional, and interpersonal skills I see as crucial to nurture in analytic candidates. While our training programs include many courses on analytic theory and practice, I have never seen a course on the thought process interpretive work entails or the emotional strengths analytic practice requires. Supervisors may mention these capacities, but in my experience this is a hit-or-miss process. I think it would be useful to spell out more clearly just what it takes to function analytically so prospective applicants can more clearly assess whether they think they have the "right stuff."

More specifically, I consider some of the talents we need to think interpretively, use countertransference emotions therapeutically, and relate to patients so as to maximize the treatment's potential to make a valuable difference in the patient's life. While I am aware that I cannot address all the qualities analytic practice entails, I focus on those I think most crucial. It seems likely to me that my interpersonal theoretical background colors my priorities. I would be very interested to compare my thinking with analysts who come from different theoretical points of view.

Chapter 8 begins with qualities I consider mostly cognitive, such as the talent to be able to make analytic connections between genetic and transferential material. Chapter 9 addresses specific emotional strengths, such as a capacity to bear the loneliness inherent in conducting treatment. Finally, in Chapter 10, I consider some general interpersonal strengths, such as the ability to keep one's boundaries relatively clear. I am not trying to suggest how much each of these qualities is a product of "nature" or "nurture." I assume we bring varying levels of innate talent for each of these tasks when we present ourselves for training, and each capacity can be enhanced during training to some degree. "Nature–nurture" debates are, I feel, usually less helpful than an assumption that both play some role.

To preview, I suggest that we study more closely what enables a developing analyst to connect material previously unconnected, create a shared language with each patient, reframe and recontextualize some of the patient's life experience, and recognize and work with preconscious material. Then I consider the capacity to distinguish emotional nuances, stimulate curiosity in oneself and the patient, bear and therapeutically use sorrow, anger, shame, loneliness, envy, and other feelings. Finally, I address some more general interpersonal strengths such as stamina, the delay of gratification, boundary clarity, the capacity to contain feelings and thoughts, and the ability to avoid burnout.

8

Thinking Analytically

Analytic Listening

A woman reflects on a meeting at work, vaguely uncomfortable because she senses she has alienated her colleagues. It started off as an amiable meeting, with ideas generated by the newer members as well as those who, like my patient, have a great deal of professional experience. The conversation turns to the use of new equipment the group recently acquired. Its allocation has not yet been determined. With what sounds to me like a jovial tone, people suggest ways the equipment could be distributed. In what I hear as a jarringly contentious rejoinder, my patient comments on how little experience seems to count in this world. What was lively repartee becomes awkward silence. The group soon disbands to go back to their duties.

As I listen, I hear the details of the incident, asking for clarification when I am not sure I understand what happened. I also encourage the patient to reflect on her feelings and on the meaning of her comment, for herself as well as for her colleagues.

So far, I could be any listener. She might tell this story to many friends, who could hear it and ask similar questions, although the purpose behind their inquiry is likely to differ from mine.

But what I am thinking about as I listen should be uniquely psychoanalytic. Simultaneously, I should be attending to:

1. The details of the story
2. What the patient may, defensively, be leaving out and just *how* she is able to miss these aspects (the analysis of defense)

3. Connections between this story's essential nature and events in the patient's early life that give the incident its particular meaning to her
4. Characteristic patterns of behavior in the patient that the story could illuminate
5. Relationships between what this story reveals about the patient and insights I have gained from the psychoanalytic literature
6. Meanings of the story that my countertransferential experience of the patient might suggest

I have often described psychoanalytic functioning as unusual because in ordinary conversation we would make obvious connections such as the relationship between the patient's comment and the group's response. In my language, this is connecting "c" with "d." That is, ordinarily when we talk, we connect events that are related to each other in a clear-cut way. But psychoanalytic thinking requires us to be able to connect "c" with "q."

Taking this clinical situation as an example, I had to be able to hear, in the patient's rendition, that she has probably left out how the tone of her voice contrasted with everyone else's. My guess would be that she was unaware of the irritation in her voice at the time of the interchange, failing to register that it was harsher than any one else's. I made a mental note to ask her if she remembers her tone of voice, and how it sounded to her.

As I listened, I thought about what I know of the patient's father, the sadism in his humor, and how frequently she felt mercilessly teased by him. I imagined that what the colleague meant as an off-hand joke felt more like a deliberately cruel taunt to my patient. I reflected that, of course, by frequently making this kind of rejoinder my patient makes it likely she actually *will*, at times, be treated with hostility.

Thinking about many other incidents when the patient took as hostility what was (consciously) intended as humor, I reflected that, this time, her interpretation could be right. As Freud suggested, humor can be hostility's scaffold. But we may never know what her colleague's original feeling was before the patient's angry rejoinder.

I then reflected that, for this woman, how she feels treated is a measure of her (low) self-worth. Narcissistic wounds have left a legacy of vulnerability to further injury. Everything becomes a personal assault. The behavior of others reflects on her (and not on them) and *her* behavior *also* reflects on her. The psychoanalytic literature on dealing with longstanding narcissistic deficits came to my mind.

But I also thought about the literature on obsessive power struggles. Rather than to directly address her colleagues, the patient tried to insinuate her message that they are unappreciative and unfair to her. Using what I like to call communication at a 45-degree angle away from talking directly, she mentioned the general lack of credit for experience in this world of ours. I see in this the essence of the obsessive conflict between saying what is meant vs. saying what will be acceptable to others. Obsessive language tries to do both at once, frequently accomplishing neither.

These thoughts led me to examine my countertransferential attitudes toward this patient. Am *I* unappreciative of her strengths, her many years of experience in her field, as well as in my office as, in a way, *my* team mate? Are we enacting something about whose ego will be served? Do I drive points home conscious of my wish to help her, unaware of my own hostile motives? Have I become her sadistic father?

I envision thinking psychoanalytically as similar to picking up a piece of a jigsaw puzzle (e.g., the event at work) and trying it out in various places. A jigsaw puzzle piece might have a blue corner, suggesting it might fit near the top of the puzzle where blue shading already exists. Similarly, the work incident has some of the earmarks of situations I remember from the patient's past, so I "hold it up" near them in my mind. I also compare the story with my own experiences with the patient, as well as situations with the patient's husband that I have heard about and her dreams, to the extent that I remember them. I am seeing where the "piece of the puzzle" might fit. If I put it down way in the right-hand corner, will it match its surround?

Unlike a piece of a jigsaw puzzle, a patient's experience might fit in many places equally well. Nevertheless, I still find this analogy useful. It prompts me to think about qualities of the incident that correspond to the color and shape of a jigsaw puzzle part. For example, what can be said about the outline of the story? Does it conform to the usual shape of obsessive battles? In other words, is it a conflict between what the patient should say vs. what she wants to say? Can a theory about obsessive power struggles help me in my next session with this patient?

Frequently, people don't understand how hard we work. Analytic focusing is nothing like the casual listening that may entertain us at a cocktail party. It is an intense process of concentration where many activities occur at once. We are trying the "jigsaw puzzle piece" in various locations, seeing where it fits and where it does not fit. We are making new connections, attempting to see the relationship between "c" and "q," as well as "c" and "d." We are hearing literally, symbolically, theoretically, genetically, and dynamically. No wonder we (frequently) talk to each other about our exhaustion at the end of the work day.

Being able to listen analytically requires us to attend to many layers of meaning simultaneously. Although for purposes of explication I have separated this task from the emotional and relational aspects of the work, of course all are going on at the same time. The capacity to concentrate for many hours a day, perhaps with few breaks, clearly requires more than just cognitive skills. But a way of thinking is part of the process. When candidates think on parallel levels simultaneously, especially if it is early in their training, we see them as naturally talented. I don't know to what extent this is a skill that can be taught, or whether it is a way of functioning that some people are innately better equipped to do. I certainly talk about this skill in supervision, but what supervisors emphasize is such a catch-as-catch-can process that it seems possible to me that there is great variability in how much this, or any other aspect of the analytic task, gets supervisory attention.

Pattern Recognition

Many tasks in life, including some aspects of the psychoanalytic process, require the immediate recognition of a familiar pattern. The tennis player sees the setup of a backhand stroke and automatically begins to position himself for a backhand. He does not have to stop and evaluate this decision. It is bred in the bone. His whole body knows when and how to prepare for that stroke. Similarly, as experienced analysts, some information comes to us automatically, based on the recognition of a familiar pattern. I think of depression or paranoia or defenses such as splitting or projection as presenting patterns we would recognize, although we may not consciously register that pattern recognition during the session. In the presence of paranoia, for example, I am likely to selectively focus on material that touches on issues of interpersonal trust, the negative motives others have toward the patient, and what is "real" underneath peoples' masks or socially sanctioned appearances. Like the tennis player, pattern recognition helps orient me. Without missing a beat, without wasting time on consciously thinking about it, I ready myself for paranoid themes just as tennis players ready their bodies to return a backhand well before the ball nears their racquet.

Of course, pattern recognition has its dangers as well as its advantages, in that it makes it easy to stereotype or even create expected behavior iatrogenically. Some analysts have argued that we are better off starting each session open to whatever we see, without "memory or desire." I think this stance has great advantages in that it leaves our minds truly free to follow the unfolding material. But, for beginners, I would say it might be too anxiety provoking. Candidates who have little clinical experience may find it so difficult to work without any sense of what they are doing that they don't really profit from their early experiences with patients. They are just "getting through" sessions, rather than living them fully.

As Sullivan (1953) famously said, anxiety is like a blow on the head. It precludes many cognitive processes. For example, a candidate presents a patient who seems to be "stuck" in an unhappy relationship with an abusive alcoholic husband. The patient is in her mid-40s, is unable to get a job, and has many medical problems and a long history of troubled relationships with family members. It is a pretty bleak picture. The candidate reports that whenever a way the patient might improve her situation is suggested, the patient becomes extremely resistant, angry, and accusing, and often misses the next session. In one particular hour they have what sounds like an argument, with the patient complaining that the treatment makes her feel worse, that she feels "thrown off balance." While this session could be understood in many ways, I hear in it an increase in the patient's *paranoid* anxiety. I believe she wonders whether the candidate is deliberately "throwing her off balance." My suggestion to the candidate in supervision is to take any possible opportunities to focus on the issue of her own motives toward the patient. It might help to make it very clear to the patient that the candidate's aim was to help her have some hope that she could improve her situation. I find that what often happens clinically is that when the clinician suggests making a change it evokes the paranoid anxiety that, as the patient might put it, "You think it is all my fault, and if I wanted to I could have a better life."

Listening as the supervisor, I heard the pattern of paranoid anxiety in the patient's complaints. For her, the most important question was whether the clinician's intentions were bad. Since the patient felt blamed and criticized, is that what the clinician meant to make her feel? Recognizing and naming this pattern enabled me to suggest an approach. I think that seeing the material this way also facilitated a change in the candidate's attitude toward his patient. The patient's criticism was taken less personally, and the candidate realized more fully that he was expecting more "progress" than was realistic. This patient is struggling to hold on to her sanity and feels genuinely endangered by some insight-oriented interventions. Out of a need for self-preservation, among other reasons, she has to fend off what the candidate is trying to offer. Seeing it this way enabled the candidate to find an acceptable role in the treatment. As always, it is important to realize the limitations as well as the advantages of pattern recognition. Of course, this patient is not just someone who suffers from paranoid anxiety. She has many other issues, and, like the rest of us, is a complex human being. But seeing the part paranoid anxiety was playing was helpful, so long as we recognized that it was only one aspect of the situation.

Levels of Abstraction

In his witty essay "Follow the Fox," Levenson (1981) suggests that one of the reasons the supervisor often sees the treatment with greater clarity than the analyst is that their experience is at differing levels of abstraction. The supervisor is considering a *type* of clinical situation, or patient, or symptom, while the clinician is interacting with a *particular* patient. At higher levels of abstraction clarity is easier to achieve.

I suggest that at times analysts change the level of abstraction for themselves and their patients without necessarily formulating it in these terms. For example, in an initial consultation, a male patient described the sulky behavior of his teenage daughter. She ruined family outings, pouting about nearly any activity. I asked a number of questions and learned that the patient is divorced from this girl's mother, has remarried, and has created a new family with his second wife. I asked when he had divorced, how his problem teenager had reacted to her parents' marriage ending, and how she now feels about the patient's new wife. My questions contained and expressed assumptions, inevitably narrowing possibilities for inquiry as much as I might be attempting to widen the focus. A question about the length of time since the divorce implies that adjustments to these changes can take time. It may matter whether the divorce was recent. I am viewing this teenager as a member of several classes of people. She is likely to bring to my mind other girls, teenagers, and children of divorce. Much as I may make conscious efforts to remain open to all possibilities, I will inevitably bring my own experiences to bear as I listen to this material. For me this child (who I will never actually meet) instantly evoked certain assumptions that shaped my questions, which affected the material I elicited. From the vantage point these assumptions helped to shape, I hypothesized some reasons that she might be unenthusiastic about "family outings."

Although, as an analyst, I am not trying to give the patient advice about how to manage his teenage daughter, I am hearing the material and responding to it in some way (even if I say nothing). My mind is shaping questions that affect the session's focus in ways that are conditioned by my previous (personal and professional) experiences. I bring my attitudes about teenage girls to this session, whether I want to or not. In some ways this may be helpful, but it can also limit what I am able to hear and see. However, I believe that no act of conscious will can change that. As I listen, I think of this girl as a member of various groups, while to her father she is a more specific person, perhaps with dimples I will never see. She is the child whose first attempt at baking turned out either delicious or disastrous. She pouts with an almost discernible faint smile. I will never know her this specifically, partly because I wouldn't know what questions to ask to get this particular information, but also because my mind doesn't hold years of memories of her. I have not known her in my dreams. It may help our work that, for me, she is a member of various classes and, of course, carries less meaning than if she were my daughter. For these reasons I may be able to imagine her differently from the way her father sees her. Perhaps I can wonder if she is torturing him for leaving her mother, while he can't imagine that. But I have known teenage girls who torture their divorced parents and I can imagine her in that way. While it is unlikely I would immediately make reference to this hypothetical conception of her, I am sure it will have some impact on my thinking in the session, whatever I consciously intend. I see her at a higher level of abstraction than her father can because I do not really know her, in all her particularity. I am both handicapped and helped by this in my efforts to understand.

I want to stress that much of this would probably remain unformulated, for me as well as the patient. But what I ask, how I hear, what

I don't focus on since I take it for granted, what I remember about all of this next session, and so much else rests on where this girl fits into my array of interpersonal experiences. I see this as unavoidable. I believe it is likely to give me a greater feeling of clarity than the patient has about the situation he describes.

Like so much else, being able to think at a higher level of abstraction can be helpful, even though in practice it may also mislead. But in a good analytic relationship, where both patient and analyst are participant observers, the issues it formulates can be of some use. Another way to think about this is that we recontextualize the patient's experience. The questions I asked the teenager's father enabled him to try out seeing her from new angles.

Participant Observation

I picture the process of participant observation, as described by Sullivan, (1953) as a kind of rocking motion. While Sullivan formulated participant observation as part of the role of the "expert" "psychiatrist," I see it as a crucial aspect of the work of both people in a treatment. The image of rocking from one side to the other enables me to think of constant motion, rather than discrete, separable actions. Another analogy I have used is a comparison with driving a car, where we frequently have to adjust the car to veer more toward the right sometimes, and toward the left at other moments. Similarly, as analysts, at times we find ourselves taking a too detached, observing stance, not "mixing it up" enough, while, at other moments, we feel lost in an enactment we are unable to observe. Analysts and patients are always inclined in the direction of observing or participating and, at the very same time, trying to "correct" for this slant. At least in my view, this constant motion does not have to be consciously formulated in order to be effective. Sometimes one or both people don't see themselves as moving from participating in something toward observing it until later in the process. I don't see it as always necessary to formulate this at the time it is happening, although sometimes I think it can be helpful.

A patient takes care to protect my ego during a session, using words that carefully tone down criticism of me. I point this out, gently and very carefully. Each of us may then think about the role of "carefulness" in our relationship with the other, and in our interactions with others. We have moved from enacting, or participating, toward observing. But in how we observe we may, for example, talk less carefully with each other than usual. We have changed our participation as a byproduct of our observations. We are now enacting something else, a bit different from the initial interplay. We rock back and forth, participating in an observed process that leads to modifications in how we interact. If we tried to freeze one frame of this rocking motion, we might see ourselves as enacting without much observing at a particular moment. But this is misleading, since we are always doing some of both. It is difficult to express the simultaneity of participation and observation and how they actually constantly modify each other. More aware of how he protects others, a man may speak to his wife a bit differently over dinner. Possibly she may sense and welcome the change or resent it. In any case, she may react a bit differently from usual, and this incident may play some role in the next analytic session. This example is meant to suggest the enormous complexity of participation and observation in analysis and its potentially profound impact on many lives.

Creating and Maintaining a Private Language

Many intimates use a private shorthand language to communicate. When one of my patients tells me that he expressed no objections to his wife's plans for their vacation, I comment, "Another passive choice." We both know what those words mean to us. In a flash a whole history comes to both our minds. At the forks in the road, he has always gone along with someone else's wishes, inwardly resented it, dragged his feet, and made them pay, sooner or later.

But when I say these words I am not just linking this choice with all the others. I am also implying "I know you." I am affirming that there is a "we." I am also expressing my own willingness to make a choice that might be seen as active, rather than passive. I could have said nothing and "gone along." I didn't.

Part of the reason I like to focus on getting a chronological history early in treatment is to facilitate the creation of a shared language. When the patient mentions an aunt I would like to know who she has been to my patient at various phases of life. But a shared language does more than inform. I think it modulates the loneliness of the work for both participants. Without the shame that (at least in our culture) can come from asking for comfort, it gives comfort. Without having to articulate it, it allows me to say, 'I'm the one who has been with you before, and I am with you now."

Languages don't maintain themselves. They take work. Just as most of us forget the French we learned in college if we never use it, a shared language must be practiced. I take notes and try to read the most recent one just before the patient arrives. Visually, I see this as surrounding myself in our words, the words of the patient's history, the words from the last time we met, the words of recent dreams. Surrounding myself with these words situates me.

Working at a Preconscious Level

Interpretive work has to aim to make fully conscious what is presently preconscious. If we focus on material that is already within patients' consciousness we add little that is new to what they already know, though we may help them make connections and see patterns they didn't see on their own. On the other hand, if we focus on what is profoundly outside the patient's awareness our interpretation will not have resonance. It will seem like a foreign, alien idea, too strange to be true. The most useful insights in treatment and other creative processes seem obvious once they are stated, because they have been dwelling near, but not within, awareness.

During sessions I actually often visualize trying to hit a target or zone. When an interpretation "clicks" there is that same feeling of rightness we have when playing tennis and the ball leaves the racquet so solidly that we know where it will land before it gets there. This "groove" has to be rediscovered every session. Often I have to find it more than once within a session. At least in my clinical experience, I cannot assume we will be able to work at a preconscious level tomorrow just because we were able to work that way today. But when we do it is exhilarating. I don't think there is any magic way to make it happen. It is easy to know when the material is at such a conscious level that there are really no new insights being discovered. The air is less alive, and time hangs rather than dashing forward.

While I strongly believe there is no recipe for preconscious insight, I think we increase our chances of finding it when we evoke more than we say. Poetry and analysis have this in common, which is one reason I believe that writing and reading poetry is helpful for

us as analysts. In poetry each word has to do a lot of work. Being succinct is valuable in both fields. In treatment, patients often remember
a succinct phrase and attach more meaning to it. Analytic theories
have benefited from pithy phrases such as Winnicott's (1971) "good
enough mother," or "transitional object." They pack a great deal
of meaning into a few words, enticing our minds into projecting
our own experience into them. When T.S. Eliot (1943) says, in the
poem "East Coker," that "In my beginning is my end," I am drawn
to ascribe my meanings to his words. The line itself skirts the distinction between inside me and outside me, as does any transitional
object. A more familiar transitional object, the teddy bear, is brown
because the factory dyed it brown, but only the child's inner experience projected onto the bear can make it delicious. In the poem,
the words "my beginning" have meanings intended by T.S. Eliot,
but they are vague and evocative enough to prompt me to ascribe
my own internal experiences to them. I help to create a personally
meaningful line out of the poet's words in what I ascribe to them.
Similarly, when I say to the patient who didn't complain about his
wife's vacation plan, "another passive choice," I am:

1. Connecting a pattern we have clarified in the past with the
   patient's behavior in the present. In effect I am saying something
   like, "You and I know what happens when you hide your resentment and seem to go along with others. You end up miserable and
   make them pay for it."
2. Reinforcing our feeling of connection by implying that we have
   our own language, and this is one of its phrases.
3. Affirming the value of prediction. If a way of interacting interpersonally has always had bad results, it is reasonable to assume it
   may work out poorly again.
4. Trying to speak succinctly and evocatively enough for the patient
   to hear his or her experience in my words, just as we do with a
   poet's words.

As analysts, our target, like the poet's, is to evoke more than we
say. This makes it more likely that phrases that resonate with the
patient's inner experience will be cocreated. The culture the patient
and I have in common provides a dictionary that exists "outside"
us. From it we create a kind of poetry by using highly evocative language. Layers of its meaning come from experiences we have had
with each other, or talked about. Like all poetry, its function, aside

from giving us joy and helping us feel connected, is to prompt us to think just a bit beyond what we have already consciously known.

I believe there is something powerful about one person's creating a phrase that captures multiple layers of another's experience. For example, when I tell one of my female patients that I think her current behavior is (in part) an effort to make her (long dead) mother smile, it has some meanings that are immediately apparent and would occur to most people hearing the phrase. But only she and I understand some of its more personal implications. The phrase refers to many earlier sessions in which we explored why this was so vital to her, what she was willing to do to evoke that smile during her mother's lifetime, and how their emotional bartering went on, uninterrupted by her mother's death. Using this phrase implies much more than it overtly states, and is meant to evoke echoes on a preconscious level. To the extent that it succeeds, she is likely to remember the phrase after the session, and it may help her bring together experiences she has never before connected. As she spends the evening trying to please her husband she may think of the phrase "making mother smile," and realize that she is playing out, with him, something from her own past. Of course I could have said, "I think you are still trying to please your mother." But I believe that would have been less effective. It would be less likely to call up images from her childhood, in which that smile was such a treasured reward. In referring to her mother's smile I am trying to capture an image that can help the patient coalesce her present conscious and preconscious experience, her memories, and interpretive work we have done together. She is aware of her wish to please her husband, but links between that and her history with her mother are not yet available to her on a fully conscious level. I think that if the patient is struck by the phrase, "making my mother smile," she will remember it, and it is more likely to facilitate consciously connecting many past and present experiences.

In another example, a male patient was severely neglected and abandoned in his childhood. In essence he grew up alone, though surrounded by his family. Even major events like changing schools and illnesses were hardly noticed. Whenever something emotionally similar happens to him now we are likely to call it "no big deal," echoing his own first description to me of these events in his childhood. But I have given the phrase an ironic twist by pushing it to caricatured extremes. Each time something reminds me of it I will say something that indicates that the quality of his entire life is "no big deal." With many patients I would not rely so heavily on irony, sarcasm, and a kind of teasing, but I believe that with this person the humor allows him to hear me. The phrase "no big deal" has come to signify his way of minimizing the importance of the events of his life, so he can ignore how his family neglects their significance. If he, himself, sees them as "no big deal" it should not hurt him that they are treated as unimportant by others.

The phrase "no big deal" allows me to evoke more than I say, and contributes to our having a special language that affirms our bond. In more than one sense it declares that the quality of this patient's life *is* a big deal to me. It is worth bothering to capture in words, to think about, joke about, and, in our own way, mourn.

"No big deal" also helps us work on a preconscious level, since the link between his childhood and a current minimized event is often potentially conscious, but as yet unavailable. When I say that something that just happened sounds to me like "no big deal" I am suggesting, in as few words as possible, that he is defending himself in his characteristic way against the pain of feeling abandoned.

I think the phrase will outlast the treatment, which I see as a good outcome. Both during and after treatment I believe that most of the work occurs outside the sessions in the patient's growing capacity for self-observation. Phrases promote this work by giving familiar "tags" to categories of experience. I hope that this patient will find himself calling something "no big deal" 20 years from now when our formal work is long over, but the ruefulness of the phrase reminds him of some of what we accomplished.

The Nexus of Theory and Practice

As we work, how does psychoanalytic theory inform our thinking process and shape our clinical choices? How do I operate differently with my patients if I believe in what Sullivan wrote? What do I listen for, respond to, say differently if I think of myself as Kohutian? I think these questions are of great importance to people in training but they often feel inhibited about asking them, as though it would be putting the instructor or supervisor on the spot. These are, however, among the questions that I believe should be asked repeatedly and addressed as often as possible.

Thinking about the nexus between theory and practice is the province of courses as well as supervision. I have always felt that nexus to be my principal focus in postgraduate teaching. It seems obvious to me that people at this level do not need me to help them read, but rather to bring my experience to bear on the question of how theory can be translated into practice in sessions with patients. Near graduation, many candidates feel painfully inadequate in this area. They have an understanding of some theories and theoretical differences, and they may feel some confidence in their clinical acumen, but when it comes to applying theory to practice they still feel lost.

This is where it is probably more effective for instructors or supervisors to talk about their own work, rather than trying to respond to the candidate's presentation. I can illustrate, for example, what Sullivan's idea of participant observation means to me and how I might use it in a session, if I talk about my own practice. Since it is a genuinely meaningful concept to me I believe that my work has been guided by it, so it will not be hard to find moments when it actually shaped my behavior. I will not feel I am artificially forcing the clinical data to fit the theory, or the theory to fit the clinical exchange. There will be a natural fit.

I think it can be especially helpful to present my work to a candidate when it illustrates how different theories would point us in different directions clinically. For example, a patient persists in remaining unwilling to look for a job despite economic necessity and his wife's mounting fury. Conflict theories might make a good case for the patient's Oedipal issues. He did have an openly competitive father. There is a good deal of evidence of unresolved feelings of not wanting to outstrip, and therefore, in some sense, kill this rather aggressive, threatening father. Seductive aspects of the patient's mother are also in evidence. I could conceptualize the patient as stuck in Oedipal conflicts that render him inhibited, sexually as well as in the area of professional ambition.

But deficit theories also fit the information I have about this patient. Self-esteem injuries abound in his life history. I could easily see him as lacking in the confidence it takes to apply for work and risk rejection.

What difference does it make which theory I hold? If I see the patient as in an Oedipal conflict I will conceive of the goal of the treatment to be to resolve the conflict, freeing him to compete. A deficit theory, on the other hand, would focus me on helping him develop a stronger sense of self.

All this is fairly straightforward and, I think, clear to most candidates. What may be less evident is the difference in the emotional attitude each theory evokes in the analyst. With a conflict theory the analyst can create a new triangle—the patient, the analyst, and the "bad" parents. Implicitly, the analyst becomes the "better" parent, just by trying to free the patient from the clutches of this conflict. Righteous anger is a frequent accompaniment. We arm ourselves with theory, ready to do battle with the damaging forces from the past.

With a deficit theory our anger is less useful, since we do not feel as though we are pitching a battle so much as healing wounds. Softer protective urges are elicited. We are sad about the lost opportunities self-esteem damage costs. We are eager to avoid further damage to the patient's ego, quicker than usual to recognize potential triggers of shame. We focus on what can nurture the patient's sense of self. We are not armed with anger, but rather strengthened by a resolve to be helpful.

The conflict model makes the patient's defenses into obstacles in the quest for freedom from inhibition. For example, with the patient who wasn't looking for a job, his repression of evidence of his father's competitive behavior could be seen as blocking progress. The patient's repression can become the focus of the analyst's eager attention. I think most patients are aware of this process, and come to feel that their analyst sees them as sacrificing their own welfare to protect their parents. They have to choose. The conscious choice to help the analyst build his case recursively recreates a triangular situation. Now, rather than father, mother, and patient, we have parents, patient, and analyst (or, perhaps, defenses that protect the parents, patient, and analyst). The patient who decides (on a conscious level) to join forces with the analyst is likely to share in the anger that is necessary to fuel any ongoing battle. How dare his father create an unfair competition with a helpless child, guaranteed to harm his son's chances to succeed in life?

The deficit model can certainly evoke anger too but, I think, creates a somewhat different interpersonal situation, with the potential to elicit other feelings just as easily as anger. While the parents may be blamed for failing to support the patient's self-esteem, therapeutic growth will be achieved through repair. Anger at the parents may accompany the process, but it is not necessary. Repair (unlike battle) can be accomplished without it. Healing and repair probably require more tenderness than anger. There also may be feelings of regret at what has been lost. The patient's shame and anxiety about inadequacy can evoke the saddened empathy one can feel in the presence of a debilitating handicap. We feel called upon to (re)build and inspire (re)growth.

Thus each model asks the candidate to develop a set of interpersonal skills, cognitive patterns, and emotional strengths. Given that there is no one model, now, that dominates psychoanalytic thinking, all candidates have to consider which model is right for them, given who they are, rather than which represents the "truth." Each candidate must ask whether they are the kind of person who can go after defenses in a reconstituted triangular conflict, or the kind of person who can tend unmet need. Of course no treatment is purely conflict- or deficit-based. But I think it is time to evaluate theoretical positions with our own emotional strengths and weaknesses in mind, rather than debating which theory has the ultimate truth about human experience.

Avoiding Splitting

How many times have you heard the build-up toward a conclusion that a particular candidate isn't confronting enough, or is engaged in too many power struggles, or is not able to sense his patient's anger quickly enough, or too intensely wants to help, or underestimates pathology, or is too trusting or too suspicious of the patient? These are some of the issues that attendees at case presentations, training committee members, and conference participants often dispute. I have frequently observed that at case conferences there is usually one bad guy. If the patient is not judged as "not analyzable," then the supervisor or the analyst is seen as functioning inadequately. Once one of these issues has been taken up, a snowballing process can evolve. Everyone lines up on one side or the other of the emerging split.

Personally, I feel these discussions are generally not useful and often have harmful results. Someone becomes the scapegoat. We lose the appreciation of nuance that characterizes our better moments. Instead of conflicted individuals we see advocates of artificially dichotomous points of view. We choose sides, like school children deciding whether to join the popular crowd or the nerds.

Whenever the temptation to participate in this jockeying threatens to overtake me I try to remind myself of the lessons that can be learned from studying the history of our field. Factional splits waste everyone's time, energy, heart. Ultimately, like the battles between "nature" and "nurture" they always result in the answer that "both of the above" have merit. Recently (Shapiro, 2006) the question was raised as to whether we have veered too sharply away from the values of neutrality, abstinence, and the worth of the classical analytic frame. Attitudes swing from one extreme to the other, with adherents denying that the "other side" has a point. Where is the sensitivity we would (hopefully) show when listening to a patient's history and hearing of clashes between what sounds right and what sounds also right? Where is the wisdom about human limitations we would (hopefully) have when counseling a troubled couple, each of whom genuinely believes she or he is fighting for Truth and Justice?

Supervisory Attitudes That Nurture Analytic Development

How the supervisor's attitudes can contribute to the candidate's general development is a vast subject. I will touch on only a few points as they relate to the evolution of the candidate's capacity for what I am calling "thinking analytically."

To me, the attitude that has the most powerful overall impact is how the supervisor feels about the integration of life experience and clinical experience. Usually this is not a subject that supervisors talk about in a conscious formulated way. But I think each supervisor communicates beliefs about the degree to which we should be guided by our own life experience as we navigate in a session. Put another way, each analyst has (usually unformulated) attitudes about how much one's behavior in a session ought to be guided by analytic theory, or insights gleaned from one's own personal life, or lessons learned during training, or from other sources. When analysts become supervisors they bring these beliefs to their supervisory work and communicate them to candidates.

I think candidates are often afraid to reveal to supervisors that they rely on their life experience to guide them in sessions, because they are worried this will be judged as not sufficiently "analytic." I can't tell you how many times people entering training have seemed to me to be apologetic about former careers, being parents, or having interests other than psychoanalysis. Perhaps the cumbersome jargon analysts often use tells them they don't belong in analytic training unless they are willing to act as though they were just born and had no clinically useful experience at all. I believe it is crucial to communicate that when we come to work as analysts we are still parents, readers, art lovers, etc. We bring our whole selves to the office in the morning and we had better learn to call on all our resources for our difficult task.

Another attitude that has profound impact in supervision is the sense that countertransference is vital information about both treatment participants. By now we all know this intellectually, but I think the supervisor's attitude can play a major role in whether this attitude is really internalized in training. Very often when people enter supervision they feel as though some of their countertransference is a secret shame, a response that would disqualify them from the profession if it were found out. The change during training that is often helpful is to become better able to use countertransference as information, not as self-castigation.

The Internal Chorus

Elsewhere (Buechler, 1998, 2004) I have developed the concept I call the clinician's internal chorus. These internalized voices help us bear the strains of our work partially, I would suggest, through memorable phrases that capture their special brand of wisdom. My own internal chorus includes many of my teachers, analysts, and supervisors, as well as theoreticians who have influenced me through their writing, such as Freud, Guntrip, Winnicott, Sullivan, and Fromm. But it also includes the poet Rilke, the writer Dostoevsky, the painter Rembrandt, and my grandmother, all of whom taught me something about living life as a human being.

I believe that having an internal chorus, a kind of assembly of wise elders, can sometimes help. At the very least it can make us feel less lonely in those dark moments when we know that how we respond clinically may make a difference, but we feel lost or conflicted. What if every response, including silence, seems potentially problematic?

In other words, what if a session closely resembles a good deal of the rest of life?

Supervision is, then, akin to a rehearsal hall where a developing clinician can listen to how another voice sounds. The values enacted in the supervision and whether they are consonant with the supervisor's stated approach are core to the supervision's impact. Thus, a supervisor who preaches kindness to patients but, in the supervision, behaves contemptuously, will confuse, at best. On the other hand, hopefully, we have all experienced the powerful effect of supervisory integrity, that is, wholeness or consistency between word and act. Supervisors make a mistake, forget something, need help, etc. Do they live the moment palpably valuing self-discovery and clinical effectiveness over their own pride? Is there evident courage, tactful truth, in *how* they teach? Does intense clinical purpose impassion the supervision? Do these supervisors embody realistic hope? Can they gracefully bear losses, including the end of the supervision process itself? In other words, supervision should manifest the meaningfulness of clinical values (Buechler, 2004). In the best supervision, an internal shift occurs as a new voice joins the clinician's inner chorus. In the future, most of the time it will blend in seamlessly. But once in a while it will be called upon to lead. In those special moments clinicians remember a phrase, or an attitude, or a theoretical belief, or a flavor of the supervisor's style, and are fortified by it as they move toward making it more truly their own.

Like analysts, supervisors are remembered (at least partially) because of their memorable phrases. When a phrase captures something about what it was like to be with that person, we remember it and find our own uses for it. Even the analyst whose training provided a resonant internal chorus feels lost in sessions, at times. Words, phrases, attitudes sometimes come back at those moments. Like a beacon, they light the path, driving away some fears of the dark but not always telling us which way to go.

Some voices from my own internal chorus may make this clearer. Sullivan has long been a member of that chorus. In fact, for me, his voice is often distinctive enough to earn the part of a soloist. A phrase that inspires me is his statement (1954) that the patient should expect to derive benefit from each session. This puts the bar very high, asking from me a keen attention to each session's potential contribution. It also reminds me how important it is to sustain hope in both participants. Without sufficient hope that the treatment can lead to a richer life, neither may be able to mobilize the stamina it takes to see the process through.

Erich Fromm often bolsters my determination, by lending me his spirited zeal. I think of his distinction between the biophilic, or life-enhancing forces in us, and the necrophilic, death-loving pulls. It is, in large part, the opportunity to fight for life, for more life, that enticed me into this field in the first place, and that still sustains my intensity. Fromm had a unique way to describe the human need for self-realization. For example, in *The Revolution of Hope* (1968) he says:

> The dynamism of human nature inasmuch as it is human is primarily rooted in this need of man to express his faculties in relation to the world rather than in his need to use the world as a means for the satisfaction of his physiological necessities. This means: because I have eyes, I have the need to see; because I have ears, I have the need to hear; because I have a heart, I have the need to feel. In short, because I am a man, I am in need of man and of the world. (p. 72)

To me, this is extremely valuable clinically. It means when I am faced with a depressed woman a slew of questions occur to me. Is there something lying dormant, some unused potential in this person? Is she, at least partially, depressed as a result of an unlived life, like, I would argue, so many of Freud's patients, who were so desperately constrained by a society that severely constricted the role of women?

Henry Krystal (1975) has contributed many apt phrases to my work. He has called calamity "opportunity in work clothes" (p. 202), reminding me that most emotions, however intense, generally pass just like storms, and suggesting that we are more afraid of our reactions to life's catastrophes than the objective consequences. Thus, if I believe what is most important is how I deal, for example, with aging or loss because I can have some control over my style of coping with these human predicaments. I will be less anxious.

Winnicott has given us so many useful concepts that it is hard to choose one, but I would vote for the idea that what we are most afraid of has, in some sense, already happened. For example, a female patient was terrified of ending up in a nursing home. I, with my own experiences of working in nursing homes in my 20s, felt this fear was so natural, so understandable that for years I failed to adequately question it. At long last it dawned on me that the patient had been a sickly child, and some of her early experiences of helplessness were activated when she thought of nursing homes. The terrible position of extreme need and unbearable loneliness that she associated with nursing homes had already happened to her and this greatly intensified her fear.

Stephen Mitchell forever changed our field with his passionate curiosity and inspiring intellectual generosity. To cite one of his ideas seems almost absurd to me, but I will have to be content with mentioning how he frequently said, "You can never interpret outside the transference and countertransference." This often serves to remind me that, for example, however much I might try to convince a distrusting patient that I am trustworthy, he will hear my effort to convince him in the only way he knows how to hear. In other words, he will experience my words through his prism.

I frequently think of Edgar Levenson's oft-repeated phrase that has come up before in this book, that the last one to know about water is a fish. That is, as human beings, we cannot see the assumptions we have always taken for granted. If someone's life experience has consistently shown life to be extremely fragile that person does not recognize this as a basic assumption. Thus, the person never questions it or even sees that there could be other attitudes. For me, this suggests that in each session my own unexamined assumptions shape what I hear, what I don't retain because it is something I take for granted, what I remember, focus on clinically, respond to passionately, formulate as pathological, feel pulled to modulate in myself or the patient, etc. I don't see the water that has always been my medium or the "givens" that have always been assumed.

My chorus also includes Freud, with his distinction between mourning and melancholia, Guntrip and his description of the need–fear dilemma, and Dostoevsky with his challenge that without God everything is permitted. Dostoevsky is, I believe, telling us that we need some kind of anchor to center us. For some of us it is a notion of God, for others it may be a philosophical vantage point or a more personally derived belief system. I also took in the work of Fromm-Reichmann, most especially her poetic, posthumously published paper (1959), "On loneliness," with its important distinction between aloneness and loneliness. She says that in aloneness, rather than the more painful state of loneliness, we often feel a sense of purpose and a belief that our present state is not permanent. Clinically, this sometimes suggests to me to focus on the patient's sense of whether he or she will always be lonely, and why.

Jay Greenberg has contributed the extremely useful idea that, as analysts, we must be equally the old object, neutral enough to allow the patient to experience transference, and a new object, facilitating change. My own version of this, discussed more fully in another chapter of this book, is that we must provide contrast, catalyst, and relational challenge. That is, we provide contrast in that we help patients see the water that, as fish, they have always taken for granted. As catalysts we are often new objects, in that we openly encourage experimenting with life outside the treatment. As relational challenges we make it hard for patients to do "business as usual" with us within the session. We are blunt enough to make it difficult for them to fail to see their own obsessive indirectness, we are passionate enough to make it hard for patients to be schizoid and depressed without noticing it, and we are willing to openly risk shame so that the narcissistic patient experiences someone who is not afraid to be wrong or look foolish, who values having life more than looking good. Most of these ideas suggest ways to be a new object for many patients, but I also greatly value Greenberg's (1991) warning that we have to be neutral enough for the most significant transferences to occur. This means to me that I cannot allow myself, for instance, to fight so passionately for patients' willingness to live that I discourage them from expressing their self-destructive urges. They may then be forced to dissociate these urges along with other transferential feelings that could rob us of vital treatment opportunities to work with these important legacies.

I often remember the voice of Ralph Crowley, my first analytic supervisor, who would frequently remind me to focus on what I already know about my patient, rather than on what I don't yet know. I think part of why this had such a profound effect on me was that it was an attitude that he embodied as well as recommended. He focused on what I knew, more than on what I didn't know, so when he suggested that I do the same his words had great impact.

Many other contributors suggest themselves to me, but I must mention the inimitable voice of Alberta Szalita. Her blunt, direct style is a significant part of her legacy. When she spoke at a meeting, for example, she often made her point in such clear language, with a simplicity that challenged us all to try to match it. When I listened to her, I wondered why we couldn't all talk like that. Still a candidate, I volunteered to present a patient to her in a day-long public forum. Details of the event have faded for me, but the feel of it was unforgettable. The image that came to mind then, and is just as vivid now, was that I was clear water she could look straight through. She saw the essence of my experience with my patient and could capture it in a few words. Aside from the clarity of her thinking, she had a way of communicating that whatever is true can be faced. Her stance toward life was, itself, inspiring. Her forthrightness was, somehow, contagious. It was as though she was able to get across to everyone, even strangers in an audience, that time is too precious to waste, so let's just get to the truth. We can do it, if we are determined enough.

In 1997, Amnon Issacharoff interviewed Szalita for the journal *Contemporary Psychoanalysis*, and asked her how her work had changed over the span of her long analytic career. Szalita said, "I'm not thinking about whether it's analytical to say it or not analytical to say it, and I'm not bound by it" (p. 627). Expanding on this statement, Szalita made it clear that her work felt freer now than it had been earlier on. She no longer worried about what the analytic establishment would say if they heard how she conducted sessions. She said what she believed would help the patient. By embodying that freedom and not merely talking about it, Szalita became an important member of my own internal chorus and, I am sure, of many others.

On the same page as this statement, Szalita summed up her philosophy about what really matters in doing analysis, "It boils down to one thing: to what degree you are concerned with yourself and to what degree you are, as a therapist, concerned with the other person" (p. 627). I think Szalita was referring here to the way analysts have to be able to focus exclusively on what might make a difference in the patient's life experience. I take from this the belief that the most important task we have when we train analysts is nurturing their capacity to concentrate on the patient. The thinking process we are facilitating in training is the ability to focus on the patient in the pure, intense, clearsighted way Szalita focused on me. Whatever we do in training is good if it enables the trainee to singlemindedly focus on the patient without a selfish preoccupation with whether the candidate sounds smart.

The internal chorus facilitates this process in that it helps the analyst feel solid, secure, backed up by elders. With this ballast, analysts can weather whatever happens, still believing in the analytic process and in their own basic competence.

The chorus sometimes provides a compass, too. Phrases I remember from my own training often point me in one direction in sessions. For example, just as I was deeply immersed in proving a much beloved point to her, my own training analyst (Rose Spiegel) would often ask me, "What else is true?" I can still hear her voice, tinkling with merriment as she interrupted my diatribe. I took her tone to mean that I might be better off if I could loosen up. What was so very crucial about making my point? Her voice can still steady me when I get wrapped up in having to prove something. It also suggests a direction I might take when patients lose their sense of perspective as they passionately argue *their* point. Rose's humor is a comfort to me now, as it was so many years ago. To whatever extent I can keep my perspective even when passionately involved in an interaction, it is because of her indomitable spirit. What I took from her, more, I believe, than anything else, was her absolute, palpable dedication to our work. This attitude that I have tried to emulate still plays a significant role in how I think and interact in sessions.

This personal chorus, replete with members who frequently play solo parts, supplies me with possibilities for what I might say in a session. I am sure it also shapes what I focus on, given that there are always myriad possibilities. As I have already said, the chorus offers me a sense of security and backup. It helps me feel less lonely. But, much of the time, its most significant gift is that it lends me its spirit.

9

Emotional Preparation for Practicing Psychoanalysis

It is late at night and I am tired. A close friend who chose a very different career path calls with family news. As we range over familiar topics, we grouse a bit about our long work days. She asks, playfully, what I want to be when I *really* grow up. It doesn't take any thought. A psychoanalyst.

When I began analytic training I had a feeling of having come home. I belong here. I may complain about the long hours, the wider culture's prejudices that endanger our field, and, inevitably as I age, how wonderful things were in the "old days" compared with now. Probably not unlike every generation as it faces a world shaped by younger people, I may long for less technology and simpler, less bottom-line-driven times. I may selectively attend to their glories and forget their disheartening aspects. I may bemoan the political atmosphere and the "doom and gloom" predictions about analysis' future. Like the theatre, analysis is always being pronounced dead. To borrow from Mark Twain, the rumors of its death have, in my judgment, been greatly exaggerated.

On a more personal note, I may complain of the sorrows of the work—constant exposure to all of life's greatest woes and the ever-present potential for yet another empathic failure. But if you ask me what career I would choose if given a "do-over," I know that I would be an analyst.

In this chapter I reflect on the emotional qualities I think analytic work requires. Who must we be to work in this field? What emotional capacities are necessary prerequisites for avoiding burnout as an analyst? How can these qualities be nurtured in analytic training? I explore several emotional challenges of the work from my own perspective. I concentrate most attention on the humility that terminating treatment gracefully requires. This focus obviously reflects my own personal feelings. Others may experience more of an emotional challenge saying "hello" than saying "goodbye." I think it might be very useful for us all to explore our differences in what we find most emotionally challenging about the work.

In pursuing this subject I have several hopes.

1. As I have already suggested, I hope to elicit discussion about what emotionally challenges other practitioners.
2. I would like us to be able to recognize what the work takes out of each of us so that we can take steps to better avoid burnout if possible.
3. I think there is a tendency to externalize our own particular discouragements with our work and envision the field itself as barren, dying, empty of meaning, etc. Perhaps if we better understood the feelings stirred in each of us, every hour, we could avoid this misleading tendency.
4. Nurturing the strengths an analytic career entails is the primary task of training. In Chapter 8 I addressed some components of the analytic *thinking* process. Here, I look at what I believe analytic *feeling* requires. In the next chapter I consider some of the interpersonal strengths I also see as prerequisite to the work.

Before beginning this discussion of the development of analytic emotionality in the candidate, I would like to define it as clearly as I can. I am aware that others might well define it differently but, once again, I think exploring these differences could be profitable for us all.

What I mean by "analytic emotionality" is very similar to the attitude of the dilettante in the work of the Indologist Heinrich Zimmer. Aside from his studies of Indian symbolism, Zimmer wrote a series of philosophical stories drawn from both Eastern and Western literature and published in the anthology *The King and the Corpse* (1948). In Zimmer's introduction he described the dilettante as follows:

> … one who takes delight (*diletto*) in something…. The moment we abandon this dilettante attitude toward the images of folklore and myth and begin to feel certain about their proper interpretation (as professional comprehenders, handling the tool of an infallible method), we deprive ourselves of the quickening contact, the demonic and inspiring assault that is the effect of their intrinsic virtue. … Delight, on the other hand, sets free in us the creative intuition, permits it to be stirred to life by contact with the fascinating script of the old symbolic tales and figures. … The true *dilettante* will be always ready to begin anew. And it will be in him that the wonderful seeds from the past will strike their roots and marvelously grow. (pp. 2–6, italics in original)

In my opinion, Zimmer captures the spirit of pleasurable curiosity that is the analyst's most positive emotional state. Of course we don't go through our days in continuous rapture. But I think the spark he describes is necessary, at least to my own survival. The "demonic and inspiring assault" that a patient might present to me tomorrow is part of what keeps me going. The "creative intuition" that is occasionally "stirred to life" in me helps to sustain me.

Elsewhere (Buechler, 2004) I have discussed the emotional balance that I think is a necessary prerequisite for the work of the patient and the analyst. Briefly, I suggest that, for both participants, loneliness, anger, anxiety, shame, guilt, sadness, and other painful feelings must not be so intense that participant observation is precluded. Both patient and analyst must be sufficiently interested in themselves and each other to turn ideas around out of curiosity. They must also have enough of a sense of the purpose of the treatment, and enough hope, kindness, courage, and integrity to be willing to exert the effort it takes to pursue the truth. This active pursuit is, in a sense, a gift they give each other. Sometimes each will have to be willing to go an "extra mile" for the other. There is, at least in my experience, a kind of generosity in that willingness. But some intense emotional states preclude finding enough generosity to effectively support the treatment.

Zimmer's dilettantes must be free enough of painful affect to enjoy themselves. Similarly, analysts need to be able to take some pleasure from their work. As Maroda (2005) and I (Buechler, 2005) have suggested, many "legitimate gratifications" and "secret pleasures" are inherent in being an analyst. The intimacy, self-healing, opportunity to be of help to another human being, enhanced self-awareness, and intellectual and emotional challenges are some of the gratifications of an analytic life.

Coltart (1996) was emphatic about liking her job, "We enjoy the ever-new fascination of traveling deep into inner space, both ours and the patients'" (p. 23). I suggest that to function as analysts we must be able to sustain curiosity and some joy in the face of the tremendously difficult, painful life circumstances we encounter with our patients. We need tensile strength to bear doing treatment. Some strength comes from adequate gratification. When a patient and I come upon a long-sought insight I feel as though something has clicked into place. I don't think I would have become an analyst without experiencing some of these pleasurable moments.

General Emotional Strengths

Hearing the Information in Emotional Experience

I see one significant goal of the patient, analyst, and supervisor as essentially the same. We all strive to remain open to learning from new experience. What does this require? I think it is not simply a matter of sufficient curiosity and sufficiently modulated negative emotions. I believe at times it requires information from one or more of our emotions, including shame, guilt, and anxiety, as well as anger, sadness, joy, envy, jealousy, loneliness, surprise, and disgust, among others. But both popular and analytic culture promote what I call "pus" theories of emotionality. On subtle and less subtle levels, we often communicate that it is best to get negative emotions out and get past them. In contrast, I am suggesting that our emotions are a significant source of information and, rather than get past them, we should strive to have them and know them as well as possible.

One obstacle to this goal is the attitude that candidates are "healthy" if their emotions are not too intense. A very angry, or anxious, or guilty candidate is, I believe, often suspected of being unstable. This communicates that feelings are dangerous, or sick, at least at high intensities. Under these circumstances how will we help candidates develop into analysts who are minimally afraid of learning from their own emotions and their patients'? At conferences and in classes we often contrast the "bad old days" when countertransference was a taboo subject with our more enlightened attitudes. Neutrality is dead, along with other outmoded analytic ideals. But do our attitudes match our words? How do we respond to emotional intensity when we are wearing our hats as analysts, supervisors, teachers, administrators (as well as patients, parents, etc)? I suggest that intense emotionality is often felt as a threat and, in some situations, this is appropriate. For example, very intense anger at a patient, impulsively expressed, can certainly pose a danger to the work. But it is not *just* a danger. It is also vital information. And no matter how high its intensity there are still alternatives as to how it is expressed.

In effect, I think we promote some schizoid and obsessive features in analysts by selecting people who have these trends and rewarding these patterns during training. I would contend that it is easier to graduate as an analyst with a schizoid, obsessive character than with any other tendencies. I think much about our field reflects this, and it provides both strengths and weaknesses. On the positive side, this may enable us to bear hearing the many painful human sagas we encounter every day. But, on the negative side, our literature can be dry, overly intellectualized, and not close enough to actual, lived, interpersonal experience. Our conferences cater to an elite that is facile with the latest buzz words. To me, this is not unlike the obsessive's use of words as instruments of magic. As Humpty Dumpty says in *Alice in Wonderland*, a word means what I say it means, no more and no less. Thus, for example, by treating experiences we label "transference" separately from those we call "character" or "personality," we draw magic lines around them or compartmentalize them.

What would our field look like if we didn't prize and privilege analysts with schizoid and obsessive tendencies? Is that possible or preferable? I think we can't know. But if we see our field as increasingly isolated and marginalized I think we should look within ourselves, as well as at the usual external suspects, such as managed care and the wider culture's limited understanding of our skills.

Training is one place where we could cultivate analysts who stay close to lived emotional experience, who mine it for its information, who are relatively unafraid of it, whose superegos serve as helpful allies, who can write what they feel, and feel what they read. To whatever extent we penalize emotional intensity in training, we nurture analysts' maintenance of defensive avoidance of intense feelings in themselves and their patients.

Emotional Resilience

Patients often ask me how I can instantly switch from listening to the last person to attending to them. Sometimes I feel they are really asking whether I can really hear them under these circumstances. Occasionally I feel they are voicing outright criticism, sure I must be faking interest.

I can understand all of these reactions. Not infrequently, at least for me, the transition from one session to the next takes a conscious act of willpower. I can only speculate as to how much of my less than conscious attention is really still focused on the previous session. As Leslie Farber (1966) so convincingly demonstrated, willpower is effective only in certain limited domains. And yet I do feel that I owe the next patient my attention. What does it take, emotionally, for me to cope with this dilemma, and how can we train candidates to be able to handle these transitions?

Mechanical solutions such as scheduling brief rest periods between sessions may help some clinicians. But I think the problem is not so easily solved. A clinical interaction can be too intense for us to count on its fading from our minds within a 10-minute break.

Some days I open my *New York Times* with some trepidation. I know that if it has published a piece on psychoanalysis one of my patients will use it to lambaste the field. With an intensity I imagine reigned during hunting season in some cultures the patient zeroes in for the kill. Unable to wait until the session begins, the diatribe commences as the patient crosses the threshold. Did I see it? What did I think of it? Did I think it "nailed" psychoanalysis's self-serving hypocrisy? Why did it leave out some of the most telling points, like …?

If I presented this moment to some of my colleagues, I think their advice would sound to me as though being aware of the transference implications of this interchange should automatically render me perfectly able to respond adroitly. To me this seems simply untrue. I am quite aware of the barely veiled contempt for me encapsulated in the patient's pointed cross-examination. I think I have some understanding of our sadomasochistic enactments, and the role(s) I play in them. Unlike the magician's wand, these insights work no miracles. The patient is likely to hear any attempt to discuss the transference as yet another clever analytic ploy. Each of us sees the world through our personal prisms.

Usually I have a strong dislike of coasting through time. To me, merely getting through the hour, the day, my life, is tremendously disheartening. But when the *Times* publishes something about psychoanalysis and I am seeing this patient, getting through that hour seems accomplishment enough. I cannot believe that my other hours are unaffected by these feelings.

A woman brings me her sorrow, that a cancer that had been in remission for years is back again, full force. Is it realistic to think that after that session I will spring up good as new, like an analytic version of the child's Slinky toy? Am I really fully capable of snapping back, fresh and ready for the next hour?

I listen to her tremulous voice as she reviews all the preventive work she and her medical team have done to try to stave off this recurrence. Has the effort been a mistake? Should she have used this cancer-free time to travel, instead of spending much of it in her oncologist's waiting room? My own thinking starts to splinter. What role did I play in her decision making? I never told her what to do, but did I focus selectively, privileging certain factors over others? What will happen to her now? Will it be like the last time, or worse? What will I do to help? The buzzer announcing the next patient's arrival sounds louder than usual. As the session ends our eyes meet, our thoughts probably not too different. I need to say something, so I end with a vague "I'm sorry." Certainly I am sorry that this happened. But am I also apologizing for it? Will she hear it that way? I think of an image I have often had, of the hungry staring into a busy restaurant. Some of us are warm and well fed; others are not. On January 1 some ring in a rich new year, while for others there is no more time left. I am shaken by these thoughts and their many personal meanings and associations.

The next patient is waiting. She is bursting to recount the latest in a long line of narcissistic injuries meted out to her by her unfeeling boss. She demands that I explain his behavior. I sense she really wants to replay the injury, but this time with me as the recipient. She says she is asking for an "explanation" but shoots down anything I say, as though proving to herself, and to me, that the boss should have behaved differently. I feel distracted, tired, unwilling. How much is that about my relationship with this patient, and how much is it about sorrow for the one before her?

Sometimes I have more resilience than I do at other times. At the end of some days I have the image of a fighter clinging to the ropes. Other days have better endings. But I cannot assert that I am in such conscious control that what happens in one hour has no impact on the next. Elsewhere (Buechler, 2004) I have suggested that the greatest and most costly gift analysts give patients is our effort to switch our attention to them. It is costly to us because it can take great effort (at times). But, more importantly, it also can cost us some of our connection with ourselves. I believe I am not alone in feeling that I often have to leave behind unprocessed, unrecognized countertransference feelings in order to move on to the next patient. I may lose a thread that could be important to my self-understanding, as well as to the treatment I am conducting. I can't allow myself to have all the insights, associations, moments of reflection that I might need. I have to rob myself of this, to "move on" to the next person. I may not be able to recapture this potentially useful self-reflection.

What do I need, in the balance of my emotions, to transition from one session to the next? Is there a way to prepare candidates for coping with this task?

I suggest that certain emotional strengths are necessary prerequisites for developing this ability:

1. Perhaps the most important prerequisite is the capacity for comfort with the unfinished. One way to think about this strength is that it entails moderate enough obsessive pulls toward neat or perfect endings. In order to deal with transitions between sessions the analyst must be reasonably comfortable with leaving things up in the air.
2. Connected to this may be a capacity to contain some chaotic experience. I think of the painter Wassily Kandinski, who I see as creating splintering images that just barely hold together.
3. To bear living with the unfinished seems to me to require some faith in the future or, perhaps, a faith that there will *be* a future. This renders the unfinished merely temporarily unfinished. Perhaps this is just another way to refer to object constancy.

I can imagine the candidate cultivating this strength in many ways. I have often suggested to people in training that reading and writing poetry is one of the best ways I know to prepare for clinical work. Listening to poetry asks us to bear the ambiguity of the unfinished thought. We have to wade into a poem, letting it wash over us, feeling it out. If we demand that it immediately surrender its meaning to our forces of reason we are likely to get nowhere. I would suggest that poems are not unlike dreams in this regard. A tight, military approach to their capture inevitable fails.

Incidentally, poetry can also cultivate our ability to be succinct. In a poem we make each word do a great deal of work. We choose words that can evoke much more than they say. These skills can be invaluable in the development of the analyst's capacity to interpret (I discussed this at greater length in Chapter 8).

Another approach to developing the capacity to transition from one session to the next might be identification with teachers, supervisors, and one's own analyst. During our training we watch these people make transitions from one session to the next or one class to the next. Transitions occur within sessions as well, from one topic to the next. I believe that the candidate's facility with transitions may be enhanced if supervisors, teachers, and training analysts are willing to be transparent about their own experiences. As I have suggested earlier, by transparency I mean an openness about one's own experience and a willingness to share it. I think this can be helpful in many ways, including that it acquaints the candidate with the fact that transitions are sometimes hard for everyone, even the most seasoned analyst.

In being transparent the supervisor, training analyst, and teacher are auditioning to become part of the candidate's set of internalized supervisory objects—the internal chorus that I have described at several points in this book. Hopefully, the candidate leaves training with many models of how one might approach clinical work. These inner "objects" will sometimes modulate remnants of graduate analysts' self-criticism. As they move through their careers, they will think of these models when they feel at a loss clinically. They may remember a phrase from their supervision or just its general texture. Perhaps they retain something even more inchoate but tremendously precious: faith in themselves as clinicians. I think that in order to have such faith in ourselves we must first have sensed someone else's faith in us. To my mind this is similar to how Ferenczi (in Dupont, 1988) understood our development of a capacity to take care of ourselves. We are not born with this capacity but, rather, develop it through interpersonal experiences of being cared for by others.

Stamina

I discuss two aspects of clinical stamina: (1) retaining analytic functioning throughout long work days, and (2) retaining analytic functioning throughout long stretches of the treatment of a particular patient. For both we might make an analogy to a long distance runner, for whom pacing is key to survival. But what does it take to be an analytic long distance runner?

To face and move through a long work day I think we can't be too depressed. This may seem too obvious to mention. But I believe it is worth reflecting on some of the many forms depression can take and their impact on the clinician. Another way to frame this discussion is as some personal reflections about burnout.

Here I discuss "depression" in much more muted forms than we usually consider. I am not talking about the analyst who is clinically depressed, with little energy for work or, more generally, little zest for life. In this unfortunate situation the depressed clinician is likely to be painfully aware of the problem.

I am alluding to a much more prevalent, though less drastically debilitating, handicap. I would bet that we all feel drained at times. During a gas shortage I remember having the fantasy that I owned a gas station. After taking care of a long parade of cars I have nothing left for my own.

The form of depression, or burnout, that I am referencing can feel like a resistance to expending any more effort. Samuel Beckett's (1995, p. 476) line that ends *The Unnamable*, "I can't go on. I'll go on." comes to mind. Of course any depression has personal sources and meanings. But for the moment I am limiting myself to looking at its manifestation in the clinician's experience of the work day. I see this resistance to clinical activity as most similar to schizoid depression, which I have previously (Buechler, 2002) described as a heavy-limbed effort to lumber through the day, expending the minimum of energy needed to just get by.

What can analytic candidates develop in training so that their careers (and personal life) will be less likely to be marked by schizoid depression? Certainly there are no magical antidotes in analytic training or anywhere else. Of course the work the candidates do in their training analysis is crucial to modulating their schizoid depressive tendencies.

But I think that schizoid depression (or burnout, as it may be characterized in regard to one's career) results (partially) from an insufficiently strong sense of purpose. Elsewhere (Buechler, 2004) I have addressed the development of the clinician's sense of purpose and how it differs from any specific goals. Here I suggest that a strong sense of purpose promotes the kind of stamina that is necessary to carry the clinician through a long hard day. I have often speculated about the effect of aging on clinical stamina. My own experience is that while aging decreases overall stamina, clinical experience has actually enhanced my stamina. I believe that the work simply takes less out of me. This might be because my superego has softened over the years, or because greater experience has given me more facility, or for many other reasons. But I would not like to leave out the impact of a strong sense of purpose. I am sure that this is something I always had to some degree. But for many of us, myself included, the need to have some impact on patients and on colleagues definitely increases with time. I think I have greater clarity about what I am here to do and an enhanced appreciation of the limitations of time. Perhaps in an Eriksonian sense, generative needs (among others) help pull me through the day.

Training can contribute to the analyst's development of a sturdy sense of purpose. For one thing, we could focus more on the importance of this attitude. Supervisors, teachers, and training analysts could talk about their own sense of purpose. It can be difficult to differentiate our overall sense of purpose from our more specific goals, such as helping patients become more conscious of their motivations. But I think a sense of purpose, however elusive to define, is nevertheless a necessary ingredient of analytic stamina.

I don't think anything matches personal experience in its ability to convince us of the potential analysis has to transform lives. Whether in our personal lives or in the lives of our patients, early experiences of profound change can make a great impact, persuading us for all time that change is possible and can be extremely meaningful. Is there any way to capture in words or measure how much effort a better life is worth? Of course not. There is no substitute for the impact of watching the fearful begin to dare, or the withdrawn begin to relate. In training we learn, hopefully, that we can participate in our own and others' growth. "Good enough" supervisors enable candidates to get some sense of their own talents for contributing to patients' lives. Of course supervision has to focus on the candidate's weak areas as well as strengths. But I think training enhances clinical stamina to the extent that it helps candidates develop a strong sense that treatment is a potentially meaningful activity and they know some of their resources for doing this work, as well as the shortcomings that are worth further attention. In other words, I think we should emerge from analytic training clearer about the potential benefits of analysis than we were when we entered it and clearer about our own strengths and weaknesses as clinicians. While knowing that our professional development is a lifelong project, I think we should feel that the training contributed to it. With this in mind, I am advocating the demystification of analytic training to the fullest possible extent. There will always be some mystery in the preparation for an analytic career, as there is in any process of human change. I don't think we should try to reduce analysis, or analytic training, to a "cookbook." But I do believe that the only way we can encourage people to become analytic candidates or analytic patients is for them to believe the process is viable, accessible to them, and transformative.

This belief in the transformative power of analysis is integral to our stamina regardless of whether we are thinking of the stamina it takes to see a long treatment through to its conclusion, or the stamina it takes to see a long work day through to its end. But I think that the stamina to keep working in a very long-term treatment takes more than just a strong sense of purpose and belief in treatment's transformative potential. I think it also takes a capacity to modulate one's own shame and guilt. A patient wails, asking why he should believe our work can help him if he feels the same as he did years ago when we first started to work together. Of course this question has many layers of significance. It is a cry for help, a jab at me, an expression of despair, and a question about trust, among other meanings. But, for the moment, let's just take it at face value. Why should he believe in treatment's potential to transform, when it has not transformed him?

I would suggest that this moment requires me to be able to modulate my own guilt and shame. Why have our results been, in the patient's view, so meager? When I encourage him to continue in treatment is this because of my own self-serving need to keep him as a source of income? Or am I unwilling to admit defeat? Am I acting out of my own narcissistic needs to deny failure?

Analysts' capacity for the stamina to withstand this kind of questioning requires them to have a helpful superego. They must be able to bear the possibility that their own shortcomings have delimited the treatment's progress. How can they face the powerful impact of their limitations on the quality of other lives without some vulnerability to shame and guilt? In a sense, we would not want analysts to be impervious to these feelings of responsibility. And yet, when the patient's faith in the long-term outcome of the treatment falters, if the analyst loses faith and hope too, the patient may terminate and they may never get to know what could have been accomplished.

I would suggest that several factors contribute to the clinician's stamina for long term treatments. After naming these factors I will briefly describe each.

1. The capacity to accept what I call life's "necessary ruthlessness"
2. The ability to function as a semipermeable membrane
3. The capacity for positive feelings, such as curiosity, to provide balance for painful emotions
4. The capacity to see a situation from more than one perspective

From my point of view, each of these attitudes is generally acquired after some years of clinical experience. Certainly my own early years were colored by unrealistic ambitions. If I had the younger Sandra Buechler here today she would have dismissed notions such as "necessary ruthlessness." What I mean by this phrase is that some of life and much of clinical work require an attitude of being willing to put one's foot on the accelerator and stop at nothing. A forceful ruthlessness may sometimes be necessary in order to take a strong stand advocating long-term treatment when the patient and others are focused on what may happen this week. The ruthlessness required of us at these times seems to me no different from that of the physician who gives unwelcome news—that a difficult procedure will be painful or inconvenient, but should be done. I would not say it is imperviousness or lack of empathy but, rather, a privileging of long-term health as a priority. I have often suggested that we must accept, and even welcome, the patients' concern for the quality of their present lives, rather than contemptuously labeling it a lack of the ability to "delay gratification." I still think that concern for one's present life is frequently what gets and keeps people in treatment, and, more generally, invested in self-improvement. It is a precious source of motivation, and should be cultivated. But there are times when long-term health must be prioritized, even at the expense of short-term satisfaction.

"Semipermeable membrane" is my phrase for analysts' ability to be affected by the patient but still remain themselves. While we may feel what it is like to be in the patient's shoes, we are still wearing our own. It is possible to have the stamina to bear long treatment days and treatments with some patients that extend over decades, because our own lives serve as our ballasts. The pain I feel hearing about what happened to a patient is circumscribed by this self-awareness. What I think I would not have understood when I was younger is that this limitation in empathic merging greatly contributes to my stamina.

I would include in this concept of the analyst as "semipermeable" the strength we need to bear the contagious aspects of the patient's emotionality. For example, a patient of mine often enters her session in a state of palpable agitation. Her words tumble out in an angry-sounding staccato. She hardly pauses to take a breath. I feel myself tensing. Although I absorb some of this energy, at some point it will contribute to my stamina if I can delimit its contagion. Similarly, in other hours I am confronted with truly sad losses sustained by my patients. Their imprint should alter me, or I am not fully present. Yet if I lose my self to their impact I will not have the stamina to keep working for the many hours of a long work day, or for the many years some treatments take.

Like the parent of a teenager threatening to leave home, sometimes clinicians have to find a balance between the impulse to panic and the urge to help them pack. Something in between totally joining the patient's intense emotionality and entirely distancing from it is often called for. Without this containing, stabilizing centeredness the clinician will be too often "thrown" to last over the long haul.

Analysts' curiosity makes every hour, no matter how painful, a potential source of their own growth and the patients' growth. To treat an intensely paranoid person, for example, knowing that at any moment we may be classified by the patient as an enemy, takes stamina. Often, we have to have the grace under pressure that was Hemingway's definition of courage (as discussed in A. Alvarez, 1973, pp. 228–229). We have to willingly embrace living with that pressure for long periods of time. Curiosity can help us bear it. Our curious mind's eye watches, knowing one false move can tip the patient's scale toward distrust of our motives. Did we go too far with that interpretation? Or have we prepared the ground well enough, so that the patient can hear today what she would have rejected yesterday? Curiosity about how human stories end helps drive many of us into the field, and keeps us involved.

When I was very young I took driving lessons. The instructor told me not to concentrate on the space immediately in front of the car, but rather to look "far, high, and wide." Even in those days I knew this was applicable to many aspects of life besides driving cars. Perspective, in many senses, allows us stamina. A patient complains that the treatment is taking too long. I ask how long it took to develop the problems we are addressing. Or, how much effort is a better quality of life worth? Looking "far, high, and wide" means to me contextualizing the present moment in time, space, and experience. In a one session consultation, a candidate presents a very troubled and troubling patient. The patient appears to have made very little progress over a long period of intensive treatment. Listening, I hear how close to psychotic I think this patient is. I suggest that the "progress" they have made is that the patient has managed to stay out of a mental hospital despite life's increasing burdens. This perspective may help the clinician have the stamina to continue the treatment. Perspective lent the effort new meaning, which may enable both participants to continue working together.

A Specific Strength: Emotional Preparation for Treatment's Termination

I got ready for my last session with a young woman I had treated for many years. "Got ready" in this context, means that I asked myself what I thought my aim was for this, our last session. How did I want to say goodbye? Was there some thought, or insight, or feeling I wanted to give her? Did I want something for myself?

Over the years of our work together each of us had talked about our fantasies of being mother and daughter. She was a strong, exquisitely sensitive person, and I would have been proud to have her for my daughter. But ours was a more nebulous relationship. Within its extreme restraints I knew her as well as anyone else ever has, and maybe as well as anyone ever can. For many years she gave me her dreams, her regrets, the dark hatreds she shocked herself with, the tears she was ashamed of. I watched her heart break as every idealized romantic partner disappeared into a hazy silence. I listened to her "morning after" self-recriminations as she searched for what she might have done wrong to make him able to refrain from calling her again. She was more mystified that he was *able* to forget her than she was hurt that he chose to move on. I was the only one she could tell, because, unlike her family and close friends, I wouldn't tell her what to do or suffer personally along with her. Or so we both wanted to believe. Others thought they were being "supportive" by telling her she was too good for all of those men. But I knew how lonely it made her feel to be thought too good for anyone real enough to put his arms around her.

What a strange relationship we have with our patients. We are such intensely intimate strangers. I know what made her cry the most when her parents separated, and she knows next to nothing about me. I know her childhood struggles with shame. Her family had to leapfrog from one neighborhood to the next to avoid their creditors. She was always the poorest child around, and learned early how to shop frugally and how to dress so she looked casual but not tattered. She kept her family's clothing clean, because arriving to school in dirty rags was one humiliation she could avoid. How can

I carry all this in my head (and heart) about someone I will (most probably) never see again?

Recently, her dreams came true more often than her nightmares. One of those beautiful dreams required her to move away. I cared enough about her to be happier for her than I was sad for myself. As the last session approached I remembered how I have always taught people to work toward some "closure" during the termination "phase." Were we having a phase? Were we avoiding it? Was this bad? After so many years of teaching clinical technique I forgot what I was supposed to say or do as we say our last goodbye.

As I bought her a gift I felt like a parent sending her daughter off to college. I wanted her to feel it was okay to leave me, that I would be all right, that she could think only about herself. I didn't want her to turn around, or, if she did, I didn't want her to see me cry.

We had been together a long time—a very big chunk of her life, and not such a small part of mine. Will I ever hear from her again? If I do, how can I respond? When I think of her and I don't know what really happened to her, what should I imagine? Does it matter?

Elsewhere (Buechler, 2000, 2004) I have suggested that analysts do not focus enough on how the loss of all our treatment partners affects us. Through abrupt or planned terminations patients leave and we may never see them again or know what happened to them. We become experts at loss, in a sense. But termination is often "in the air" long before the actual date of parting. How we handle this issue can have great impact. What is its legacy in the lives of both treatment participants?

When this patient terminated treatment I could not diminish the pain of the moment of parting by reminding myself that she was not my life partner. I knew who she was and who she was not. I don't think of her, or miss her, in comparison with someone else. I believe that sometimes analysts act as though we can replace one patient with another and move on from our losses as though they don't affect us personally. For me, this is simply untrue.

I would say that, at least for me, bearing the constant flow of losses of patients, supervisees, and students takes considerable fortitude. I have certainly tried to find ways to limit the loss to what I feel is truly unavoidable. In my previous work (Buechler, 2000) I suggested that human beings can bear necessary losses if we limit the loss to what cannot be helped.

While I know some might disagree, I feel strongly that I should not make any attempts to contact previous patients, so, for me, termination leaves a (possibly permanent) question mark about the patient's future. It seems fine for patients to contact me to let me know how they are doing. But for me to initiate contact would, I believe, exert pressure to respond, whether or not the former patient desires further interaction, especially if she feels gratitude for our previous work together. Another concern I have is that contact with former patients may complicate the process if they wish to return to treatment in the future. While it is true that they could go to another analyst, some would rather go back to an analyst who already knows them. This opportunity can be lost if we allow the relationship to become a friendship after the treatment has ended. For myself, I have decided that I will not initiate contact with former patients and I limit my response if they contact me.

Given these boundaries, the end of treatment is really a loss that is likely to be forever. Knowing this makes bearing the loss a very complicated emotional challenge. I have tried to isolate some of the requirements of this task.

1. Among the emotional constituents of the capacity to bear this loss, I would put love at the top of the list. Sullivan's (1940) definition of love is, "When the satisfaction or security of another person becomes as significant to one as is one's own satisfaction or security, then the state of love exists" (pp. 42–43). To the extent that I have come to love the patient in Sullivan's sense of the word, I will be better able to bear losing her. When the patient I referred to earlier left treatment, I believed she was creating a new, exciting chapter of her life. I wanted her to have this chance. To the extent that I could love her, I was able to care about this more than I cared about my own loss.

2. The analyst's ability to bear losing patients also requires humility. I think we have to have a realistic perspective on the place of analysis in a person's life. Treatment is not the only way people grow. Hopefully, patients will continue to work on themselves after they leave. I have always believed that life is what really "cures" people, but treatment may facilitate having more life experience. While treatment can be a vitally significant experience, other events also can have tremendous power to promote change. I remember a woman I treated for many, many years with little shift in her paranoid style. She married and had a child. I do believe that our work together facilitated her being able to make these choices. That is,

the "success" of the work is that she *could* do these things, rather than that she did do them. But I believe that the most significant changes she made in her ways of operating in the world came as a result of being a parent. She was one of the most devoted mothers I have ever known. She would, quite literally, do anything for her child. In his interest, I think she would have overcome any fear she still had. Nothing in her treatment was as powerful as becoming a mother. Treatment may have enabled her to have this life experience, but it was the life experience itself that most changed her. I believe that this is as it should be. To grasp this takes humility. I have to hold onto awareness of the limits of my role. There have been times that I have actually encouraged patients to leave treatment if I have felt that we had accomplished a great deal of the work we could do, and there were other important life experiences waiting for them elsewhere. I am aware of the ever-present possibility that this is an enactment of transference and countertransference. No doubt to some degree it is. But I believe it may also be an acknowledgment of the limitations of my role in their lives and of their role in my own life.

3. Bearing loss takes confidence in one's resilience. In order to let myself fully experience the loss rather than defensively deny it, I have to believe I can live through it. My experiences of living through other losses may help me. I feel that attempting to bypass grief is what often makes it unmanageable. Patients often pull toward avoiding saying goodbye. They may "forget" the last session, withdraw emotionally, try to diminish their investment in the work, call it an interruption or "break," rather than fully facing termination. Some try to distract themselves, and me, with other matters. I think it takes confidence in oneself as a "going concern" to fully embrace the reality that this is the end of something. Often, I suggest, it is the analyst who must lead the way in this process.

4. I am convinced that ending treatment asks both participants to have what I would call "energetic resignation." I am aware that resignation is not usually thought of as energetic. But I want to be clear that I am not describing a depressed, vanquished resignation, but, rather, an active, fully alive state. Ideally, termination should celebrate as much as it mourns. Resignation, in this sense, is a graceful acceptance of the limitations that are inherent in every walk of life, including treatment. It is an attitude, rather than a statement or action. Many analysts become adversarial around termination, as though it were an insult, or, perhaps, as though the economic and emotional loss to them was what was

paramount. Energetic resignation says to the patient that the analyst can continue to value their experience together after the treatment ends. It is another way to express the ideal of only losing what is inevitably lost. Through energetic, rather than defeated, resignation, I tell the patient that our effect on each other will survive the termination. While we will lose having each other as physical presences, that is all we will lose.

5. Terminating well requires that we find peace about our impact on the patient. This is another way of referring to the analyst's need for a loving superego (Schafer, 1960; Schecter, 1979). Elsewhere (Buechler, 1997, 1998, 1999, 2004) and in Chapter 8, I have developed the notion of the analyst's "internal chorus" of internalized supervisors, teachers, analysts, and others that accompany us throughout our professional lives. If we didn't have these internalized models, we might be too painfully lost and lonely to continue working. Even with this ballast we can burn out, as has been amply demonstrated (see Arnold Cooper, 1986, for an incisive discussion of burnout in analysts). Surviving and even thriving (Coltart, 1993) as an analyst requires us to have the humility to gracefully accept our lapses, failures, and other limitations. As termination approaches and the limits of what will be achieved in this treatment become clear, we need to be able to forgive ourselves for what we could not accomplish. This challenge can further test our humility.

Elsewhere (Buechler, in press, a) I wrote about the analyst's search for self-forgiveness. I compared our "atonement" with more traditional religious beliefs about what brings human beings a feeling of being forgiven. Atonement, or being "at-one" requires us to be able to integrate what might otherwise create unbearable shame, guilt, sorrow, envy, anger, or depression. I include in "depression" the many forms of burnout that can express themselves in the analyst's inability to fully invest in the work with the next patient. Like any other human beings, analysts can react to repeated loss with a diminished ability to invest. Integrating the loss of the physical presence of the patient with the "gain" of the sense of the treatment's accomplishments, and the guilt and shame over its deficits with celebration of its strengths, may help us retain our ability to invest in future treatment relationships. If we can have realistic expectations of the treatment and of the termination itself, rather than insisting on a "complete" analysis, we have a chance to achieve peace.

Rigors of Training and Practice

How do we enhance the candidate's overall emotional fortitude during the training process? I think we might first examine how some of our attitudes may inhibit, rather than enhance, the candidate's emotional development. Elsewhere (Buechler, 2006) I have discussed the shame-inducing aspects of analytic training and their unfortunate legacy. Briefly, we might shame candidates when we make implicit comparisons between their clinical acumen and our own, or between one candidate's skills and another's, or one class of candidates and another. We exacerbate and complicate candidates' shame when we communicate that they should not feel it. Even though it is an understandable response to the constant examination of their psychic functioning candidates undergo, we imply there is something wrong with them if they feel uncomfortable. While being evaluated for their adequacy in their chosen profession, supervisees are expected to remain at ease examining their countertransferential defenses, enactments, unconscious slips, and other material. I think this is not always humanly possible. By creating shame about having difficulty with this requirement, the unrealistic expectation may, itself, hinder rather than enhance the candidate's development.

On a more positive note, candidates need their training to prepare them for the emotional rigors of an analytic career. I have written (Buechler, 2004) of the curiosity, hope, kindness, courage, sense of purpose, emotional balance, capacity to bear loss, and integrity required of the analyst. Developing these emotional strengths is a significant part of becoming an analyst. In this chapter, I discuss another capacity I see as central to the work. The analytic task requires facility at reframing or recontextualizing life experiences. For purposes of clarity toward the end of this chapter, I consider emotional and interpersonal reframing separately although, of course, in lived experience they are interwoven.

As an example of the role of context I will once again mention Joseph Albers, the Bauhaus artist whose series "Homage to the Square" demonstrates how context shapes and colors experience. The "same" colored square against different backgrounds looks different and, in a way, *is* different. In a similar vein, the analyst must become adept at the transformation of experience that recontextualization makes possible.

I suggest that recontextualizing or reframing is key to human survival. We act on our (most often unformulated) understanding of this in many ways. We remind a woman who is lamenting her failures that she has also had successes, thus putting the failures in context. A parent, complaining about his son's malady, saw bald children in the pediatrician's waiting room. He deduced they had leukemia and were undergoing chemotherapy. Suddenly, his son's malady seems too minor, and too temporary, to complain about. He is ashamed, wishing he could retract his complaints, and so very grateful for his son's basic good health.

Perspective changes experience, in treatment and elsewhere. Oedipus' "sin" is, in a sense, a failure of contextualization. Marrying a woman and killing a traveler, he failed to apprehend who they were. Had he kept his own background more prominently in mind the story might have come out differently. He failed to make vital connections because, in a sense, he experienced the present as though it could exist in a vacuum, rather than against the backdrop of the past.

Emotional Recontextualization

Contextualizing is an emotional, and not merely a cognitive capacity, that has the potential to transform human experience. In my judgment, during training the analyst must become especially adept at this task. It is not just a matter of learning the more obvious ways of verbally reframing what a patient is saying. For example, a patient of mine starts our session in an anxious, rushed, frantic, high-pitched tone. In response, my tone is slow, measured, calm. The contrast is, to me, the interpretation. Without saying anything directly about the tone I have used contrast to recontextualize it. In the context of my tone, the patient's stands out even more than it did before, just as Albers's orange square stands out differently against a black background than it does against beige.

In this example, recontextualization requires a contrasting, rather than a mirroring, emotional tone. We understand the power of emotional contexts on an intuitive level. Children cry in the dentist's office. We tell them how brave they can be. Thus, we reframe bearing the pain and fear as an emotional *challenge*, rather than just a misfortune. We have privileged *how* the children bear their feelings, not just what they feel. Does this actually change what the children feel? Does Albers actually change the orange square? I would say he does.

Patients so frequently ask me whether treatment will help them feel different or just change how they handle their feelings. I think that often the way life feels actually does change. The patient on the couch is (at times) alone in the presence of another. In a Winnicottian sense, this may transform aloneness. It changes its meaning, its feel, or texture.

Some patients are unable to avail themselves of the transformative potential in recontextualizing. They are vigilant against what they would call "fooling themselves" with "bullshit." I have asked one such person whether this means the most painful explanations are always the truest. This patient has no difficulty agreeing with this conclusion. Anything short of the hardest version to bear must be "soft-soaping." Thus, for this person, reframing means lying. This patient's is a harsh world.

In recontextualization a feeling changes its texture because of its cognitive/emotional context. Anger about an injustice in the context of fighting for what we think is right may be experienced as a strength. But if the "same" anger is contextualized as an out-of-control temper, it can feel like a weakness. Curiosity can feel like intrusive aggression or enlivening stimulation. Ongoing mourning over a death can feel like deep loyal attachment or a sign of psychological disturbance. Repeated moments of terror after trauma can become occasions for self-soothing or self-flagellation. I emphasize that this is not just about the cognitive meaning attached to the emotion. It is also about the other emotions, along with cognitions, that form an overall context.

Interpersonal Recontextualization

To bear the feelings the patient induces, analysts may recontextualize them. This can then become an alternative available to the patient (at least unconsciously). This is one of the functions the analyst can serve. For example, very early in my career I treated a man who had been a member of a violent political group. His group's beliefs were especially repugnant to me on a personal level. I wondered whether it would be possible for me to treat him, given how I felt. But I stayed with it long enough to hear of his terrible, lonely childhood. The abuse and neglect he was subjected to touched my heart. In my own mind I began to reframe his membership in this group. I am not saying that his political beliefs could or should be reduced to a function of his childhood. I am aware that it is much more complex than that. But reframing them allowed me to work with him over the long haul, and I do think my understanding of why he belonged to this group was part of the truth. An acutely alienated, drifting young man had found a new "home" and "family" where he could belong, have shared perceptions and goals, and find meaning for his life.

Eventually, when my reframing became ours, he saw himself in this light, along with other ways we understood his history. At first I kept my reframing to myself. It allowed me to feel empathy for a man I might otherwise have hastily written off. Later, when it made sense to him too, it helped him have more empathy for himself.

Interpersonal reframing can be initiated by either participant. A supervisee tells me about a patient who was subjected to sexual abuse by her older brother. For the patient, episodes of the "abuse" constituted her happiest, most exciting childhood moments. She had finally found a way to get her dazzling brother to pay attention to her. Of course, for her analyst, it had a different meaning. I felt it would be helpful if the analyst could try to understand the patient's reframing from "inside." That is, I asked the analyst to imaginatively enter into the patient's experience as much as she could: "Be 13. You followed him around all your life. He was always more interested in his friends. They made fun of you, and wouldn't let you play with them. Now he wants you, alone, just you."

How are candidates helped to learn how to engage in this process? Modeling is certainly one approach. In addition, the supervisor learns to be attuned to what could function as an obstacle to the reframing process in the supervisee. Obstacles have to be named, at the very least, and may then be focused on in the supervisee's personal treatment, if it does not seem appropriate as a subject for the supervision.

Emotionally reframing often requires a modulation of an intense feeling. For example, with the patient I mentioned who was a member of a personally repugnant political group, it had to be possible for an emotion to modulate my feelings about his group membership. If I couldn't see past that membership, if my feelings about it were so intense it was all I could hold in my awareness, I could not have reframed and treated him. Another way to say this is that I had to be capable of shifting my priorities, from passionately representing my dislike of this group to equally passionately trying to understand this individual.

The "transparency" of the supervisor is key to this work. I have dealt with the issue of supervisory transparency at many points in other chapters. Here I merely mention that, for supervisees to develop the ability to reframe, supervisors must be open enough about their own reframing process to manifest it.

Transformation

The "magic" of treatment can be described as a process where unintended changes accompany intended changes. While this plays out in different ways with different patient–analyst pairs, personally I have found some interesting consistencies. It is, for example, a common observation that patients often look different, at least to their analysts, over time. It may be that some of the tension of the facial muscles relaxes.

Certain subjects, initially in the center of the patient's consciousness, seem to fade in importance. The "presenting problems" are often an example of this. Patients who come into treatment with clearly stress-related physiological symptoms, such as headaches, experience them less often. Sleep may improve. But less concrete regularities also come to my mind, like changes in the main subject matter of sessions. Patients who enter treatment (especially as young adults) preoccupied with their families of origin find this subject gradually receding into the background of their thoughts. Or career concerns are initially pressing, but become less central over time. I have found, fairly regularly, that some patients seem to suffer less from minor ailments, for reasons I have never been able to clarify. Perhaps there are lifestyle changes that partially account for this. One patient, for example, stopped taking as many airline flights, and seemed to suffer less frequently from respiratory illnesses.

Of course, these sketchy and obviously subjective impressions are not meant as scientific findings. I am suggesting that there is a process of transformation, at least in some treatments, where changes beyond those aimed for regularly occur. We may be ostensibly "working on" why the patient cannot seem to sustain intimate relationships. I call treatment "transformative" because, unlike a didactic course, its results cannot be predicted and are not limited to those obviously related to the focus of our attention.

What emotional preparation is necessary for candidates to engage in transformative processes with their patients? Of course, each candidate enters supervision with a different set of personal strengths and limitations. But on the whole, I would say that, in a supervision where the relationship is good, what usually occurs is a decrease in the supervisee's feelings of shame, guilt, and anxiety. Perhaps this is just another way of referring to the softening of superego functioning. Or, another possibility is that I, as a supervisor, am entering the supervisee's internal chorus.

Engaging in transformative treatments means, to me, being able to suspend disbelief as one would in the theater, but in a real-life situation. It also requires being able to be a transitional object, open to moderate alteration by the patient, but still retaining one's own basic contours. Being transformative, in other words, requires being transformable, to some extent, but only to an extent.

I think of the analyst as a transitional object, in Winnicott's sense. (In other contexts I have written about the patient as *my* transitional object. I think both occur). We have our own contours, just like the teddy bear. There are limits to the ways we can adapt to patients' needs. But, within those limits, there is a wide range of possibilities for transforming us. Children can project soft warmth onto the bear, and feel warmed by the bear. Or, they can project the delight of a playmate, and feel eagerly partnered in play. In other words, there are limits to reality but, within those limits, a great deal is possible.

In a similar sense, patients have a great deal of impact on what I would call textural aspects of the work. By "textural" I mean something like the *feel* of it. I like to say that the analyst must be firmer in contour than in texture. That is, somewhat like the transitional object, analysts as material for transitional relating must have their own properties, so that they seem real enough to the patient, but the feel of being with them should be, in large part, the patient's creation. More specifically, I mean that patients affect the frequency of my interventions, the tone of my voice, the direction of my gaze, the posture of my body, the length of my sentences, the pace of the interchange, (from rapid-fire staccato to slow and measured) and the use I make of silence. I am calling these elements "textural" to emphasize their relationship to the feel of the experience of being with me. Other variables include the extent to which I rely on theory when I am with a particular patient, the intensity of my empathy, the degree of focus on dream and other unconscious material, whether I privilege transference and countertransference interpretations, the extent of the focus on genetic material, and the centrality of the analysis of defenses and resistance. Of course the texture, or feel of the work is also shaped by whether the patient is on the couch or sitting up, the frequency of sessions and their spacing during the week, and the degree to which we "float" in a freely associating mode or maintain a more linear back-and-forth discussion.

As material to be molded, I have limitations like the blanket or bear. For example, if a patient tries to get me to passively, unresponsively receive who he or she is, I will be unlikely to meet this requirement. Just as the teddy bear can probably morph into a jungle tyrant or a helpless baby bear but will not make a convincing waterfall, my malleability will only go so far.

Some patients are able to get me to stretch more than others. With some, for example, I can be a relentless inquisitor some days, with a staccato cross-examining style. But on other days I am their poet-in-residence, softly shaping our mutually created thoughts into images. I think I take more varied shapes with them than I do with most people, for reasons we have not yet made clear. People bring out different aspects of what I am capable of but, of course, I cannot stretch beyond that limit. I think of my personal limitations as my contours, much as the blanket or teddy bear has an intrinsic shape and a range of possibilities.

From my point of view, treatment is successful to the extent that the analyst is able to become something useful to the patient. At the termination I should still recognize myself in that my overall shape has not changed. There are stretches I am capable of, and others I will never manage because of my personal limitations and life experiences. But I should also have been transformed enough to recognize the difference from my usual demeanor. I feel successful, on any particular day, if I have been able to be both theme and variations.

So, for me, the distance between my usual ways of functioning and the way I come to operate with a particular patient is the measure of the transference/countertransference. In other words, each analyst/patient dyad creates an ambiance, a texture of experience. While ambiance varies some from session to session, the hours with a particular patient should have much in common with each other, and something (but less) in common with all my hours with all my patients. Hopefully, I am sufficiently, but not infinitely, malleable in terms of the ambiances I am capable of cocreating.

Watching an infant with its mother tells me that a basic human interchange is the experience of having an impact on the face, gesture, and vocal tone of the other. While we must be careful about analogies between the processes of early development and analytic work with adults, I do believe there is some overlap. Much research (e.g., the work of Beatrice Beebe and the literature on attachment styles) contends that some patterns of interpersonal relating are ingrained early in life (see Goldberg, Muir, and Kerr, 1995, for an overview of this literature). The rhythm between people in which each responds to the other, partially adapting, is fundamental to human experience. The wooden person whose features are invariant is as ill-equipped as Woody Allen's chameleon-like Zelig, who continuously morphs but has no consistent self.

By being sufficiently malleable, I hope to facilitate the patient's participation in the mutual creation of a texture of experience. This is another way to say that to facilitate patients' transformations we have to be sufficiently transformable. How does our training prepare us for this task?

Becoming Transformative

Analytic training is, to me, a process of expanding and clarifying what one can imagine oneself to be. I would not go so far as to say *nothing* human should be alien to me. I still do have my contours, my limitations as a transformative and transformable person. But my training helped me imagine more potential selves than I could before. Put another way, the analysis of defense enabled me to connect with aspects of my humanness that I had failed to recognize up to that point.

While, hopefully, any analysis should have this result, I think the training analysis should emphasize the development of a wider range of potential selves. This will increase the range of human experiences candidates can enter empathically. It should also broaden and deepen candidates' capacity for transforming themselves with each patient. With this greater latitude in who I can become for a patient, comes greater range in who I can treat.

In my own training, a supervisor played a key role at one point. He felt I could treat the patient more successfully if I could enter more fully into the adolescent aspect of this young adult. It quickly became clear that my own adolescence was spent mainly behind desks, rather than in malls or on dance floors. Could I reach far enough into myself to find someone who might have enjoyed hanging out at the mall? Could this patient and I coconstruct enough (but not too much) of a teenage rhythm? Could I be molded enough so I sufficiently matched her style, but not so much that I entirely lost mine?

I had enough fun at it to make it lively, and I think my work was better than it would have been without this supervisory suggestion. I would say that my curiosity was strong enough, and my anxiety/shame/guilt was at a low enough level to enjoy this assignment. It seems to me that the emotional preparation for being adequately transformable includes low enough intensities of self-critical feelings and high enough intensities of curiosity. The kind of curiosity relevant here seems to me to be the type Schachtel describes (1954) as a form of openness to the world, in which we turn something on its side just to see what happens.

But high enough curiosity and low enough anxiety/shame/guilt are not enough. I think analysts also need the right kind of aggression with (and on behalf of) the patient (Chapter 7). I understand anger/aggression as a continuum of human emotions, from the more assertive forms through the more violent versions. One theoretical expression of this is Fromm's discussion of the forms of aggression in his 1973 book *The Anatomy of Human Destructiveness*. Fromm differentiates those forms of aggression that are actually life enhancing (or biophilic) from the necrophilic variants. Clara Thompson (1955) also contributed the idea that assertion is a form of aggression. In this sense I think I have to have enough assertive energy to actively participate in the transformative process with the patient.

How do candidates develop this emotional profile? As is true about so much of training and treatment, I don't think we can directly aim to raise the candidates' curiosity or lower their shame. Like human happiness, some feelings are a byproduct of living well (whatever that may mean) rather than targets we can aim for. Trying to raise or lower the candidates' emotions would make training into an artificial exercise. But we can try to be cognizant of the immense emotional challenges that sustaining an analytic career requires, and focus some of our attention in training on cultivating candidates' emotional resources.

10

Developing the Personal Strengths of a Psychoanalyst

In the two preceding chapters I have considered some of the intellectual and emotional resources candidates must develop in order to become analysts. In this chapter, I describe personal qualities and interpersonal strengths that I believe the role requires.

The Capacity to Set the Frame

A supervisee discusses his work with a young man in a demanding profession who came into treatment to talk about the death of a grandparent. But soon, other important issues arose, such as recurring relationship difficulties and ambivalence about his unending professional responsibilities.

Not long into the treatment the patient began to miss many sessions and come very late for others. Sometimes he would call just before the session should have ended to say he was sorry, but would have to miss the session due to urgent work deadlines. At about this time, the patient also began talking about his tendency to lie when he thinks telling the truth might make him "look bad."

From the beginning of the treatment, the patient compared the supervisee to his previous therapist, whom he idealized. No one would ever understand him as well. His complaints about the current treatment increased. It was going nowhere.

The supervisee felt stymied. He was being held responsible for the treatment but prevented from doing it by the patient's negative transference and unwillingness to attend regularly. But he was afraid he would lose the patient entirely if he became too confrontational. In supervision he expressed intense self-doubt. As the supervisor,

I began to focus on the challenges to the supervisee's self-esteem. I suggested that this patient had a need to diminish the supervisee's self-confidence, believing this was the way to bolster his own. I suggested that how the supervisee dealt with his *own* sense of self in the sessions would be crucial to the outcome of the treatment. He needed to feel entitled to the patient's respect and reasonable adherence to the frame of the work. He also needed the treatment's goals to be realistic enough for them both to have some hope that the treatment could, possibly, succeed. This supervision highlights several important issues, in my view. I believe that in the treatment the supervisee had to have sufficient self-esteem to carry himself in a way that offered the patient a contrast to his usual experiences. The supervision had to help the supervisee accomplish this. It had to enhance the supervisee's capacity to feel entitled to decent working conditions and reasonable, realistic expectations.

It has been useful to me to think of setting the frame of a treatment as including establishing expectations as to what can be accomplished (Levenson, 1981). In my experience, vast differences often lie between the expectations of the patient and the expectations of the clinician. This cannot be avoided. One of the most important tasks is clarifying, rather than eradicating, these differences. Early phases of treatments often seem to me to be seductions in which the clinician tries to persuade the patient to have "healthier" goals. For example, one female patient wants to feel better about herself when she leaves the session than she felt entering it. But her therapist wants her to value new insight into herself above momentary increases in self-appreciation. Or, another patient wants to feel her treatment will help her extract better behavior from her husband. But her therapist wants her to focus on herself and not on her husband's behavior. Clinicians ruefully complain to each other about patients who enter treatment to perfect their neuroses, not to change. At first, we sometimes appear to accept the patient's goals hoping gradually to seduce them into embracing ours.

Elsewhere (Buechler 2004) I have dealt with these situations as clashes of hopes for the treatment. In this chapter, I address the interpersonal strengths the clinician needs to participate in setting the frame. Degrees, certificates, credentials are not sufficient to render us able to function clinically. There is also *an internal process* whereby we appoint ourselves as therapists or analysts. What interpersonal strengths does this require?

It seems to me that it takes a sufficient sense of entitlement to be able to see oneself as a clinician. We have to feel that our time and expertise sufficiently warrant our charging a fee. Perhaps more vitally, we have to feel entitled to our own point of view about the material the patient presents. Early in their careers many clinicians seem unable to do more than reflect back what the patient has said. They feel safe slightly reframing the patient's ideas, but not expressing any differences. Partially as a result, they encounter skepticism from their patients as to whether treatment offers anything new and valuable. Their patients' negative attitude can further diminish the clinicians' confidence.

Reflecting and reframing are significant activities in psychological treatments. At times they provide something meaningful. But I believe that every clinician must be prepared to take a point of view about the material (whether or not it is formulated and expressed to the patient verbally). This requires comfort with our separateness and a sense of being entitled to having a point of view. What enables this to happen?

The life histories of clinicians and their characterological development are relevant. Especially significant is the strength of their self-esteem. Candidates enter training with varying degrees of personal preparation for the task of clinical self-appointment. But I think training can also play a role in facilitating this growth.

For example, with one male supervisee I find us frequently returning to questions about the more concrete aspects of frame setting. How do we deal with fees, policies about cancellations, and patients' lateness to sessions? What do we do with patients who have nothing to say? How do we keep patients from quitting treatment before it has really gotten underway? After lengthy discussion I find out that the supervisee feels rather uncertain about what he has to offer patients. This contributes to his difficulties in setting a frame and having clear expectations. I ask myself, and then I ask the supervisee, why we keep coming back to these issues. What is he looking for from me? In other words, what are his expectations from the supervision? In the amazing way material tends to be recursive, we then discuss the goals of our supervisory work. This gives me an opportunity to work on the question of how two people set up expectations for their collaboration. That is, as we discuss our expectations for the supervision, we are also enacting how two people can negotiate about goals in supervision, treatment, or any other relationship.

To whatever extent the supervisee's character issues are involved, this interchange will not transform them, in and of itself. But it might alert him to address entitlement issues in his own treatment if he is engaged in a personal analysis.

Self-appointment as a clinician is frequently under fire, challenged by managed care, patients themselves, and patients' relatives. Perhaps nowhere is this more apparent than in clinical work with children. Child therapists must have an especially strong sense of healthy entitlement, in my opinion. They are often completely alone with their sense that the treatment may prove valuable to the child. They must believe in it *before* it has proven itself valuable to anyone else. Ultimately, I think, that means they must believe in themselves.

How does this come about? My own notion parallels a position taken by Ferenczi, who asserted that we all learn to cherish our lives through experiencing their being cherished by a parent. Contrary to Freud's notion of an inborn drive, Ferenczi (1929) suggested that we must have certain interpersonal experiences in order to feel welcomed into life and to take adequate care of ourselves. Similarly, I believe that clinicians have to have the experience of someone believing in them, in order to believe in themselves. This faith, by definition, needs no proof. It is a conviction of promise, not a perception of accomplishment. And yet it will do no good (and, possibly, great harm) if it is blind faith. It must be based on real observations of nascent clinical strengths. Candidates who are obviously talented at (self- and other) observation have an ingredient that is a crucial component of clinical acumen. Perhaps they have not yet had enough experience to hone their natural observational ability into a clinical strength, but the potential is there and should be accorded recognition.

I can isolate some significant experiences in my own professional development that told me someone believed in my potential. I imagine that I had to have sufficient self-esteem in order to take in these votes of confidence. For example, I remember the psychiatrist who referred a very troubled outpatient to me at a time when I had almost no clinical experience. When I questioned the appropriateness of the referral, she said something (I don't remember what) that indicated that she thought it would work out. I remained uncertain, but ready to try. Or, many years later, I remember the analytic supervisor who encouraged me to reflect on what I already knew about my patient, rather than joining the patient in carping about what was not yet clear. More than his words, his attitude toward me lent me conviction until I could develop confidence on other bases.

As supervisors, our own eagerness to have something valuable to teach, or our own anxiety about mistakes the candidate might make, could dull our appreciation of the importance of helping the candidate develop adequate clinical entitlement. No less than in treatment, in supervision our job includes acute (self- and other) observation. Of course we should notice weak areas as well as strengths. But I believe we must be alert to opportunities to strengthen self-appointment when they occur. Developing clinicians have to feel they have something potentially valuable to offer in order to create a viable frame with their patient.

The Capacity to Identify with the Analytic Enterprise

One of the situations where this capacity is necessary is when candidates have to propose an analytic treatment to prospective patients they want to convert from psychotherapy to psychoanalysis. Frequently, this is how candidates find control cases.

Unfortunately, it can be very difficult to find suitable patients who are willing to commit to sufficient time in analytic treatment to qualify as control cases. It is often necessary to offer a financially advantageous arrangement. The patient gets relatively low-cost treatment in exchange for committing to the necessary regimen of a control case. The supervisee gets credit for conducting the case and advances further toward graduation. The supervisor and institute benefit too, in that, with active candidates, they remain viable.

There are no losers here. This arrangement generally works well for everyone involved. But, to enable it to work, the supervisee has to identify with the analytic enterprise enough to present this "deal" to the patient with conviction that it is in the patient's best interests to consider it. If the candidate can't muster this conviction, I think it is unlikely that the patient will become convinced he or she should enter the agreement.

Prescribing analysis requires an ability to see oneself as a professional and an authority. To present analysis as worth the patient's investments of time, effort, and money, candidates have to believe that treatment with them can be effective. Frequently, for both candidates and prospective analytic patients, a leap of faith is required.

I would suggest that patients have to believe in the *personhood* of candidates before they can believe in analysis. That is, patients have to accept something like, "This person has integrity and would not suggest analysis for me if she did not think it would work." Only after some positive experiences in analytic treatment can the patient feel confidence in the process itself.

Candidates, on the other hand, need faith in the process from the very beginning. To feel that they are talking patients into doing analysis solely because they need a control case to fulfill their own requirements, whether or not it is in the patients' best interests, is a terrible feeling for many candidates. It can be experienced as a hypo-critical betrayal of the patients. Only when the candidates identify enough with analysis to expect it will be beneficial for the patient as well as for themselves, can they be comfortable recommending it.

Elsewhere, I have written (Buechler, 2003, 2004) of the necessity that analysts experience themselves as having integrity, and that patients perceive it. Integrity, or the sense of wholeness, entails a feeling of bringing one's whole self to each moment. To work with a sense of integrity, analysts would have to experience themselves as functioning clinically according to their deeply held values.

When candidates present the option of working analytically, they need to believe in its potential efficacy in order to have and convey integrity. The patients' willingness to collaborate, hopefulness, and sense of purpose are at stake. As Sullivan indicated years ago (1954) the patient must "expect to derive benefit" from the treatment.

I am emphasizing some qualities I think candidates need to retain their integrity when they begin treating control cases: confidence in themselves as clinicians, sufficient development of their voices as authorities, and adequate identification with the analytic endeavor. Without any of these components the candidate's trying to convince a patient to go into analysis can feel like a charlatan. It can be a hol-low, awful feeling that leaves a permanent legacy.

Analysis, like a great deal of life, requires both participants to believe in something before there is proof it will succeed. Not unlike the leap of faith necessary to become a parent, for example, patients become patients and analysts become analysts without any guarantees.

To add to the complexity, candidates are often the very people who would most suffer from talking a patient into entering an unhelp-ful process. Values (Zeddies, 2002; Buechler, 2004) such as honesty and dedication to the patient's welfare are embedded in the analytic culture and we choose candidates we believe are capable of holding these values.

I would suggest that the candidate's faith in the process is generated in a way that is similar to the patient's belief in the process. Faith is, at first, trust in the integrity of someone who represents the analytic enterprise. In candidates, faith may come from their personal experience of their own analysis as meaningful to them. But, in addition, I think some aspects of faith in the work usually evolve from experiences in supervision. While the personal analysis can manifest the potential utility of analysis as a process, only in supervision can candidates develop a sense of analysis' potential when *they* conduct it.

Just as the prospective analytic patient needs to believe the analyst has integrity and would not be recommending analysis if he did not think it could be of benefit, so the candidates have to believe supervisors have integrity and would not mentor them without some faith in their potential to become analysts.

This is a rather complex process. I am suggesting that candidates need faith in supervisors to develop faith in themselves. The supervisors' "vote of confidence" in them would be meaningless otherwise. If the candidates feel the supervisors are just going through the motions rather than carefully assessing strengths and shortcomings and addressing them, adequate self-appointment seems to me unlikely to develop. Thus, although the process is one of *self*-appointment, it is still interpersonal.

For example, a female candidate is in need of an analytic patient to fulfill her requirements. One of her twice-a-week psychotherapy patients has been calling her between sessions, on occasion, to ask questions about their schedule and other procedural matters. The candidate considers whether she can propose that the patient add a third session and become an analytic patient. She is asking for my opinion and, in a sense, for my permission. But I believe much more than that is involved (although it probably has not been formulated on a conscious level). She is also asking whether I believe in her ability to treat this patient analytically enough to "back her" decision. If she presents to the patient the option of working analytically is she being self-serving at the patient's expense? Is it hypocritical, perhaps even a fraud? Only if I, as supervisor, have faith that she is more likely to help the patient analytically can I help her develop adequate self-appointment.

Adding to the complexity of the situation is the financial aspect. Candidates often offer prospective analytic patients lower fee treatment than they offer psychotherapy patients. This makes sense, in that the patient is contributing to the candidates' professional development. But the candidate often feels uneasy with this quid pro quo. It seems a bit too commercial, like an under-the-table deal. It does not fit our idealized notions of our own motives, and it seems to contradict the belief that the process is, essentially, for the patient.

Candidates often develop an attitude that they have to make a few of these tainted deals in order to graduate, but after that they will become honest practitioners. The ends justify the means. This is obviously harmful in several ways:

1. It encourages an attitude that training is something to be gotten through, rather than fully lived.
2. It presumes that we can have such experiences without their leaving a permanent imprint. Upon receiving our analytic certificates, we can return to our moral, ethical selves. Training is just a temporary hiatus.
3. It is unlikely to serve as a foundation for conviction in the efficacy of analysis. It is remarkable to me that practitioners express doubts about the efficacy of analytic treatment without reference to their own training and how it may have failed to instill conviction. In what I think of as an act of externalization, we can project our doubts about our own work and see the whole field as ineffective. I would suggest that it takes a strong development of conviction during training to withstand the pulls toward burnout from our cynical wider culture, as well as from within the profession. The tremendous difficulty of life as an analyst facilitates burnout if our training has not adequately inoculated us against it.
4. It gravely endangers the candidate's sense of integrity, sense of purpose, and hopefulness. This is a personal as well as a professional loss.
5. It can create a self-fulfilling prophecy, in that the analyst who has not developed adequate conviction in training will not elicit it in patients, and, consequently, may not have the kind of experiences that foster belief in the process.

Many candidates enter supervision with two basic questions: (1) Is psychoanalysis viable as a profession, and (2) Am I fit to be an analyst? Unless they trust that a supervisor who has integrity genuinely answers both questions in the affirmative, I don't think the paper credentials they receive have much meaning.

Analysis can take decades. Patients will, naturally, express doubts along the way. If the analyst does not develop genuine conviction during training, burnout seems inevitable.

The Capacity To Bear Treatment's Limitations

It is not uncommon for beginning analysts to suffer guilt or shame about how little they are able to help their patients. What the patient needs feels so much greater than what we can provide. Patients, of course, can contribute to our sense of falling short. For clarity I discuss the resulting guilt and shame separately, although, of course, both can occur in the practitioner. How can training contribute to the analyst's capacity to modulate these feelings?

While theorists differ in how they separate guilt from shame I frequently explain the difference by using a common experience as an example. A girl scores 40 on a school examination. If the student studied, she might well feel inadequate and, consequently, ashamed. If she did not study, but believes one should study, she is likely to feel guilt for having failed to live up to a standard she holds.

Applying this to analysts, we often feel shame when we sense our efforts to help the patient fall short. We wonder whether the patient could benefit more from working with another analyst. We may go so far as to question our career choice. In training, shame may be manifested in a reluctance to talk in supervision or in classes. We feel guilt, on the other hand, if we believe we have failed to live up to our own professional standards. An example might be the feeling of guilt if we have let our attention wander during a session. Of course, we can also feel shame about this, but it is likely that guilt would play some role if we believe analysts should focus on their patients during sessions and we have failed to do so.

In another publication (Buechler, in press, a) I have discussed analysts' need for atonement and the importance of limiting our guilt to occasions when our actions were conscious choices. Faulting ourselves because of our focus in a session seems problematic to me. How much is inattention a conscious choice, and how much, therefore, at least in my view, does it merit guilt? I think we can be overly harsh toward ourselves and colleagues about the issue of focus, sometimes treating any deviation from absolute attention to the patient as though it were a kind of betrayal. I think our standard can resemble the old-fashioned ideal of the ever-attentive mother.

Some patients seem to have a talent for eliciting shame and guilt in their analysts. For example, a male candidate tells me (as his supervisor) about a female patient whose symptom array includes self-mutilation (cutting). This patient holds over the candidate's head the threat that if she is narcissistically injured in the session she will go home and cut herself. The candidate is locked in a complicated bind. He knows he should not allow himself to be "blackmailed" into avoiding any possibility of narcissistic injury to the patient. This could hamstring the treatment and render it meaningless. But he does find it hard to stop himself from weighing whether each intervention is worth the risk. Of course, in the supervision, we can examine what makes this so hard, and the candidate can take up some of the more personal aspects in his analysis. Examining the meanings of the situation to him should help. But I think the situation with the patient will still be difficult.

Candidates' guilt and shame about the limitations of what they can provide may be exacerbated by the shaming aspects of the training process as a whole. Elsewhere (Buechler, 2006; in press, b) I have discussed what evokes shame in analytic training. Briefly, I think we elicit shame in candidates when we create subtle, unfair comparisons between the candidate's capacities and our own, or one candidate's capacities and another's. We also shame candidates unnecessarily when we fail to adequately acknowledge that they are required to expose their character issues while being evaluated, and this is an inherently insecure position. The candidates' shame about having shame is an unnecessary, unfortunate result. I believe some shame is inevitable in analytic training, given that it often combines psychological exposure and evaluation. But shame about shame is avoidable, if those of us involved in training appreciate what this situation feels like for the candidate. I think we can often be too cavalier, implicitly suggesting that candidates should be able to surmount shame through adequate employment of their willpower. Those unable to do so may be seen as lacking courage, too sensitive, narcissistically vulnerable, or insufficiently dedicated to analysis, which may further exacerbate their shame.

I think supervisors can help candidates with their feelings of shame and guilt by adopting some of the following practices:

1. Providing examples of one's own work. Frequently, candidates present their process notes or tapes in classes and supervision. While teachers and supervisors may illustrate points with vignettes they do not have to do so, and can pick and choose which ones to expose. Seeing the dilemmas faced by supervisors in their own clinical work can help candidates feel less shame in several ways. It demystifies the treatment process, manifests its inherent difficulty, models comfort with being limited, and communicates the truth that we are all struggling with the challenges of being human.

2. By having integrity (consistency between what supervisors advise candidates to do and how they themselves behave in the supervision) we make it possible for candidates to internalize aspects of us as part of their internal chorus.

3. By making one's thinking process transparent. Transparency is a very valuable concept to me, as a supervisor as well as in my work as an analyst. I first formulated it for myself when I worked with adolescents. I came to believe that if I could take some of them through each step of my own thinking process they might develop enough trust to enter treatment. Since then I have found it especially useful in working with paranoia, whatever the age of the person. In retrospect, it may be seen as my version of Renik's (1998) idea of "showing all your cards." I think it is equally useful with supervisees. In supervision I may attempt to be transparent as an analyst, telling candidates as much as I can about my own thinking process during a clinical interchange I am describing to them. Or, I might try to make my process in the supervision, itself, transparent. In either case, I think the more we can be transparent the more likely we make it that we can be internalized.

4. By being open about how you balance shame and guilt with other modulating emotions that your work evokes in you. The concept that the emotions form a system, with each modifying the intensity of all the others, can be as helpful in supervision as it is in treatment. One meaning I think it can have is that, when we feel we are failing, our shame and guilt may be balanced by our sense of purpose, our curiosity, our courage and other feelings and values. For example, a candidate became exasperated with a patient and, essentially, the candidate lost her temper. Subsequently the candidate felt both shame and guilt, probably exacerbated by feeling compelled to tell me about it. I think that talking about other aspects of the work and focusing on why the patient came into treatment provided perspective. The candidate's shame, guilt, and residual anger were balanced by other, equally strong feelings of dedication and empathy. It seems important to me to emphasize

that the shame, guilt, and anger did not disappear. They were balanced, recontextualized, but not negated. We didn't try to get rid of them, but to acknowledge that other feelings were also true.

The Capacity To Bear the Extent of Treatment's Impact

It might seem as though it should be harder to bear the limitations of what treatment can do than to bear its power. But my view is that dealing with our potential impact is an extremely complicated achievement. Hopefully, training readies the candidate to bear this responsibility.

A male patient tells me, with evident pride, that he was finally able to turn down a career opportunity. A year ago he would have taken it. But thanks to "the treatment," he was "able" to refuse it. He assumes I will see this as cause for celebration. And, indeed, in many senses, I do. Of course I never told him to turn down job opportunities. But he and I have worked hard to increase his awareness of the price of his lifestyle. As we have come to describe it, he works 200% of the time. This is our shorthand for referencing the stringency of his work ethic. My understanding of my role is that part of my job is to help him become more aware of the part denial plays in his psychic functioning. I assume that a gradual decrease in his need for this defense, and an increase in his awareness of when he uses it, will give him greater conscious choice over how he lives his life. At that point, I have fulfilled my function and it is up to him to decide how to arrange his work and nonwork life. This is my bargain with neutrality. Strictly speaking, I cannot claim the "even hovering" among id, ego, and superego that the original concept required (A. Freud, 1936; Poland, 1984). I am not neutral in that I am moving against, or in the opposite direction, from the defenses. What repression renders unconscious, analysis works to make conscious. We focus on integrating what splitting separates. When patients project their motives onto others we help them see their internal basis. I have argued (Buechler, 1999) that it is impossible for the analyst to be neutral, in the classical sense, toward the defenses.

However, I am neutral in the sense that I do not know how the aforementioned patient should juggle his work and home life. People struggle with this challenge in a variety of ways, and I don't believe I have an ideal answer. However, it is true that our work together has resulted in the patient's allocation of more time to his marriage, social, and cultural life. He is not wrong that I have promoted this change. I think there is meaning to the distinction I am making, that I am not neutral toward defenses but I am neutral about lifestyles. However, I doubt it would make much difference to the patient. He (correctly) assumes that I think he is moving toward greater freedom and health. To him, that is what counts.

Although I am glad about this result, it does remind me of the enormous impact analysts have on other peoples' lives, and the tremendous responsibility this confers. Another example comes to my mind. Years ago I treated a man who had been jailed many times for criminal sexual behavior. Clearly in the grip of a compulsion, this man was putting himself at grave risk and endangering others. An aesthetic, sensitive soul, he had become a favorite target in jail. I could not bear to imagine the tortures devised for him by unsympathetic fellow inmates. Each time he came up before the local judge his sentences were more severe, and the judge warned him that he was losing patience and next time he would be even more punitive.

At that time I had very little clinical experience and almost no acquaintance with theory. I had no real understanding of his behavior, but only knew that this man's life was quite literally at stake. An accomplished practitioner of several art forms, his hopes for any kind of career were dwindling. He had a wife and young daughter who were still remarkably attached to him, but I wondered how many jail terms they could survive without losing their faith and love.

I felt the weight of the situation quite keenly. I was acutely aware of my limitations as a clinician. I knew how unprepared I was. But I still had to do something. I opted for a stab in the dark. I suggested that he give up all artistic endeavors and take a job that had nothing to do with them. I was betting on the observation that when he was in the midst of his creative efforts he often engaged in the compulsive criminal sexual activity. I had no theory as to why the artistic and sexual activities might be linked. All I had was my observation that one seemed to follow the other.

So far as I know, it "worked," in that he stayed out of trouble for the next several years. I left that geographic area, so I don't know what has happened since then. But I do know some of the impact of this experience on me. I still think of him. I wonder how I would work with him now. I feel very bad about the outcome of this work, although I have some positive feelings as well. I hope that he was able to return to pursuing some of his artistic ambitions and that he found an expression for his gifts. And I hope he was able to refrain from the criminal behavior that endangered his own life and the lives of others.

Of course this work was not, in any sense, a neutral analysis, in that (for one thing) my attention was not evenly distributed toward the patient's id, ego, and superego. But I think it still illustrates the position of the analyst, perhaps in extreme form. In that we cannot be neutral toward defensive and symptomatic behavior our impact on patients' lives has a particular slant. Even in an analytic context I am not neutral about whether, for example, a patient spends an hour washing his hands in the morning. I may or may not express my feelings openly, directly, consciously, or otherwise. But I do have feelings. It would be dishonest and inauthentic for me to say otherwise. In this instance, if given the choice of his symptoms' continuing vs. my taking a vigorous stand against their expression, I would not take as firm and forthright a stance as I did with the patient whose behavior resulted in his incarceration. A hand-washing patient is damaging the quality of his life, but not endangering his existence and that of others. I will "bet" on the treatment in this case, hoping that, eventually, he will not need to spend an hour this way. But even though I would be less directive, I am still not "neutral" in that my attention does not evenly hover. I am looking for ways to understand why he needs to engage in this symptom, with the hope that we can make it less necessary. My heart is in the same place it was with the patient who engaged in criminal sexual behavior. But I am more comfortable relying on exploration without explicit direction.

My awareness that each of these judgment calls I am making is inherently subjective and value-driven means to me that who I am has a huge impact on the people I treat. I think this cannot be questioned. We no longer believe in the analyst's applying a neutral technique in a replicable standard fashion. But the consequence of this has, I suggest, been hard for us to absorb. We are responsible for our impact on countless patients' lives as well as the lives of their partners, children, and others. Considering how much we really can't know about "healthy" living, how can we bear having this much influence?

Another way to frame this question is, how do we develop a helpful enough superego to bear having this much influence when we have also fully grasped the limits of our knowledge? This is one of the challenges our field has struggled with since we have become more skeptical about the certainties of classical analysis. The postmodern shift, the movement away from Cartesian splits and enlightenment dictums, and the post-1960s questioning of authority have forced us to examine our assumptions. If where id was, ego should or should not be, how can we feel satisfied with our impact? Or, put another way, if our conception of psychological health is unclear, how can we define analytic progress?

And yet patients still come to see us, pay money for our time, and hope for the best. Our training has to prepare us to take responsibility for our role in treatment. I suggest that a good deal of training is frequently a kind of recalibration of the candidate's superego. It becomes more watchful and less punitive. It goes from part-time rigid standard-keeping to full-time kindly surveillance. It is harsh less often but gives feedback more often. Countertransference yields more information but less condemnation. In my view, this is the movement of training. It is not unlike the movement of treatment itself and, perhaps, many other processes of growth.

The Capacity To Interpret Transference

Boundary Clarity

Interpreting the patient's interpersonal patterns requires clarity about who did what to whom in the treatment interaction. To appreciate one of my favorite phrases in this regard you have to know that I am quite short in stature—under 5 feet. The phrase I use is that, "No one can hurt me by calling me too tall." What I mean by this is that our own clarity about our boundaries and identity can help us deal with some interchanges with patients. Human beings are always struggling with the distinction between what comes from inside us and what comes from outside. That seemingly early acquisition really occupies a lifetime of self-examination. Am I angry at my (patient, husband, friend, etc.) or are they angry at me, or both? Did I hurt their pride or have they wounded mine? The phrase about my stature is meant to indicate that if I know and accept my own attributes I will be better able to recognize and respond to transferences.

If a patient were to call me "too tall" (which has never really happened) could I know for sure that this is "purely" transference? No. I may have been acting "tall" in some way. But I could probably withstand inquiry about this more easily than if the patient characterized me as having qualities I can't let myself know I have. I don't feel "too tall," so I think I can consider the issue more fully than if I lived every day mourning or regretting this aspect of myself.

Hopefully, training helps us cope with distinguishing "outside" from "inside" in several ways.

1. The training analysis and other forms of self-exploration acquaint us with aspects of ourselves we may have defended against fully knowing.
2. The training analysis and other forms of education acquaint us with *how* we are able to keep from knowing about ourselves (the analysis of defense).
3. The training analysis, the supervision, and other influences modify our guilt and shame about ourselves enough to allow us to examine our contributions to interactions more comfortably.
4. Through all aspects of the training, including interactions with our patients and with colleagues, we learn how others often perceive us.
5. We develop more acquaintance and comfort with an "as if" stance. That is, if someone calls me "too tall," instead of immediately correcting them (or feeling like doing this) I can wonder what it would be like if I were "too tall." Or, I can wonder what makes me seem too tall to this person. I can wonder how tall is "too" tall, etc.

Boundary clarity is a much broader issue than I have considered so far. In that nothing really comes entirely from outside or inside, boundary clarity is an illusion, but, I would say, it is probably a necessary one. For Kernberg (1975), the capacity to distinguish outside from inside oneself is the essential difference between psychosis and all nonpsychotic states. I would suggest boundary clarity is an extremely complex concept, in that much creativity and empathic immersion involve blurring of a boundary. But I would agree that a *capacity* for boundaries is a strength, and an important one for the analyst.

A highly experienced, accomplished analyst presents a "difficult" patient in private supervision with me. Patient and analyst greatly contrast in their ways of interacting interpersonally. The analyst is a very articulate, quiet, sensitive man who tends toward obsessive carefulness. The patient is a loud, brassy, street-smart woman who overwhelms others with her aggressive, wild, raunchy humor. She often expresses her wish that he would "chase" her. She chastises him about the last session, "I needed you to talk to me, and you were just sitting there and writing your fucking notes. I was miserable after I left, suicidal." After the last session the patient had left an angry message, saying she has a right to be cared about. Other therapists have hugged her when she left. It wasn't much to ask. She has been asking for love all her life. She is sick of it. She has to take care of herself by quitting this therapy. "You can hardly even listen to me. You can't wait for me to leave. You would rather see any of your other patients. You are too careful, uptight, stuck up for me. I am a jealous lunatic. Why do I have to leave after 45 minutes? What do you have to do that is so important? Go home to your fucking wife, have your fucking dinner. ..."

Is it worthwhile to try to have "boundaries" in this situation? Aren't they just a protective device for the analyst, a way to retreat from this patient's aggression without kicking her out of the office? Isn't she right about a great deal of what she is saying? What should the analyst do with that? Admitting it would probably be demystifying and a relief, perhaps for both of them. But it might further the patient's table-turning. The treatment might become nothing but an exploration of the analyst's rigidities. Though uncomfortable for him, might this be helpful for the patient?

When I consider the analyst's boundaries in this clinical situation, I mean several qualities I think he needs to have.

1. He needs to be aware that some patients are likely to *create* in their analysts the very feelings they are accusing them of having. That is, by the end of the session, the analyst *would* rather see just about any other patient. They really can't wait for such people to leave. Searles (1986) wrote about this uncanny ability in some patients.
2. I think analysts need to be able to remain available to each patient psychologically. To do this, they must be aware of the ways they tend to defensively withdraw.
3. Analysts need to feel entitled to draw some limits to the patients' access to them, so that they can remain comfortable enough to continue the work.
4. While not overly preoccupied with what is "true" about themselves vs. what is "not true," I think it is important for analysts to recognize that their personal limitations play a role in this interchange.
5. I favor a stance that, in effect, says, "You can get some things from me, and not others. Personally and professionally I will give you what I can. I will be sorry for the deprivation that remains, but I will not be coerced into pretending I feel things I don't feel, just

to keep you quiet. I may or may not be moved by you, but I will not be blackmailed. I don't mean that you have the intention to blackmail me, but just that it might be easy to try to buy you off, by pretending to feel more than I really do. I will not do that."

Thus, many "boundaries" are involved in this clinical interaction. There is the boundary between analyst and patient, available and unavailable, and what feels "true" vs. what feels "not true," or what seems to be coming from inside vs. outside. Analysts must claim the right to enough comfort for themselves that they can continue the work. This means, to me, that they should protect themselves from unbearable anxiety, guilt, shame, loneliness, rage, and any other feeling state that precludes functioning. If their effort to protect their ability to function occurs on a (relatively) conscious level I think the treatment can continue, perhaps with real benefits to both participants. Hopefully, their training and other experiences have enabled them to feel entitled to take appropriate care of themselves.

The Capacity To Be Blamed and Blameworthy

When we evaluate the development of analytic candidates we are frequently judging how well they can bear criticism. I have often been reminded of Henry James's novel *Washington Square*, in which a father coolly appraises whether his daughter can or can't "stick it out." Can she take his less than gentle provocations? Is she made of stern enough stuff?

Let me be clear. I am not defending supervisors' becoming sadistic toward their supervisees. This can verge on, or actually become, an abuse of power. As such, it is unacceptable. But there is, I would say, a place for encouraging candidates to be open to hearing anything about themselves with more genuine interest in what they can learn than self-protective investment in what they look like to themselves and others.

The philosopher Seneca once remarked that we spend our whole lives preparing to die. Far from a morbid comment, I hear this as a statement about the work we each need to do to accept aging gracefully. Our own narcissism must be actively encountered and balanced with other needs. While I would like to think well of myself and have others think well of me, I hope I am even more interested in doing some good on this earth while I have the chance. The opportunity to "do some good" requires me to engage in an interpersonal search for truths that will not always be flattering to either or both of the participants in a therapeutic relationship.

Returning to the patient and analyst above where the angry patient accuses the analyst of depriving her of his love, I think he has to bear being blamed and blameworthy (to some extent). Another way to say this is that we must be able to be blamed in a way that feels fair, and in ways that feel unfair. For example, the artist who engaged in criminal sexual behavior could have accused me of being too willing to help him sacrifice an important aspect of himself for the sake of conformity. He would not be the only patient who has blamed me for being, in the words of another, a "doctor of adaptation." Perhaps if I were more of a risk taker I could have helped him come to a better integration of the various aspects of himself. I will never know, in some senses, what came from "inside" me vs. what came from "him," or, what was necessary vs. what I thought, at the time, was necessary. Could he have continued his artistic pursuits and stayed out of jail if *I* had been more daring, or more patient, or more strongly against an adaptation that sacrificed such a precious aspect of himself?

In this instance I have to live with being blameworthy, although I don't recall actually being blamed (by the patient). But in many other cases I have been both blamed and blameworthy. A patient whose mother died many years ago is still, in her own words, unable to believe it or mourn the loss. This has been going on for quite a while, in a several-decades-long analysis. As I reflect on it, I feel that earlier on I was impatient with her. I wanted her to get "past" this issue and move on, whatever that really means. One day, this usually unassertive woman rather angrily accused me of being unwilling to accept her feelings about her mother's death. It was, for her, still unthinkable. I recognized she was right, and said so. Since then (not coincidentally, I am sure) I have made something of a study of mourning. I think I have been able to examine my own impatience and see some of its components. Here, I believe I was both blamed and blameworthy.

To be able to bear being blamed in a situation where it feels grossly unfair is a challenge we all face at one time or another. Many analysands accuse their analysts of failing to help, though these patients may miss more sessions than they attend, arrive late, have nothing to say, and generally make the work difficult. This position, of being held accountable yet prevented from working effectively, is probably all too familiar. Sometimes it takes considerable grace to deal with it honestly, without a pretense of self-blame but also without becoming defensively self-protective and emotionally closed off.

The Capacity To Choose To Interpret Defense/Resistance

A supervisee presents her analytic work with a patient who would not have been assigned to a candidate in earlier eras. The patient's severe narcissistic vulnerability renders the treatment limited as a learning experience. It is extremely difficult to learn about the art of the timing of interventions while under a real threat that the patient may decompensate or leave at any moment. As the supervisor, I cannot as easily explore the candidate's countertransference issues when I feel that concern about the patient's basic functioning is well warranted.

More than anything else, this situation limits our ability to work on the candidate's comfort with analyzing defenses. As analysts we are always deciding whether to interpret defense or what it is defending against. This judgment call is part of every moment of every analytic session, though we may not focus on it as a conscious choice. I believe that this decision-making process is always implicit, if not explicit.

The narcissistically vulnerable patient just mentioned is a man who has limited every aspect of his life, in part to avoid all possibilities of failure. He has almost no social life, no partner, little contact with his family of origin, and a job that utilizes few of his talents. His considerable artistic sensibility remains an unrealized potential. By his own admission, he just gets through each day.

While the candidate has done a superb job of engaging this patient, earning his trust, and establishing a good working alliance, their unspoken pact is to avoid topics that might challenge the patient's self-esteem. I have often found that when candidates treat narcissistic patients the most intense countertransference is often expressed by the *supervisor*. It is much easier for supervisors to get fed up with the patient's entitlement than it is for candidates, who have to withstand the injured patient's fury first hand and need to find a way to keep the patient in treatment to complete training (among many other reasons). This patient is a past master at finding fault with others. No one is immune, but (so far) the candidate holds the record for lasting as a good object. In supervision we have explored the price of this détente.

It would be inaccurate to say that I have always expressed more impatience than my supervisees. There have been times when their anger has suddenly ignited and actually threatened the work. My supervisory experience tells me that it is not uncommon for analysts to bend over backward to satisfy difficult patients (especially if they are control cases during analytic training) only to suddenly lose all tolerance over a seemingly minor act of entitlement on the part of the patient. Sometimes this feels as though the analyst would like to "fire" the patient on the spot. At this point, as the supervisor, I have tended to interpret this as the analyst's response to his or her own accumulated irritation, rather than a response to one particular moment. This can lead to useful exploration of the treatment dynamic.

But in the case just mentioned, this candidate has always rallied from moments of irritation, unlike her patient, who seems to run out of tolerance for everyone. He is without a friend in the world and loses or quits every job, because sooner or later he finds every human being and every interpersonal interaction too flawed to bear.

Many moments in this treatment provide clear opportunities for deciding when to focus on defense vs. what is being defended against. For example, the patient gets into an all-too-predictable altercation with another employee, who has failed to perform up to the patient's standards. The managers of the firm must be alerted to this breach! It cannot continue! Conflict between the two employees escalates, and it looks to the candidate as though her patient is about to lose yet another job. He will once again be unemployed, penniless, alone, prey to his greatest fears. The life of the treatment, along with the life of this potentially suicidal patient, will be at risk.

What should be the treatment's focus? The analysis of defense might proceed with an inquiry into the patient's way of projecting his own shortcomings onto others. Or the inquiry could center on the patient's use of splitting, with everyone divided between the competent (the patient) and the incompetent (everyone else). This focus would emphasize *how* the patient comes to see the world as he does, rather than *what* he sees.

But the analyst could also focus on the content of the patient's perceptions and their meaning. Who, in the patient's early life, failed to live up to standards, and what were the consequences? How did the patient become fixated on the witch hunt his life has largely become? What would it mean to the patient to ignore or tolerate imperfection?

Another possibility would be to center on the interpersonal situation in the treatment. What is the meaning of the patient's way of reporting the situation to the analyst? What is he hoping will be her response?

My point is that I believe:

1. There is here, as always, a choice between focusing on the defenses vs. what they are defending against.
2. Choosing the analysis of defense is likely to elicit more negative responses from the patient. He wants his perceptions to be understood and treated as veridical, not as defensive maneuvers.
3. The analysis of narcissistic behavior is, itself, potentially narcissistically injuring. We enact the content in the process (as always).

While I believe there is no "right way" to analyze, one of the objectives of training is to make more possibilities available. I think the candidate should be capable of deciding to analyze the defenses, whether she chooses to do so or not. Of course, this sounds as though analysis could proceed as a series of deliberate, conscious choices on the part of the analyst. I think we all know that this is far from true. Analysis (perhaps like much of the rest of life) can be understood only in retrospect by both participants—to the extent that it is ever "understood" at all.

But, at least some of the time, analysts are consciously considering various possibilities for the direction they might take in the session. To whatever extent they feel genuinely able to bear the patient's (potentially negative) response to a focus on his or her defenses, this choice becomes more available.

The Capacity To Say What Usually Cannot Be Said

The analysis of defense can be considered an example of a broader category. Analytic work differs from other conversations in its freedom to explore territories that would usually be forbidden. We have all benefited from Freud's stroke of genius in his liberating direction to the patient to censor nothing. I think he linked freedom of expression with hope implicitly. More recent analytic traditions increasingly accord that freedom to the analyst as well as the patient. While no analysts would, I think, feel they should say whatever comes to mind, we do allow ourselves ever-expanding leeway. At the cocktail party, tact generally vies with directness for jurisdiction over what is said out loud vs. merely silently thought. In our work as analysts we are still aware of the requirements of tact and timing, but, increasingly, we privilege our own spontaneity and freedom of expression.

This requires candidates to become comfortable with their own aggression, trusting it will have limits that will serve the treatment well. To be able to say what is usually forbidden one must believe in one's own capacity to modulate aggression. I have to trust that even before I have had a chance to think, I will not (usually) act out destructively, although I will be given countless invitations to be sadistic. In short, I have to trust my capacity for *unconscious* modulation of my *unformulated* aggressive, competitive, sadistic, retaliatory impulses.

Years ago, I worked in an outpatient clinic seeing young children. In one case I felt the need to speak with a girl's father who, by all accounts, was unfriendly to psychotherapy in general and me, as his daughter's "shrink," in particular. Nevertheless, I felt there were some things I should tell him directly, so I asked him to come to my office. I felt very certain I would have only one chance to make some impact on him, that might give my patient more room to grow up without the extreme restrictions he was now imposing. In the waiting room I met the gruff, angry, barely contained tough guy I had expected to find. I don't remember the details of what I said, but my impression was that I held nothing back. As he was leaving, he turned back for a moment and paid me what I have taken to be one of my greatest compliments. He said that he wanted me to know that I must be very good at my job, because anyone else who tried to make even half of my points to him would never live to see another day.

Looking back, I believe that the freedom to say what usually can't be said is a privilege vital for both participants in treatment. Candidates must develop the strength to claim this privilege as theirs. They must trust their own aggression regulation enough to know they will not (generally) become sadistic, even when provoked. Perhaps most of all, they must believe in their own capacity to recover and to inspire recovery from the interpersonal injuries that are inevitable when two people have license to express what they think and feel, rather than what they *should* think and feel.

Certain aspects of the work, such as the saying of what usually would not be said and the analysis of defense, require us to value long-term growth over our own and the patient's short-term comfort. They also take courage. In another publication (Buechler, 2004)

I have addressed the issue of the courage treatment requires of both participants. In this chapter, I am specifically considering the courage it takes to say what would usually be left out.

How is this capacity cultivated in candidates? It is my opinion that sometimes, in the current analytic climate, the ability to confront is not merely nurtured as one among many strengths the analyst must have, but is, rather, treated as a kind of fetish. It is glorified, idealized, prized above all else. Meetings about candidates' training can become macho displays of everyone's ability to be "tough." Confronting is privileged over other forms of communication, as though it were the supreme function of the analyst, and every part of training should groom the candidate for this role. Ironically, I think this sets a tone that can discourage the development of analytic courage. If the training process itself requires the candidate to submit to the order to be confrontational with patients, whether or not this seems to the candidate to be therapeutically indicated, it seems likely to me that the candidate will learn how to submit, more than anything else. What will be inculcated will be deference to authority or, perhaps, a sense of inadequacy, rather than the development of each candidate's strong, clear, separate voice.

Setting a frame, self-appointment, developing an analytic identity, bearing treatment's limitations and power, interpreting transference, setting boundaries, being blamed, being blameworthy, interpreting defense, and saying what usually goes unsaid all require us each to claim the right to have a separate point of view. The world looks a little bit different from my vantage point than from yours. I must feel as entitled to express my opinion as I remain respectful of the opinions of others.

The Capacity To Persist: Working Through

I have often found Henry James's description (in the short story "The Turn of the Screw," 1898) of the circular and upward motion of the turning screw to be a useful model for the middle phase of analytic treatment. A central issue in the patient's life is understood, although it may not yet be clearly formulated by either participant. If it is initially explored during an inquiry into the patient's early life, eventually it will be necessary to understand how it plays out in two other major arenas: the patient's current relationships outside the treatment, and the transference (among others, Levenson, 1981, spells out that thorough understanding of an issue includes its genetic, transferential, and current relationship expressions).

A deepening awareness of the impact of this issue in the patient's life evolves. The insight develops three-dimensionality. Thus, for example, we see how one patient's mother required him to devote himself to her exclusively. Over time, we clarify how his resulting expectations have affected his marriage and his transference to me. I think it would not matter if we had started with an exploration of the issue in one of the other two arenas. Eventually, we would have to clarify the origin of this interpersonal template and its legacies. The middle period of treatment, by far its most lengthy phase, can be seen as both a circular movement and an upward movement. It is circular in that it explores how the same issue plays out in the three arenas. It is upward in that new issues are engaged as the work proceeds.

Obviously, this takes enormous persistence. When I am able to make a clarifying interpretation, patients, as well as supervisees, will sometimes ask me why I did not point this out before. Why was I able to see something in November but not last May? Although I have reflected on this question many times, I generally fail to find a satisfactory answer. I usually don't know why I can formulate something now or why I couldn't do it before. This can be tremendously frustrating for both participants. The timing of when we grasp something can have life-altering consequences, but neither of us can force insight to occur.

The circular and upward movement of the process is a common description of the way analysis unfolds. It was cited many times during the course of my training. What I feel was not as fully addressed was the issue of how analysts become able to endure the length of this process. Also absent, in my opinion, was sufficient attention to how patients become able to persist, despite the high costs of analysis, in many senses. How can we, as analysts, facilitate the patients' patience and our own? Even in the best of circumstances we are asking two people to go around in circles for (sometimes many) years, at great emotional and financial expense. The concrete benefits may take a long time to discern, while the costs are often all too obvious. For both patient and analyst it is easy to give up hope and lose faith in analysis. Burnout can take many forms. I have argued (Buechler, 1999) that analysts should support their patients' desire for a good life now. It can be a powerful incentive for bearing treatment's inevitable pain. Rather than showing disdain for patients who want quick results, I think we should applaud their investment in the quality of their lives and not chastise their lack of "frustration tolerance." It is self-serving and contemptuous to judge people as immature because they care about their present life as much as they care about their future. I think analysis has paid a heavy price for this hubris. We have been branded as irrelevant, ivory-tower, uppity. Perhaps we should see this as society's just revenge for our own high handedness.

But, while I decry the privileging of the future over the present, and I am glad when my patients care about their current lives, I also feel certain that treatment can take a good deal of time to be truly meaningful and make a real difference in how a life is lived. Good intentions and active effort on the part of both participants may not suffice to shorten the time it takes. Perhaps my feelings about this are affected by where I am in my own career and personal life. As I become increasingly aware of the passage of time, of its preciousness and its limits, I deeply want to shorten the time treatment takes. I wish I could work faster. Despite my own strong feelings on this subject I often feel I have to champion the treatment's need for patience. I am, I believe, largely responsible for the health of the treatment (rather than the health of the patient). What I mean by this is that, at least early in the work, I have a clearer idea of what analysis is like, since I have studied and practiced it for some time. I am in a better position to guard its health, to "feed" it properly. I have a sense of the difference it can make to work with sufficient frequency and regularity. I have felt the difference between working passionately vs. going through the motions. I can distinguish one from the other. Aside from my feeling of professional responsibility, I feel that my experience as an analyst has prepared me to nurture the life of a treatment. Sometimes I have to represent its needs, arguing for adherence to the frame, or greater frequency of sessions. Hopefully the patient will join me in this effort but, at first, I believe it is often my responsibility. I feel tremendous conviction fighting for a treatment's life. Sometimes this task seems simpler than fighting for the patient's life. What "fighting for the patient's life" entails can be ambiguous. A patient is determined to stay in a marriage that exposes him or her to abuse. I know that the decision about the marriage is the patient's choice, not mine. Yet I sometimes feel that by listening I am condoning, and by empathizing I might be enabling. Do I make it easier to stay in the marriage if I offer a sympathetic ear? Is that a role I ought to play? Is treating this person inevitably "voting" for the status quo by making it more bearable? Is there any meaning to the term "neutrality" in this situation? These questions are inherently thornier than we would like to think. I have argued that (Buechler, 1995, 1999, 2004), especially in our work with depression, neutrality must be passionate to be effective. Similarly, supporting the life of the treatment requires of us a passionate stance.

As an example of the work in the mid-phase, I will describe my treatment of a middle-aged woman who has been in analysis for more than a decade. She tells me that she was depressed after the last session. She could hardly make her way home. She felt so dismayed that we had uncovered "yet another issue" that needed attention. The patient is a married woman who has suffered from varying levels of depression at different points. While she has never been actively suicidal I certainly think of her depression as a very serious problem. To me she seems less depressed than she used to be. Her life is less constricted, and she is more able to enjoy socializing, being with family, pursuing interests. In general, in working with her, I have found myself focusing more actively on her early life and current relationships outside the treatment than on the transference. When I have tried to address the transference it did not seem to go very far.

In my mind I have the hypothesis that the patient's depression is a form of anger (most often, lately, anger at me). That is, I think she can't let herself formulate some of her thoughts and feelings. She can't be consciously angry with me or become paranoid about my "real" motives. She can't know about any of her suspicions that I am not really trying to "cure" her, because I make money by treating her, so I have a motive to keep the process going. If she does have the beginning of this train of thought she quickly stifles it.

We could interpret this as a manifestation of her belief that her (Oedipal) mother didn't really want the patient to compete and have a more satisfying family life than the mother herself was able to enjoy. Or, it could be a manifestation of a paternal transference based on her experience of her manipulative, dishonest father.

To me, all of these ideas seem potentially useful, at least as hypotheses. But as the patient sometimes intuits and mentions, I am frequently inquiring about the relationship between her anger and her depression. It seems to me to be most important to work on how her anger gets experienced as an altered mood. In my mind, I am privileging three focuses out of the many possibilities that occur to me:

1. I want to better understand why her anger takes the form of depression (for a more extensive discussion of anger and depression, see, among many other contributions, Spiegel, 1967; Bonime, 1982; Buechler, 1995). It seems to me important to emphasize that it is a *form* of anger, rather than a result of anger. Being with the patient feels to me like being with someone who is very angry.

2. The patient's early life predisposed her to be afraid to express emotions directly, but to feel intensely, unfairly deprived, envious, and jealous. This is ground we have covered many times. We have focused on various ways it affects her current relationships outside the treatment and, sometimes, we have looked at its impact on us. What we have not done, in my view, is to inquire into how emotions such as jealousy and envy affect the patient's depressed form of anger. Without the exquisitely painful comparisons she makes between her lot in life and the fates of others (including me) would her anger take a different shape? This question is, in a sense, an outgrowth of the perspective that the emotions form a system, with the intensity of each impacting on all the others.

3. By making my own comments as succinct as possible I try to contrast with what I see as the patient's obsessional linguistic tendencies. My effort is to call a spade a spade. I am not focusing on the content so much as what I see as her defensive style. I interpret it through contrasting with it. I will, at some point, interpret it more directly. I will say the words, "I think it is safer for you to be depressed than to be angry with me," and "I think you feel deprived compared to me," and "I think you express yourself in a roundabout way because you are afraid to be more direct." But it is my belief that these interpretations, although accurate, will have minimal effect if I don't also provide palpable contrasts. The impact of the contrasts is not always formulated, at least not at the time they occur. I am not sure whether formulation of the contrast is important. I think it is the *experience* of the contrast, more than the conscious formulation of it, that eventually makes a difference. To return to Levenson's aphorism that the last one to know about water is a fish, I think providing something besides "water" gives the "fish" a chance to recognize what she has always taken for granted.

This kind of contrast is, to me, the bread and butter of the mid-phase of treatments. It is repeated in various arenas. Repetition allows us both to formulate it more clearly. As in the previously mentioned image of the turn of the screw we will circle, in that we address the patient's style of being angry with me, with her boss, with her husband, with her friends, and in her family of origin. But at the same time we are moving upward in that we are advancing toward new understandings. For example, we are beginning to see the patient's part in various conflicts with her husband. He describes himself as feeling as though he is "shadow boxing" with her. He knows they are having a fight, but he can't quite articulate the issues. I think we are moving toward a better formulation of how this occurs.

Some would say I should address the issues in the transference more directly, or that I should express them differently. Some might say I am too active in the process. I think there are very different, valid ways to focus on the material. What I do believe, however, is that no matter how the analyst engages in the process it will take time, repetition, and patience on the part of both participants. The inherently potentially frustrating aspect of this is that the patient's life is going by and she keenly feels it is being hampered by the legacies of her past. As I have often said, some people pay for the "sins of their fathers" in their childhoods, when they suffered at their hands, and then they pay for those sins over and over again for the rest of their lives because of the marks abuse leaves. This patient, who was severely abused, understands this in a particularly acute and painful sense. Since we have explored some permutations of the legacies of her past, the issues are not unknown to her. As she herself says, "Haven't we covered everything by now?" And, in a sense, we have. But "covering" everything is not the same as working it through. And yet time, life itself, passes relentlessly.

Is there any way that analytic training can prepare us to participate in this painstaking process? I have written about the courage, hope, and sense of purpose that I believe analytic careers require (Buechler, 2004). I have addressed how I think theory can fortify us and how the "chorus" of our internalized role models can inspire. But lately I have come to the problematic conclusion that another component is necessary. I think we each need an experience of a treatment that went on for an extended period and finally jelled. It might be our own personal treatment or the experience of one of our patients. It might be that significant gains were made all along the way. I am not suggesting that some specific experience has magical powers. But I do believe that it takes an actual experience to prepare us for how long some processes take before certain kinds of change can occur. I have seen some patients for more than 20 years before they were able to create significantly better lives, as they described it.

I have often expressed the thought that life, rather than treatment, is what really "cures" people, but that treatment often enables more life to happen. Treatment, which occurs only a few hours a week, just isn't usually as powerful as other aspects of the rest of life. But treatment can prepare a person to take advantage of opportunities life has to offer. Sometimes treatment allows the patient to recognize potential opportunities. Sometimes, as Shakespeare said, the "readiness is all." Treatment enables people to have enough life to become emotionally richer. If, as patients or as analysts, we have had the chance to see that it can take many years of hard work before certain gains are possible, I think we can bring conviction when we address the question, "Can I still hope for a better life, given that we have been working for so long?" Perhaps personal experience is not the only effective teacher, and some can grasp how long treatment can take without having seen it for themselves. Writing about this is my way of promoting our capacity to formulate our intuitive awareness that outcomes in treatment, like so much of the rest of life, can be dearly wanted, richly deserved, and still just out of reach for a very long time but, hopefully, not forever.

Becoming Contrast, Relational Challenge, and Catalyst

The vignette I just mentioned illustrated how contrasting with the patient can clarify the "water" the "fish" has not seen previously. But what personal strengths must the analyst have to be able to facilitate that process?

I have developed (Buechler, 2004) conceptions of our roles as contrasts, relational challenges, and catalysts. Briefly, the analyst serves as (somewhat) of a contrast to the patients' expectations. That is, only when the analyst differs to some palpable degree from what the patient expects, can the patient become aware of his or her expectations. If patients assume I will be competitive with them (based on their interpersonal experience and, perhaps, projections) the most convincing way they can become aware of this is if I am not competitive, at least at times. I believe that a verbal formulation such as the interpretation, "You think everyone is always being competitive," is not usually mutative without some accompanying experience. In a way that is very similar to the integrity that I feel is so crucial to the effectiveness of supervision, contrasts teach. For example, when people expect us to use ammunition against them to humiliate them and we don't do it, it can be a vivid demonstration of what they usually expect to happen.

Here I must stress that I am not suggesting that we provide demonstration lessons for patients. I would no more go into a session telling myself, 'This patient needs me to show him I am non-competitive" than I would go into a session telling myself to be angry or anxious. Treatment must be an alive authentic response to a lived moment, not a sterile rehearsed lesson. My sense that a patient is expecting me to be competitive will prime me to notice the contrast between his or her expectation and my behavior and, after the fact, to point it out. Contrasts are not set up in advance, but are pointed out in retrospect.

Becoming a relational challenge means making it hard for the patient to do "business as usual." For example, if a patient uses obsessive, indirect language and I translate it into a more direct expression, I am interfering in his defensive maneuver. A patient once said she was "upset" with me, and I asked if she really was angry. She realized that she had been angry, but she had called it "upset" because she was afraid that naming her anger could evoke retribution. So, unconsciously, she substituted the word "upset" for the word "anger." Sullivan (1956) described this defensive use of language as obsessive.

Being a catalyst means facilitating the patient's efforts to experiment with new ways of interacting in the world, both within and outside the treatment. I believe in active encouragement of experimentation with life. I am well aware that this is not neutral, and would be considered non-analytic by many. I do appreciate the great potential cost of this deviation from neutrality (Greenberg, 1991). I have spelled out why I believe that there are times when we cannot afford neutrality (Buechler, 1999, 2004). For example, I think depression has to be actively fought by both patient and analyst. While this may slant the transference or even prevent it from occurring, I think it can be necessary.

All three of these ways of using the analytic role are consonant with Sullivan's (1953, 1954) conception of health as the ability to profit from new experience. They encourage the patient to become aware of assumptions or defensive behaviors that usually prevent new experience from occurring. They conceive of the analyst as promoting health, sometimes through active encouragement and sometimes through more usual verbal interpretations. Eventually, being an active catalyst should result in opportunities for interpretive work. That is, once a patient is less depressed, for example, it becomes possible to engage him or her in a reflective process.

But how does the analyst become capable of being a contrast, relational challenge, and catalyst? My experience as a supervisor tells me that many clinicians are quite comfortable with these roles until they begin analytic training. At that point many start to question whether being a contrast, relational challenge and, especially, a catalyst, is "against the rules." Some candidates continue to perform these functions for their patients and try to hide this behavior from supervisors, or choose not to bring these patients into supervision. I see this as extremely problematic. Potentially, the supervision can become a kind of "false self" performance. Or it can create an artificial split between lofty analytic treatment versus lower-status psychotherapy. Sometimes candidates actually defend against their own awareness of their style out of fear of disapproval. All of these outcomes are highly unfortunate. They leave a lasting negative legacy in the individual as well as in the field as a whole.

I am suggesting that the first thing we can do to facilitate the development of the candidate's ability to be a contrast, relational challenge, and catalyst is to respect these aspects of treatment. Related to this respect is my belief that psychotherapy and psychoanalysis are not easily distinguished from one another. One is not superior to the other or more intellectually demanding. In my mind, they exist on a continuum. A treatment is analytically informed if it includes focus on transferences and defensive processes. Techniques such as the frequency of the sessions and the couch may promote analytic work but they do not define it. At conferences the most critical comment made is the judgment, "You are not doing analysis." Our profession's history is replete with stories of those who have been labeled as analytic outlaws, such as Bowlby and many of the interpersonalists. These dichotomies and political wars have done the field great harm and probably marked the lives and careers of individual practitioners as well. The accusation that a process is not analytic is destructive because it preserves belief in a mythically pure analytic process. No treatment of many years' duration can be adequately categorized. Some sessions will be closer to a conception of analytic process than others. Even within one session, what we focus on will vary. A global condemnation such as, "That is not analysis" mystifies much more than it illuminates. On some level I think the contempt in it is what is best understood by the recipient. It is a way of saying, "You have not been adequately trained," or "You do not even realize that you have exposed your shortcomings." It implies that the speaker, in contrast, has no difficulty in telling what is "analytic" from what is not. Among the many deleterious effects of this professional name-calling is, I believe, a kind of alienation. Not only has it condemned some practitioners to a lesser "caste," but, ironically, it has enshrined analysis itself.

In supervision we have ample opportunity to develop the candidate's capacity to serve as a contrast, relational challenge, and catalyst. I think a great deal of our impact as supervisors depends on our own ability to learn from new experience in the supervision. I will not effectively communicate these processes if they are not intrinsic to my practice of supervision, as well as analysis. This is not about being egalitarian. I think that a communication is not effective unless it has integrity. If I am harshly judgmental as I tell supervisees they should be more accepting of patients, I will mystify them. On some (probably unformulated) level they will become confused. They will hear that they are not accepting their patients enough, but probably they will not *feel* any more accepting.

Aside from avoiding global condemnations of the supervisee's work, and remaining open to new experiences ourselves, how can we foster talent as a contrast, relational challenge, and catalyst? I think we can help candidates by encouraging them to integrate their general experience as human beings into their work as analysts. Sometimes, for example, something we learned from Shakespeare might be useful in a session, or something we best understood through a struggle in our own lives. I have often found, particularly with women who enter analytic training after becoming mothers, that they feel their experience as parents should not be referenced while they are at work. Some seem to consider being mothers as a liability, rather than an asset, in their efforts to become analysts. This is unfortunate in my view, because it robs them of a potential resource, and because it creates a kind of internal schism. Of course, being an analyst differs from being a mother, but both are human activities, and sometimes can inform each other.

Curiosity can be modeled in supervision. The supervisor who genuinely wonders what would happen if a thought were turned on its head is fostering curiosity. More generally, I think that the maintenance of an emotional balance can be modeled. Since human emotions exist in a system, so a change in the intensity of any one emotion affects the level of all the others, becoming more curious will have an impact on my anxiety level, my shame, my joy, and other feelings. How we handle our emotions in supervision can be very informative. For example, how I react when I forget something, how I respond to criticism from the supervisee, how I deal with the termination of the supervision, and what I do with my own impatience can tell something about how I deal with my own emotionality. When I feel shame or guilt what do I tend to do? Does another emotion, such as curiosity or a joyful investment, generally put my shame in perspective?

One of the most helpful ways of doing supervision, I would say, is making your thought process transparent. Thinking out loud allows the supervisee access to how you create a link between, for example, the genetic material and a fragment of a dream. Telling the supervisee your relatively unformulated thoughts as you have them can make the analytic process much more alive and much clearer.

As to the more specific tasks of fostering development as a contrast, relational challenge, and catalyst, I think transparency is vitally important to all three. Seeing just how the supervisor's mind works can help the candidate formulate his or her role as a contrast. For example, a supervisee presents a woman who has suffered from profound narcissistic injuries her whole life. Her parents seem to have barely noticed her existence, failing to register her state of health even when she was quite ill. As I listen, I begin to feel that this patient is not having much impact on my supervisee who, I notice (unusual for this candidate), seems unable to remember basic facts about the patient's life. As I wonder aloud about this I formulate the idea that the patient is repeating her experience of having little impact. But then I ask whether there is some way she actually *has* made an impression. I believe that asking this might foster the supervisee's capacity to be aware of exceptions to the rule that, by contrast, might further clarify the patient's usual patterns.

Being a relational challenge sometimes requires acquaintance with analytic theory. For example, in order to interfere with the patient's use of obsessive language, the candidate needs some notion of what that language sounds like. Thus, supervision has didactic aspects. Of course that is not sufficient. Knowing what obsessive language sounds like does not, by itself, enable a supervisee to work with it. It is, I would suggest, necessary but not sufficient. Working well with defensive material and, especially, presenting a relational challenge, necessitates a certain kind of freedom and courage. This stance requires the supervisee to brave the patient's disapproval. Most people do not like to have their defensive behaviors pointed out. Making obsessive language obvious can elicit the patient's shame and, even, withdrawal from treatment. I generally comment on this in supervision. I believe that in treatment we are always choosing between focusing on defenses vs. what they are defending against (although, much of the time, this choice is made on an unformulated level). When my patient said she was "upset" rather than "angry," I could either point out her defensive wording or inquire into what she was afraid of (among many other possibilities). Often the choice to focus on defense evokes a negative reaction from the patient. In this case, she might feel criticized and point out that she is not there to be edited but to be treated. I feel that the choice to focus on defense is often the better alternative, even though it is inherently likely to evoke negative responses. I think the treatment process can proceed more quickly when we focus on the patient's defensive style early in the work. When this is possible, the patient can become a better equipped self-observer and do the work of the treatment between sessions as well as within them. She can, for example, wonder why she was so indirect with her husband at dinner.

Being a catalyst often takes a firm sense of purpose and courage. Encouraging experimenting with life, trying out new ways of being in the world, requires clinicians to take risks themselves. It can feel safer to follow the material more passively. We would all probably like to believe we are part of a patient-guided process. It is hard to recognize the extent to which our own values about psychological health influence what we hear, focus on, and respond to. As I have discussed at greater length elsewhere (Buechler, 2004) it would be comforting to believe that the values that shape the treatment process come from the patient. But I think it is clear that the process is shaped by the values of both participants. How we define healthy relationships determines what we ask about, forget, and formulate as a treatment goal. As we attempt to encourage the patient to take risks in life, we are taking a risk. For example, a socially isolated patient described possibilities for new interpersonal experiences. I knew that there was no way I could be "neutral" about whether she tried to venture into new territory. I also knew her to be vulnerable and easily hurt if something went wrong. It takes some courage to openly advocate taking risks. Once again, the process parallels the content, and the degree to which we practice what we preach is vitally important.

Overall, becoming capable of serving as a contrast, catalyst, and relational challenge requires being able to deal with feeling regret, shame, sorrow, anger, and other emotions. To be a sufficient contrast we may have to bear intense awareness of our separateness, and whatever feelings that recruits for each of us. Whatever it means to me to be a surprise is likely to come up in this work. All my experience of surprising people (in welcome and unwelcome ways) comes with me to the office in the morning.

Being a catalyst can test my ability to bear shame, guilt, sadness, and regret, among other possibilities. Depending on the outcome of the experiments with life that our work facilitates, my patient may feel grateful for my encouragement, or condemnation of us both, or many other emotions. I am very aware of the potential pitfalls, and I know that my role as a catalyst endangers (and could destroy) my neutrality. I am acutely aware that I don't know the right way to live for anyone, and that having the humility to embrace the limitations of the clinician's role is essential. But I also profoundly believe that life is what cures people. Life experience has the greatest power to make a difference in how being on this earth feels. So, I don't think there is any way I could or should hide my agreement with the poet Rilke (1934), who advised us to "... let life happen to you. Believe me: life is right in any case" (p. 74).

Being a relational challenge can evoke escalating anxiety in both treatment participants, among many other possibilities. Without the familiarity of "business as usual" how can we relate to each other?

Personally, I put faith in my own resilience. Clinical work constantly challenges my intellectual, emotional, and interpersonal resources. After years of facing these challenges every day, many of us go dead. We end our careers going through the motions of buzzing in the next patient or supervisee and just getting through each hour while waiting for the day to end. In my opinion, some of us project our own deadness onto the field, seeing it as doomed. I think it is our job to promote resilience in our patients, our candidates, our field, and ourselves. When Henry Krystal (1975) wrote that "... calamity is opportunity in work clothes" (p. 202), I take this statement to mean that what we fear (in sessions, in life, in our field) is not so much what can happen, but more our response to it. This attitude potentially changes our focus from something that is essentially out-side our control to something that is potentially within it. If what matters most is our response, then our central task as supervisors, analysts, human beings, is to nurture resiliency. I know that I will misstep sometimes when I point out contrasts, or function as a cata-lyst or relational challenge. What seems most important, from my point of view, is what comes next.

Clinical work calls on all the intellectual, emotional, and inter-personal resources we have nurtured over our long years of training and practice. Even though we may be heartened by those we have internalized there still will be many very painful, sorrowful times we have to face. But, for myself, I can say that the investments others have made in me have inspired me to spend the rest of my life trying to become the best analyst I can be. Just as a violinist has to take care of her instrument, I must pay attention to mine. My instrument is me. This means to me that I must spend my life cultivating my per-sonal capacity for emotional balance and resiliency.

Trying to make a difference in others' lives is a privilege as well as a great challenge. Anyone who comes this close to so many peo-ples' sorrows is likely to be saddened. But the curiosity, joy, love, and intellectual pleasure I get from my work can fortify me to fully live, and not just survive, its sorrows.

Epilogue
Making a Difference

We came into this field hoping to make a difference. Most of us believed that the treatment process would become clearer with time. When we "grew up," had enough clinical experience and training, we would have an understanding of what cures, what matters most to accomplish, and what methods work best. Such clarity still eludes most of us.

As is true for countless others, my experience tells me that insight, on its own, is simply not powerful enough to make a significant difference in peoples' lives. Lived emotional experience, formulated or not, seems to be a necessary component.

Our emotions are our principal motivators, connecting us with each other and with ourselves. Most patients come into treatment because they are too anxious, or depressed, or don't seem to feel alive enough. Something is wrong with what they feel, or don't feel. Given that the emotions operate as a system, with the intensity of each affecting the level of all the others, it makes sense that it would be an emotional experience that would have enough power to change what we feel. But ironically, the wider culture, and even psychoanalysts, seem to favor "solutions" that aim to mute emotionality, rather than relying on one emotion to modify another. We turn to pharmaceutical, cognitive, or behavioral change to make a difference in how life feels. Because we are afraid of emotional intensity we cut off our most powerful source of regulation.

Over time, I have developed faith in the three aspects of the clinician's task that I have called being a contrast, relational challenge, and catalyst. Briefly, analysts points out when they have contrasted with the patient's expectations, which heightens the patient's awareness of those expectations. Potentially, this experience can also challenge some long-held, but not necessarily consciously formulated assumptions about the way life has to be. This may free the patient to consider new possibilities and hope for more.

Being a relational challenge means, to me, making it hard for the patient to do "business as usual." Often, people have developed rigidified patterns of relating to others that they rely on for outdated reasons. These patterns may limit the joy, the curiosity, the love we can feel. They straightjacket our relationships and, in a sense, our lives, diminishing our strength. I see it as part of the analyst's role to interfere in mindless repetition of these patterns within the treatment.

To be a catalyst means, to me, to facilitate experimentation with life. In my judgment, most of treatment does not go on in the clinician's office. Changing how a life is lived takes a more powerful experience than we can usually provide in 45 minutes a few times a week. I see part of my role as helping people try out new behavior in the openly curious way we all found natural as children. Like the little child who throws a toy just to see what will happen, we encourage a stance toward life that asks, 'What would happen if I ...'"?

All of these activities require our empathic presence. But, as we would expect, empathy has been understood in many different ways. I favor an active form of empathy, one that privileges my own recovery of emotional balance as a central aspect of the empathic process. To capitalize on the power of emotions to impact other emotions I feel that something more than accurate mirroring (for example) has to go on in treatment. When we are locked in a terrible emotional state we need someone who understands our pain, but we also need that person to remain capable of offering us some hope that things can change. Only a clinician who has remained emotionally intact can hold out that hope.

Of course, my point of view is partially a product of my own character, with its strengths and flaws. But it is also steeped in an interpersonal tradition. From my teachers, analysts, supervisors, colleagues, and others, I have taken an attitude that each of us puts our unique imprint on all our experience. I extend that to suggest that we each have a history of interpersonal experience with each of the fundamental human emotions, such as shame, joy, and anger. Part of how I know myself is that I know what I tend to be like when I am angry. Each emotion, when it is intense enough, is like a separate self-state, coloring our consciousness, shaping our focus.

Because these ideas are central to my thinking, I cannot accept theories that suggest that one person "puts" their experience into another. If an interaction with a patient evokes anger in me, it is always *my* brand of anger. My anger today brings a whole personal history of angry experiences in its wake. No one can put "their" anger in me. Once I am feeling an emotion it takes on the coloring that comes from my lifetime of experience.

My interpersonal emphasis leads me to a particular outlook on the human experience of loss. While I believe there can be some consolation in retaining an ongoing relationship with the "internal object," nothing replaces the body of an alive, surprising, living, changing other. Those who have lost children, life partners, parents, or any very significant person tend to express this. They miss the touch, the smell, the sound of the other. They want to feel, again, what that person's actual *presence* made them feel. Nothing else gives them back the *self* they were when the other was still alive.

Because each emotion is qualitatively, and not just quantitatively, different, I believe that we can't talk about working with "counter-transference emotions" without being more specific. Each of five emotions: shame, regret, joy, grief, and anger, receives separate attention here.

When the patient is extremely sensitive to shame it seems to me especially important for the analyst to retain an adequate sense of self. Of course, we would each approach this task differently. I distinguish various forms of shame as I understand them, and suggest some approaches, including sharing the patient's shame, much as, I think, a Shakespearian "fool" would. Not unlike the analyst, this character sometimes softens pain by being willing to look "foolish" himself if that contributes to creating a new perspective.

Regret (and anticipatory fear of regret) can play a hidden, but extremely significant part in all our lives. It is remarkable to me how little we name it as a factor in treatment. How often does each of us look back, and wish we had picked up on a word, a tone, a facial expression that might have unlocked much more? Analysts have so many "roads not taken" every hour, since each moment comes with infinite choices as to our focus, what we privilege, respond to, let pass, remember, and so on. We have many chances for regret, but also just as many opportunities to atone. The concept of atonement has become increasingly important to me, personally and professionally. I approach it from several angles here, including the idea (taken from religious sources) that at-one-ment can be achieved through a kind of self integration as well as integration of the individual with the greater community.

Feeling a part of humankind is one way to understand what brings some moments of joy. I call joy the "universal antidote" because I believe it can play a vital role in modulating all of our most painful emotional experiences. Joy makes us feel we can soar over frustrating obstacles. It counters the paralysis in depression and the diminishment in grief. Its potential for moments of timelessness frees us from anxious constraint. Interludes of joy help us shed shame, guilt, sorrow, and fear and invest more fully in life again. As clinicians, it seems to me to be important to wonder how we can help others, and help ourselves access the power of joy.

I have already mentioned grief, but would like to add that I think of loss as an ongoing process in treatment and the rest of life. The ultimate losses crystallize our feelings about the more subtle but pervasive ones. How many times in a session does each of us lose a bit of hope of being really understood? When we open the newspaper in the morning, how much of our belief in a sane, humane world is shattered? These "micro-losses" gather at the point of termination of treatment or at other times of concrete loss. At those moments, grief is formulated partially, perhaps because there will be no more chances to recoup what has been lost along the way.

To be able to function as a person I think we need access to empowering anger, assertion, and aggression, as well as other feelings that lend us strength. But we are all painfully aware of the dangers of anger. I have long wondered what sometimes allows anger to give us strength, sustaining our fight against the desecration of our environment, for example. Is there any clear difference between empowering anger and disorienting, disregulating anger? More specifically, how can analysts tap into their own aggression and their patient's in the service of their work together?

How can we train people to be better at the task of making a difference in the lives of others? I think training can be an unnecessarily mystifying experience, where shame and a sense of professional inadequacy grows more, not less, intense. Using antiquated jargon, we have separated analytic wisdom from other sources and created schisms between what each of us knows from our life experience and what we know from clinical experience. This perpetuates our own dissociation, as well as our isolation as a field. Training will be relevant enough to undertake only if it speaks directly to people about how they can become better at their life's work.

I have tried to describe the cognitive, emotional, and interpersonal strengths that I think must be nurtured in training. Each training experience is an opportunity to take in a new voice that can be with the clinician for the rest of her career. I have called the aggregate of these voices the "internal chorus" to suggest that these voices meld. Hopefully, they sometimes guide us and always sustain us.

Doing clinical work is a daunting task. To focus on so many levels at once, to be in the vicinity of so much heartache, to bear the loss of every treatment partner, to live with the limits and the degree of our influence is an extraordinary challenge. But it is also an extraordinary privilege. Training is just the beginning of a lifelong effort to work on becoming the best clinicians we can be. Like the musician, we have to keep our instruments in top form. But for clinicians, our instruments are ourselves. We have the audacity and the humility to try to use our own cognitive, emotional, and interpersonal resources to make a difference in others' lives.

References

Albers, J. (1963). *Interaction of Color*. New Haven: Yale University Press.

Alexander, F. (1961). *The Scope of Psychoanalysis* 1921–1961. New York: Basic Books.

Alvarez, A. (1973). *The Savage God: A Study of Suicide*. New York: Bantam.

Arieti, S. (1967). *The Intrapsychic Self*. New York: Basic Books.

_____. (1972). *The Will to Be Human*. New York: Quadrangle Books.

Aristotle (4th Century B.C.). *The Nicomachean Ethics*. trans. H. Rackham. Ware, UK: Wordsworth Editions Limited.

_____. (1924). Rhetoric. In: *The Works of Aristotle, Vol. XI*, Robert Rhys, Trans. Oxford: The Clarendon Press.

Bacal, H. (1997). "Shame—The affect of discrepancy." In M. Lansky & A. Morrison (Eds.), *The Widening Scope of Shame*. Hillsdale, NJ: The Analytic Press.

Balint, M. (1968). *The Basic Fault*. London: Tavistock.

Barnett, J. (1980). "Interpersonal processes, cognition and the analysis of character." *Contemporary Psychoanalysis*, 16: 397–416.

Bayley, J. (1999a). "Last jokes." *The New Yorker*. August 2, pp. 38–43.

_____. (1999b). *Elegy for Iris*. New York: W. W. Norton and Company.

Beckett, S. (1955). *The Unnamable*. Part of trilogy including *Molloy* and *Malone Dies*. New York: Alfred A. Knopf.

Blechner, M. (1988). "Differentiating empathy from therapeutic action." *Contemporary Psychoanalysis*, 24: 301.

Bollas, C. (1987). *The Shadow of the Object*. New York: Columbia University Press.

_____. (1999). *The Mystery of Things*. London: Routledge.

Bonime, W. (1976). "The psychodynamics of neurotic depression." *Journal of the American Academy of Psychoanalysis*, 4: 301–326.

_____. (1982). "Psychotherapy of the depressed patient." *Contemporary Psychoanalysis*, 18: 173–189.

Bromberg, P. (1998). *Standing in the Spaces*. Hillsdale, NJ: The Analytic Press.

Broucek, F. (1997). "Shame: Early developmental issues." In M. Lansky & A. Morrison (Eds.), *The Widening Scope of Shame*. Hillsdale, NJ: The Analytic Press.

Buechler, S. (1988). "Joining the psychoanalytic culture." *Contemporary Psychoanalysis*, 24: 462–470.

———. (1992). "Stress in the personal and professional development of a psychoanalyst." *Journal of the American Academy of Psychoanalysis*, 20: 183–191.

———. (1995a). "Emotion." In M. Lionells, J. Fiscalini, C. H. Mann, and D. B. Stern (Eds.), *Handbook of Interpersonal Psychoanalysis*. Hillsdale, NJ: The Analytic Press, pp. 165–88.

———. (1995b). "Hatred: The strength of the sensitive." Discussion of paper by Otto Kernberg, presented at William Alanson White Scientific Meeting, New York, October.

———. (1997). "The right stuff." *Contemporary Psychoanalysis*, 33: 295–306.

———. (1998). "The analyst's experience of loneliness." *Contemporary Psychoanalysis*, 34: 91–105.

———. (1999). "Searching for a passionate neutrality." *Contemporary Psychoanalysis*, 35: 231–227.

———. (2000). "Necessary and unnecessary losses: The analyst's mourning." *Contemporary Psychoanalysis*, 36: 77–90.

———. (2002). "Joy in the analytic encounter: A response to Biancoli." *Contemporary Psychoanalysis*, 38: 613–622.

———. (2003). "Analytic integrity: A review of Affect Intolerance in Patient and Analyst." *Contemporary Psychoanalysis*, 39: 323–326.

———. (2004). *Clinical Values: Emotions That Guide Psychoanalytic Treatment*. Hillsdale, NJ: The Analytic Press.

———. (2005). "Secret pleasures: A discussion of Maroda's 'Legitimate gratification of the analyst's needs.'" *Contemporary Psychoanalysis*, 41: 389–395.

———. (2006). "The legacies of shaming psychoanalytic candidates." Presented at Mt. Sinai Symposium 2006, New York, March.

———. (in press, a). "The analyst's search for atonement." *Psychoanalytic Inquiry*.

———. (in press, b). "The legacies of shaming psychoanalytic candidates." *Contemporary Psychoanalysis*.

Cole, G, (2005). "Loss, mourning, and time." *Psychoanalytic Dialogues*, 15: 539–549.

Coltart, N. (1993). *How to Survive as a Psychotherapist*. London: Sheldon Press.

———. (1996). *The Baby and the Bathwater*. Madison, WI: International Universities Press, Inc.

Cooper, A. (1986). "Some limitations of therapeutic effectiveness: The burnout syndrome' in psychoanalysis." *Psychoanalytic Quarterly*, 55: 576–598.

Cushman, P. (1995). *Constructing the Self, Constructing America*. Reading, MA: Addison-Wesley Publishing Co.

Darwin, C. (1872). *The Expression of Emotions in Man and Animals*. London: John Murray.

Dostoevsky, F. (1968). "The double." In R. Hingley (Ed.), George Bird (trans.), *Great Short Works of Dostoevsky*. New York: Harper & Row.

Didion, J. (2005). *The Year of Magical Thinking*. New York: Alfred A. Knopf.

Ehrenberg, D. B. (1992). *The Intimate Edge: Extending the Reach of Psychoanalytic Interaction*. New York: W. W. Norton.

Ekman, P. (2003). *Emotions Revealed*. New York: Holt and Company.

Eliot, T. S. (1943). *Four Quartets*. New York: Harcourt, Inc.

Emde, R. (1992). "Positive emotions for psychoanalytic theory: Surprises from infancy research and new directions." In T. Shapiro & R. Emde (Eds.), *Affect: Psychoanalytic Perspectives*. Madison CT: International Universities Press.

English, O. (1976). "The emotional stresses of psychotherapeutic practice." *Journal of the American Academy of Psychoanalysis*, 4: 119–210.

Epstein, L. (1979). "The therapeutic use of countertransference data with borderline patients." *Contemporary Psychoanalysis*, 15: 248–275.

Farber, L. (1966). *The Ways of the Will*. New York: Basic Books.

Ferenczi, S. (1928). "The elasticity of psychoanalytic technique." In *The Final Contributions to the Problems and Methods of Psychoanalysis*. London: Hogarth Press. Paper reprinted 1988. *Contemporary Psychoanalysis*, 24: 196–206.

———. (1929). "The unwelcome child and his death instinct." In *The Final Contributions to the Problems and Methods of Psychoanalysis*. London: Hogarth Press.

———. (1933). "Confusion of tongues between adults and the child." In *The Final Contributions to the Problems and Methods of Psychoanalysis*. London: Hogarth Press. Paper reprinted 1988. *Contemporary Psychoanalysis*, 24: 196–206.

———. (1988). *The Clinical Diary of Sandor Ferenczi*. J. Dupont (Ed.). Cambridge, MA: Harvard University Press.

Fonagy, P. (2001). *Attachment Theory and Psychoanalysis*. New York: Other Press.

Frankel, E. (2003). *Sacred Therapy*. Boston, MA: Shambhala.

Frankl, V. (1985). *Man's Search for Meaning*. New York: Simon & Schuster.

Fredrickson, B. L. (2001). "The role of positive emotions in positive psychology: The broaden-and-build theory of positive emotions." *American Psychologist*, 56, 218–226.

Freud, A. (1936). *The Ego and the Mechanisms of Defense*. New York: International Universities Press.

Freud, S. (1917/1915). "Mourning and melancholia." *Standard Edition*. 14: 237–258. London: Hogarth Press.

———. (1921). *Group Psychology and the Analysis of the Ego, Standard Edition*. 18: 65–143. London: Hogarth Press.

Fromm, E. (1947). *Man for Himself*. New York: Rinehart.

———. (1964). *The Heart of Man: Its Genius for Good and Evil*. New York: Harper & Row.

———. (1968). *The Revolution of Hope*. New York: Harper & Row.

———. (1973). *The Anatomy of Human Destructiveness*. New York: Holt, Rinehart & Winston.

———. (1976). *To Have or to Be?* New York: Harper & Row.

Frommer, M. S. (1995). "Living in the liminal spaces of mortality." *Psychoanalytic Dialogues*, 15: 479–499.

Fromm-Reichmann, F. (1959/1990). "Loneliness." *Contemporary Psychoanalysis*, 26: 305–330.

Gaines, R. (1997). "Detachment and continuity: The two tasks of mourning." *Contemporary Psychoanalysis*, 33: 549–571.

Ghent, E. (1990). "Masochism, submission, surrender: Masochism as a perversion of surrender." *Contemporary Psychoanalysis*, 26: 108–136.

Glennon, S. (1995). "Psychoanalysis and mourning-two distinct views." *Psychoanalytic Dialogues*, 15: 529–539.

Goldberg, S., Muir, R., and Kerr, J. (1995). *Attachment Theory: Social, Developmental, and Clinical Perspectives*. Hillsdale, NJ: The Analytic Press.

Gorer, G. (1965). *Death, Grief, and Mourning*. Beaufort Books.

Greenberg, J. (1991). *Oedipus and Beyond: A Clinical Theory*. Cambridge: Harvard University Press.

Hanson, K. (1997). "Reasons for shame, shame against reason." In M. Lansky & A. Morrison (Eds.), *The Widening Scope of Shame*. Hillsdale, NJ: The Analytic Press.

Harden, E. (1985). *Fyodor Dostoevsky: The Double-Two Versions*. Ann Arbor, MI: Ardis Publishers.

Heisterkamp, G. (2001). "Is psychoanalysis a cheerless (Freud-less) profession? Toward a psychoanalysis of joy." *The Psychoanalytic Quarterly*, 70: 839–871.

Hirsch, I. (2005). "Clinical services meeting." Presented at the William Alanson White Institute, New York, September 20.

Hirsch, I. (2008). *Coasting in the Countertransference*. New York: The Analytic Press.

Hoffman, I. Z. (1998). *Ritual and Spontaneity in the Psychoanalytic Process*. Hillsdale, NJ: The Analytic Press.

Hornstein, G. A. (2000). *To Redeem One Person Is to Redeem the World: The Life of Frieda Fromm-Reichmann*. New York: The Free Press.

Issacharoff, A. (1997). "A conversation with Dr. Alberta Szalita." *Contemporary Psychoanalysis*, 33: 615–632.

Izard, C. E. (1971). *The Face of Emotion*. New York: Meredith Corp.

_____. (1972). *Patterns of Emotion*. New York: Academic Press.

_____. (1977). *Human Emotions*. New York: Plenum Press.

_____. (1989). "The structure and functions of emotions." In I. S. Cohen (Ed.), *The G. Stanley Hall Lecture Series* (Vol. 9, pp. 35–73). Washington, DC: American Psychological Association.

_____. (2001). "Emotional intelligence or adaptive emotions?" *Emotion*, 1: 249–257.

Jacobs, T. (1986). "On countertransference enactments." *Journal of the American Psychoanalytic Association*, 34: 289–307.

James, H. (1881). "Washington Square." In *Great Short Works of Henry James*. New York: Harper & Row, 1966.

_____. (1898). "The Turn of the Screw." In *Great Short Works of Henry James*. New York: Harper & Row, 1966.

Jones, J. (1995). *Affects As Process*. Hillsdale, NJ: The Analytic Press.

Josephs, L. (1988). "A comparison of archaeological and empathic modes of listening." *Contemporary Psychoanalysis*, 24: 282–301.

Kepinski, A. (1981). "Sorrows and joys of the psychotherapist." *Journal of the American Academy of Psychoanalysis*, 9(3): 391–398.

Kernberg, O. F. (1975). *Borderline Conditions and Pathological Narcissism*. New York: Jason Aronson, Inc.

_____. (1990). *Internal World and External Reality*. New York: Jason Aronson, Inc.

Kohut, H. (1971). *The Analysis of the Self*. New York: International Universities Press.

_____. (1977). *The Restoration of the Self*. New York: International Universities Press.

_____. (1984). *How Does Analysis Cure?* Chicago: University of Chicago Press.

Krystal, H. (1975). "Affect tolerance." *Annual of Psychoanalysis*, 3: 179–217.

Kumin, M. (1974). *Our Ground Time Here Will Be Brief*. New York: Viking Penguin.

Lansky, M. & Morrison, A. (Eds). (1997). *The Widening Scope of Shame*. Hillsdale, NJ: The Analytic Press.

Levenson, E. (1982). "Follow the fox: An inquiry into the vicissitudes of psychoanalytic supervision." *Contemporary Psychoanalysis*, 18: 1–15.

_____. (1991). *The Purloined Self: Interpersonal Perspectives in Psychoanalysis*. New York: Contemporary Psychoanalysis Books.

Lewis, H. B. (1971). *Shame and Guilt in Neurosis*. New York: International Universities Press.

Lipps, T. (1903). "Empathy and aesthetic pleasure." In K. Aschenbrenner & A. Isenberg (Eds.), *Aesthetic Theories: Studies in the Philosophy of Art.* Englewood Cliffs, NJ: Prentice Hall.

Magai, C. & McFadden, S. H. (1995). *The Role of Emotions in Social and Personality Development: History, Theory, and Research.* New York: Plenum Press.

Manning, M. (2001). "The legacy." In N. Casey (Ed.) *Unholy Ghost: Writers on Depression.* New York: Harper Collins, pp. 256–269.

Marmor, J. (1982). "Some factors involved in occupation-related depression among psychiatrists." *Psychiatric Annals,* 12(10): 913–920.

Maroda, K. (1991). *The Power of Countertransference.* Chichester: Wiley.

_____. (1999). *Seduction, Surrender, and Transformation.* Hillsdale, NJ: The Analytic Press.

_____. (2002). "No place to hide: affectivity, the unconscious, and the development of relational techniques." *Contemporary Psychoanalysis,* 38: 101–121.

_____. (2005). "Legitimate gratification of the analyst's needs." *Contemporary Psychoanalysis,* 41: 371–389.

Mendelson, M. (1988). "Empathy, self-observation, and judgment." *Contemporary Psychoanalysis,* 24: 323–331.

Merwin, W. S. (1973). *Writings to an Unfinished Accompaniment.* New York: Athenium.

Michels, R. (1997). "Rethinking shame." In M. Lansky & A. Morrison (Eds.), *The Widening Scope of Shame.* Hillsdale, NJ: The Analytic Press.

Milner, M. (1956). "The yell of joy." In M. Klein, P. Heimann, & R. E. Money-Kyrle (Eds.), *New Directions in Psychoanalysis.* New York: Basic Books.

Mitchell, S. A. (1993). *Hope and Dread in Psychoanalysis.* New York: Basic Books.

Moore, O. (1992). *The New York Times,* April 19, 1992.

Morris, W. (1969). *American Heritage Dictionary of the English Language.* Boston: Houghton Mifflin Co.

Morrison, A. & Stolorow, R. (1997). "Shame, narcissism, and intersubjectivity." In M. Lansky & A. Morrison (Eds.), *The Widening Scope of Shame.* Hillsdale, N. J. : The Analytic Press.

Nathanson, D. L. (1992). *Shame and Pride.* New York: Norton.

_____. (1994). "Shame, compassion, and the 'borderline' personality." *Psychiatric Clinicians of North America,* 17: 785–810.

_____. (1997). Affect theory and the compass of shame. In M. Lansky & A. Morrison (Eds.), *The Widening Scope of Shame.* Hillsdale, NJ: The Analytic Press.

Ogden, T. H. (2001). "An elegy, a love song, and a lullaby." *Psychoanalytic Dialogues,* 11(2): 293–311.

Panksepp, J. (1998). *Affective Neuroscience*. New York: Oxford University Press.

Penhall, J. (2001). *Blue/Orange*. London: Methuen.

Poland, W. (1984). "On the analyst's neutrality." *Journal of the American Psychoanalytic Association*. 32: 283–299.

Racker, H. (1968). *Transference and Countertransference*. New York: International Universities Press.

Rank, O. (1925/1971). *The Double*. Chapel Hill: University of North Carolina Press.

Rapaport, D. (1967). "On the psychoanalytic theory of motivation." In M. M. Gill (Ed.), *The Collected Papers of David Rapaport*. New York: Basic Books, pp. 853–915.

Renik, O. (1995). "The ideal of the anonymous analyst and the problem of self-disclosure." *Psychoanalytic Quarterly*, 64: 466–495.

_____. (1998). "Getting real in analysis." *Psychoanalytic Quarterly*, 67: 566–593.

Rich, A. (1981). *A Wild Patience Has Taken Me This Far: Poems, 1978–1981*. New York: W. W. Norton & Company.

Rilke, R. M. (1934). *Letters to a Young Poet*. New York: W. W. Norton and Co. , Inc.

Safran, J. D. (1993). "Breaches in the therapeutic alliance: An arena for negotiating authentic relatedness." *Psychotherapy*, 30: 11–24.

_____. (1999). "Faith, despair, will, and the paradox of acceptance." *Contemporary Psychoanalysis*, 35: 5–24.

Safran, J. D. & Muran, J. C. (2000). *Negotiating the Therapeutic Alliance*. New York: The Guilford Press.

Schachtel, E. G. (1959). *Metamorphosis*. New York: Basic Books.

Schafer, R. (1960). "The loving and beloved superego in Freud's structural theory." *The Psychoanalytic Study of the Child*, 15: 163–188. New York: International Universities Press.

_____. (1983). *The Analytic Attitude*. New York: Basic Books.

_____. (2003). *Bad Feelings*. New York: Karnac.

Schecter, D, E. (1979). "The loving and persecuting superego." *Contemporary Psychoanalysis*, 15: 361–379.

Schmideberg, M. (1947). "The treatment of psychopaths and borderline patients." *American Journal of Psychotherapy*, 1: 45–70.

Schwaber, E. (1983). "A particular perspective on analytic listening." *Psychoanalytic Study of the Child*, 38: 519–546.

Schwartz-Salant, N. (1983). *The Borderline Personality: Vision and Healing*. Wilmette, IL: Chiron Publications.

Searles, H. F. (1986). "The countertransference with the borderline patient." In M. H. Stone (Ed.), *Essential Papers on Borderline Disorders*. New York: New York University Press.

Seneca (1994). "Moral Epistles (*Ad Lucilium Epistulae Morales*)." In M. C. Nussbaum, *The Therapy of Desire: Theory and Practice in Hellenistic Ethics*. Princeton, NJ: Princeton University Press.

Shabad, P. (2001). *Despair and the Return of Hope*. Northvale, NJ: Jason Aronson, Inc.

Shakespeare, W. *King Lear*. In: *The Arden Edition of the Works of William Shakespeare*. London: Methuen (1972).

Shapiro, R. (2006). "Relatively relational: A critique and rationale for integration." William Alanson White Institute, New York, September 12, 2006.

Sharma, R. M. (1993). *Understanding the Concept of Empathy and its Foundations in Psychoanalysis*. Lewiston, New York: The Edwin Mellen Press.

Sherby, L. B. (1989). "Love and hate in the treatment of borderline patients." *Contemporary Psychoanalysis*, 25: 574–591.

Slochower, H. (1970). *Mythopoesis*. Detroit: Wayne State University Press.

Slochower, J. (2003). "The analyst's secret delinquencies." *Psychoanalytic Dialogues*, 13(4): 451–469.

Spiegel, R. (1967). "Anger and acting out: Masks of depression." *Journal of the American Academy of Psychoanalysis*, 21: 597–606.

_____. (1980). "Cognitive aspects of affects and other feeling states with clinical applications." *Journal of the American Academy of Psychoanalysis*, 8: 591–614.

Stechler, G. (2003). "Affect: The heart of the matter." *Psychoanalytic Dialogues*, 13(5): 711–726.

Stern, D. (1998). "The process of therapeutic change involving implicit knowledge: Some implications of developmental observations for adult psychotherapy." *Infant Mental Health Journal*, 19: 300–308.

Stern, D. B. (1990). "Courting surprise." *Contemporary Psychoanalysis*, 26: 425–478.

_____. (1997). *Unformulated Experience: From Dissociation to Imagination in Psychoanalysis*. Hillsdale, NJ: The Analytic Press.

_____. (2005). "The man who mistook his impact for a hat: Reactions to the interview." *Contemporary Psychoanalysis*, 41: 691–713.

Stoeri, J. (2005). "Surprise, shock, and dread, and the nature of therapeutic action." *Contemporary Psychoanalysis*, 41: 183–202.

Succillo, M. V. (2005). "Psychoanalysis and mourning—two distinct views." *Psychoanalytic Dialogues*, 15: 499–529.

Sullivan, H. S. (1940). *Conceptions of Modern Psychiatry*. New York: W. W. Norton.

_____. (1948). "The meaning of anxiety in psychiatry and in life." *Psychiatry*, 11: 1–13.

_____. (1953). *The Interpersonal Theory of Psychiatry*. New York: W. W. Norton.

_____. (1954). *The Psychiatric Interview*. New York: W. W. Norton.

_____. (1956) *Clinical Studies in Psychiatry*. New York: W. W. Norton.

Szalita, A. (1955). "The 'intuitive process' and its relation to work with schizophrenics." *Journal of the American Psychoanalytic Association*, 3: 7–18.

_____. (1976). "Some thoughts on empathy." *Psychiatry*, 39: 142–152.

_____. (1981). "The use and misuse of empathy in psychoanalysis and psychotherapy." *The Psychoanalytic Review*, 68: 3–21.

_____. (1988). "Epistemology: ways of knowing in psychoanalysis: Afterword." *Contemporary Psychoanalysis*, 24: 338–341.

Tennyson, A. "Tears, idle tears." In L. Untermeyer (Ed.), *A Great Treasury of Poems, Volume Two*. New York: Simon and Schuster (1942).

Thompson, C. (1955). "Transference and character analysis." In C. Thompson, M. Mazer & E. G. Witenberg (Eds.), *An Outline of Psychoanalysis*. New York: Modern Library, pp. 527–538.

Titchener, E. B. (1910). *Lectures on the Experimental Psychology of Thought Processes*. New York: Macmillan.

Tolstoy, L. (1886/1982). "The Death of Ivan Ilych." In A. Maude & L. Maude (trans.), *The Raid and Other Stories*. New York: Oxford University Press.

Tomkins, S. S. (1962). *Affect, Imagery, Consciousness. Vol. I, The Positive Affects*. New York: Springer.

_____. (1963). *Affect, Imagery, Consciousness. Vol. II, The Negative Affects*. New York: Springer.

_____. (1970). "Affect as the primary motivational system." In M. B. Arnold (Ed.), *Feelings and Emotions*. New York: Academic Press, pp. 101–110.

Tronick, E. Z. (1989). "Emotions and emotional communication in infants." *American Psychologist*, 44: 112–119.

Vaillant, G. E. (2002). *Aging Well*. Boston: Little, Brown and Company.

Wilbur, R. (1989). "The writer." In: Havens, L. , *A Safe Place*. New York: Random House, p. 23.

Winnicott, D. (1949). "Hate in the countertransference." *International Journal of Psycho-Analysis*, 30: 69–75.

_____. (1971). *Playing and Reality*. London: Tavistock Publications.

Wordsworth, W. "My heart leaps up when I behold" and "Ode: Intimations of immortality from recollections of early childhood." In S. Heaney (Ed.), *Essential Wordsworth*. New York: HarperCollins (1993).

Wurmser, L. (1997). "Nietzsche's war against shame and resentment." In M. Lansky & A. Morrison (Eds.), *The Widening Scope of Shame*. Hillsdale, NJ: The Analytic Press.

Zeddies, T. J. (2002). "Sluggers and analysts: Batting for average with the psychoanalytic unconscious." *Contemporary Psychoanalysis*, 38: 465–477.

Zimmer, H. (1948). *The King and the Corpse: Tales of the Soul's Conquest of Evil*. J. Campbell (Ed.). Washington, DC: The Bollingen Foundation.

Zweig, P. (1968). *The Heresy of Self-Love*. Princeton, NJ: Princeton University Press.

Index